DON QUIXOTE AMONG THE SARACENS:
A CLASH OF CIVILIZATIONS AND LITERARY GENRES

FREDERICK A. DE ARMAS

Don Quixote among the Saracens

A Clash of Civilizations and Literary Genres

UNIVERSITY OF TORONTO PRESS
Toronto Buffalo London

© University of Toronto Press 2011
Toronto   Buffalo   London
www.utppublishing.com
Printed in Canada

ISBN 978-1-4426-4345-1

∞

Printed on acid-free, 100% post-consumer recycled paper with vegetable-based inks.

Library and Archives Canada Cataloguing in Publication

De Armas, Frederick A.
Don Quixote among the Saracens : a clash of civilizations and literary genres / Frederick A. de Armas.

Includes bibliographical references and index.
ISBN 978-1-4426-4345-1

1. Cervantes Saavedra, Miguel de, 1547–1616. Don Quixote.
2. Cervantes Saavedra, Miguel de, 1547–1616 – Technique.   3. Saracens in literature.   4. Culture conflict in literature.   I. Title.

PQ6353.D37 2011   863'.3   C2011-902099-8

University of Toronto Press acknowledges the financial assistance to its publishing program of the Canada Council for the Arts and the Ontario Arts Council.

Canada Council   Conseil des Arts   ONTARIO ARTS COUNCIL
for the Arts   du Canada   CONSEIL DES ARTS DE L'ONTARIO

University of Toronto Press acknowledges the financial support of the Government of Canada through the Canada Book Fund for its publishing activities.

Contents

Illustrations

Preface

This book grew out of a happy misunderstanding. When Julio Hans Jensen asked me to attend a symposium on genre at the University of Copenhagen, he mentioned that the papers would be published in the *Revue Romaine*. Rather than consulting the journal, I set out to write an essay on questions of genre in *Don Quixote*. This was a topic I wanted to consider further since, in my previous book, *Quixotic Frescoes*, I had broached the topic but could not develop it as the book's focus was the art of memory, Italian art, and ekphrasis. I was delighted to finish the Copenhagen essay long before the deadline. When I sent it to Julio Jensen, he wrote a very apologetic note reminding me that the journal only published in the romance languages and that my essay was in English. Would I mind translating it? After thinking about it for some time, I felt that what I had written was best left in English. I took the months that remained to write quite a different piece in Spanish for the symposium and the journal, one that foregrounded Virgil's misplacement in Cervantes' novel. The English article, I set aside. I was tempted to publish it in a journal, but the more I read it, the more I noticed that there was much more I wanted to include – so much, that the five sections in the essay soon became so lengthy that they turned into chapters.

I was never able to make it to Copenhagen. A small accident kept me at home, and kept me writing. When the fourth chapter soon became too long, I divided it into four additional chapters. And, as I was finishing the seventh chapter, a curious use of the *Orlando furioso* in chapter 45 of Cervantes' novel led me to puzzle out a mystery. The solution comes out of the text's invitation in chapter 22 to become a detective, to follow the thread that can allow us to navigate the labyrinth of converging genres and come out with an answer. In addition to the confluence of genres, there is no greater labyrinth in the text than the mind of our gentleman from La Mancha. Genre and character, then, impelled me to recreate a scene that could answer a number of questions about the novel. Once I glimpsed the mystery, all the previous chapters had to be revised to include this second thread of argument. All these mishaps have led to this book that deals with a knight whose journey is filled with accidental happenings. These accidents lead him this way and that, just as the narrative takes on and discards different genres. The way Cervantes uses countless genres metamorphosing them into something novel, and even turning them against each other, is one of the many reasons *Don Quixote* is an unforgettable novel. Here, the Virgilian epic of the victors might be placed against Lucan's epic of the defeated; the marvellous excesses in Ariosto's *Orlando furioso* can be juxtaposed to an episode from Tasso's *Gerusalemme liberata* where, attempting to restrain the marvellous, the author is carried away by the narrative; the violence of the *Belianís de Grecia* is pitted against the concepts of Feliciano de Silva's chivalric texts. Chivalry can be furthered by the Greek romances; the clustering of Italian *novelle* can resemble the interlacing of romance; theatrical techniques can irrupt at any point, as tragedy and comedy are contrasted; Ovidian metamorphoses are everywhere, as well as names and tales from mythographical manuals. Other forms of prose are constantly contaminating the narrative: emblematic literature, hagiography, medical manuals, manuals of oratory, technical treatises, etc. Each instance deserves a detailed study. But that is far beyond the range of this book. What interests me most is how the narrative seems to defy different genres as the knight moves 'through' them. At a time when Cervantes' novel is viewed as a modern and even a postmodern novel, it is appropriate to look back, to analyse how Cervantes' work originated out of clashes of genre, many of which are of no importance to the contemporary reader. It is also important, I think, to show how the territories of genre become part of the empire of the novel; and how Don Quixote rides on, a ghostly memory of Emperor Charles V and his son Philip.

While studying the generic clashes, the imitation and parody of so many texts, I came across, quite unexpectedly, a hidden element, a secret that is, as noted above, partially revealed through the uses of the *Orlando furioso*. It is the mystery of Don Quixote's relations to the Moorish culture of Spain, an anxiety that hides a kind of maurophilia, and perhaps even more. The book's title, *Don Quixote among the Saracens*, reflects one of the names given to the Muslims through the Middle Ages and even into the seventeenth century. Ariosto refers to the Islamic enemy that is laying siege to Paris as Saracens, some say, because the name referred to all Muslims and particularly to those from Sicily and southern Italy. However, he could have been reflecting its use during the times of Charlemagne, where it meant anyone who was not Christian and was thus interchangeable with 'pagan.' In Spain, the term Saracen was used for the invading Moors from Africa as early as the eighth century. Many Christian invectives were attached to this word. Thirteen years before the publication of *Don Quixote*, for example, Petro de la Cavalleria and Martino Alfonso Vivaldo composed their *Tractatus Zelus Christi contra Iudaeos Saracenos et Infideles* (1592). My usage of the term acknowledges its historical roots. While in classical times it was a neutral term to refer to a people who lived far away from what early Europeans conceived as the centres of power, it could still mean that Saracens were but one of many types of barbarians. Later, it became a word applied to the enemies of Christianity. Even today, the expression 'sarracina' refers to a confusing contest or quarrel. In many ways, this is how Cervantes takes the episode at the inn. It includes a series of confusing altercations. Although Cervantes refrains from mentioning the word, he turns to imitate Ariosto's episode with many confusing quarrels in order to show that peace can be achieved by abiding among the Saracens. Thus, in Cervantes' novel a hybrid status is lauded as a site for harmony. In many ways, my hope is to rescue the term and foreground its connotations as a threatened Other. Indeed, I recently read an editorial by Lluís Bassets in the Spanish newspaper *El País* that was entitled 'El Cid se lanza contra los sarracenos' [The Cid Fights against the Saracens]. The essay was a complaint against policies by Nicolas Sarkozy and Berlusconi who are intent on excluding foreigners from their countries, and particularly on expelling the gypsies (2010, 13). What I am trying to show in this book is that the Saracen/Other has to be faced within ourselves. The struggle is one for tolerance, one that acknowledges and makes room for different cultures and civilizations, for different expressions of the self.

It is my contention, then, that Don Quixote is at first anxious and then at home among the Saracens. Why so? This, then, is an essential mystery that hides among the clashes in the novel. The clashes of genre and the knight's imaginings conceal a clash of civilizations and the anxieties that they produce. In this and many other ways, Cervantes' novel, although looking at the past, echoes today's clashes of civilizations as described by Samuel Huntington and many others. And since my own study functions often through allusion, I would point out that I use Huntington's provocative and useful notion of a clash of civilizations in a nuanced way that will be explained in chapter 1. And just because I take up the phrase 'clashes of civilizations' does not mean that I accept many of Huntington's other arguments.

The book is divided into ten chapters. The first serves as introduction, setting the scene. The second chapter looks at the foundations to the chivalric world that are laid in chapter 1 of *Don Quixote*. This construction is aided by Pythagorean numerology, onomastics, and a number of quaternities such as Empedocles' elements, the four humours that balance the physiology, the four qualities, and the four seasons. At the same time, parody of the romances undercuts, among others, the naming of the knight and his lady. This parody turns polemical when it hints of a mystery that involves both the knight's ancestry and the lady's lineage. These anxieties propel the gentleman to leave his home, imagining himself emperor of Trebizond – and a new Charles V. In other words, he wishes to live in a simpler world (as portrayed in chivalric romances) where Trebizond was a Christian empire that could prevail against the 'infidels'; or he can at least live in a recent past where there was the hope of a Christian *Dominus mundi* who would bring peace to the world. Chapter 3 takes up the remaining seven chapters of the first part of the novel. Here, diverse generic forms will come into play, such as hagiography, the picaresque, treatises on religious conversion, and technological manuals. But all are subservient to the chivalric and its parody as well as to the Pythagorean buttressing of narrative. The shadow of the ghostly emperor Charles V will haunt the text from its beginning since the original name of the gentleman from La Mancha is Quijada or jaw, thus pointing to the protruding Habsburg jaw of Charles V and his successor Philip II. Hidden within Pythagorean harmonies, a mysterious subtext continues to emerge as the knight 'mistakes' crosses and clerics as enemies. Chapter 4 turns to the second part of *Don Quixote* (chapters 9–14). Here pastoral paradoxically points to epic, while the intrusion of an Arabic narrator attempts to destabilize a narrative which is now buttressed by epic possibilities. And a woman is seen appropriating epic devices to counter accusations against her. A clash of epics requires the abandonment of the pastoral land in search of a new start. Epic possibilities are again reasserted in the third part of the novel (chapters 15–22). These eight chapters are the subject of our chapter 5, as they reroute a narrative that had become too complex back into the linear and chivalric mode. The chivalric is buttressed by the Carolingian cycle and the Italian romances while it is destabilized by parody and, to a lesser extent, by the 'author,' Cide Hamete Benengeli. The French and Italian models provide two magical objects, the balsam of Fierabrás and Mambrino's helmet. While the first becomes a dangerous heterodox *ensalmo*, a curative process often used by *conversos* and *moriscos*, the second emboldens the knight with the allure of invincibility and the daring of a Moorish enchantment. Together, these two objects haunt the knight with anxieties regarding his ancestry and his lady's lineage. At the same time, parodic episodes contain numerous allusions to Virgil's *Aeneid*. It soon becomes apparent that the narrative is not following the foundational and imperial epic. Although coming closer to the epic of the defeated, the episodic narrative eventually reaches an impasse when the knight decides to free the galley slaves. Is he the ghost of an ancient emperor restoring his descendant's sense of justice? Or is he impelled by Moorish/Jewish magic? Whatever the answer, Don Quixote becomes, in the words of Roberto González Echevarría, a 'fugitive from justice' (2005, 54). The epic of the defeated defeats the knight by turning him into a fugitive. At this narrative impasse, represented by Sierra Morena, the gentleman from La Mancha must find a new way ahead. The road is unstable, as neither the knight nor the commissary who leads the galley slaves can hold up their swords. Traversing these pillars, the chivalric pair comes up with a labyrinth.

Cervantes' novel does not establish a break here. Dividing it into four parts, Cervantes begins the last section of his novel in chapter 28. I begin it in chapter 23 and subdivide this lengthy fourth segment into three parts, each representing a different mystery. Chapter 6 tracks Don Quixote as he moves deeper into Sierra Morena and encounters a number of unexplained clues. This chapter shows how knight and squire beckon the reader to become involved, to become a detective, as the chivalric pair move from the mystery of the portmanteau, to the mystery of the dead mule, to the mystery of Cardenio. Clues become essential in this quasi-detective fiction. While Sancho begins as an excellent detective, Don Quixote slowly surpasses him. The topographical labyrinth is thus linked to a series of threads or clues that the characters must follow to solve the mystery. However, once Cardenio becomes the suspect and tells his story of how he went mad because of unrequited love, Don Quixote abandons all interest in sleuthing. After all, he has found his new calling, that of a knight in love. However, the search for clues calls for the discovery of hidden mysteries in the text as the shimmering visions of dromedary, Minotaur, and dragon impel readers to search for the constructions of monstrous otherness. Chapter 7 describes the mystery of the labyrinth. It shows Don Quixote alone in the mountains doing penance for his lady, while new narratives sprout all around him. Works that resemble Italian *novelle* become clustered in what appears as fragments from Greek or even Italian romances. In this section the knight loses much of his protagonism and voice as others around him recount their tales, act out their problems, and search for solutions. The tales of Cardenio and Dorotea, Fernando and Luscinda, Anselmo and Camila fill these pages. Their amorous endeavours bring humidity and variety to a dry and linear narrative. At the same time, Don Quixote becomes drier and more melancholy as he remains in the mountains. While other genres surface around him, he does not forget his own generic path, trying to decide if he will imitate the romances of chivalry (*Amadís de Gaula*) or the Italian romances (*Orlando furioso*). Although he decides on the former, some elements of the latter will contaminate his actions. These events further derange his mind and dry up his body. They also include keys to the main mystery this book explores, including a heterodox rosary and a needless penitence.

Chapter 8 finds Don Quixote at the inn. He has already tried to regain protagonism by interrupting the tale of the *Curisoso impertinente*. He now tries again with the speech of Arms and Letters. It is followed by a tale that is still not completed, but seeks a denouement at the inn. It is the Captive's Tale, one where Spain's struggle with Moorish culture is at its very centre. Mysteries of naming resurface in this story as the name Zoraida/María can be taken as clues to clashes of genres and civilizations. The tale is never resolved, and neither is the following one, that of Luis and Clara, where the epic figure of Virgil's helmsman, Palinurus, is transformed into a lover. Chapter 9 shows how Don Quixote finally regains his voice. As all is discord at the inn, he decides to invoke a passage from the Italian romances, from *Orlando furioso*, the discord at Agramante's camp during the Saracen's siege of Paris. Although the knight is successful and peace is regained, we are left to wonder why he would choose a scene at the Saracens' camp to depict Christians. This is no trick from the narrator, since it is Don Quixote who comes up with the analogy in order to insert the helmet of Mambrino among the objects of discord. This parody of canto 27 in the *Orlando* allows us to rethink much of what the knight has done. If he is indeed a ghostly remnant of the Holy Roman Emperor Charles V, he seems to choose the wrong side of the battle here. A review of a number of previous episodes in light of this one provides a theory as to the well-hidden mystery in the text. Indeed, the novel has prepared us to attempt to solve such a mystery with the detections of knight and squire and the many twists of narrative that follow. An active reader may then come up with a possible solution to this central clue. Once all is well at the inn, the narrative again takes on a linear and chivalric direction. Chapter 10, then, discusses the fifth segment of the novel (chapters 47–52). Here the chivalric is buttressed by astrology and magic. The trip home recalls Charles V's journey to Yuste after he abdicates the crown in favour of his son Philip II. Under the influence of Saturn, Don Quixote is led home. And this is as it should be since Saturn at this time was seen as a planet of delays, frustrations, incarceration, and even death. It is also a planet associated with the non-Christian Other. The protean nature of the knight is again revealed: a Saracen secret sympathizer, a gentleman who fears a *converso* ancestry, a lover who doubts his lady's lineage, and a Christian knight who vows to battle the infidel.

Although consulting both Diego Clemencín's erudite nineteenth-century edition and Francisco Rico's monumental recent edition of *Don Quixote,* I am citing from the text I use in my classes, Luis Andrés Murillo's edition of 1978. I do so because I am most familiar with its pages. When citing Don Quixote I first provide the Spanish, followed by Charles Jarvis's English translation in Oxford World's Classics. English translations from other Spanish texts are my own. Works from other languages appear only in English translation.

I would like to thank Julio Hans Jensen and all the participants at the University of Copenhagen workshop. I owe a particular debt of gratitude to my colleague Thomas Pavel, who read not only the Spanish essay for Copenhagen, but also the one that became the basis for this book. He and I have co-taught *Don Quixote* and many of the dialogues that ensued impinge upon my text. I would also like to thank Martha Roth, Dean of Humanities at the University of Chicago, for awarding me a research leave so that I could write this book. I was able to complete the final research on this book at the Consejo Superior de Investigaciones Científicas in Madrid with the aid of their Salvador de Madariaga program. To my colleagues at Chicago, who have been patient with my monomania and have provided counsel and conversation, I am in their debt: Ryan Giles, Armando Maggi, and many others. To many Cervantistas who have provided new insights or conversed with me on these subjects at conferences or at campus talks I give thanks. If

I begin naming, this will become endless, but perhaps a few names will stand for the many: María Antonia Garcés, Juan Pablo Gil-Oslé, Roberto González Echevarría, Luciano García Lorenzo, Ignacio López-Alemany, Thomas Lathrop, Charles Presberg, Steven Wagschal, and Christopher Weimer. The memory of Daniel L. Heiple, Carroll Johnson, and Edward Dudley is evoked throughout these pages. I also want to express my gratitude to the two anonymous readers of the manuscript. I appreciate their detailed and insightful suggestions. To my research and course assistants at the University of Chicago, Jesús Botello, Carmela Mattza, and James Nemiroff, I owe a great debt of gratitude. In particular, I would like to thank Felipe Rojas for his help in assembling and editing this book. I would like to express my appreciation to the editors of *Cervantes* and the *Revue Romaine* for allowing me to include material from my essays in these journals. And, my thanks to the University of Toronto Press for allowing me to repeat, verbatim at times, some of the genre discussions that appeared in *Quixotic Frescoes*. These genre discussions, concealed in a work about ekphrasis, are now expanded to foreground the parodic tone, and the clashes among different forms. They are also interlaced with the 'mystery' of the text.

1 Pillars of Genre / Ghosts of Empire: An Introduction

The 'invention' of the novel resulted from the re-fashioning of literary genres already in place, and Don Quixote stands in relation to the origin of the novel not as the invention of something radically new, but as the uncovering of new possibilities for the combination of elements that pre-existed it.

– Anthony Cascardi, *The Cambridge Companion to Cervantes*

We know that Henry James's secret . . . resides precisely in the existence of a secret, of an absent and absolute cause, as well as in the effort to plumb this secret, to render the absent present . . . We might go further and say that in order for this ever-absent cause to become present, it *must* be a ghost.

– Tzvetan Todorov, *The Poetics of Prose*

At the very ends of the world, where the sun sets, lie the paradisiacal gardens of the Hesperides, where three maidens, daughters of Atlas, tended to the tree with the golden apples. One of them was called Erythea. She gave her name to a little island situated just south of Hispania very near to what is today Cádiz, then Gades.[1] The island, some said, was home to Geryon and it was there, according to Seneca, that Hercules was sent to steal his cattle.[2] To be able to reach this remote place, Hercules had to break a mountain chain that stood in his path.[3] The remnants became two huge rocks separated by a new watery path, an opening through which the waters of Oceanus flowed. These are the Straits of Gibraltar, and guarding the path to Oceanus are the Pillars of Hercules, be they promontories on either side of the straits, or an island

1.1 Spanish nobles lead a riderless horse with the motto of Emperor Charles
V *Plus ultra* in the funerary procession held in Brussels in 1558. Watercolour
in a book printed by Plantin-Moretus in Brussels. Location: Bibliothèque
Municipale, Besançon, France. Art Resource, NY.

in its midst.[4] The pillars served as a warning to sailors not to venture
beyond. Alternately, they protected the Mediterranean from the monsters and floods at the edge of the world.[5]

Centuries passed and Hispania was no longer at the end of the
world – it was becoming the centre of European power, and it was
about to welcome a Habsburg ruler into its midst. The future emperor,
Charles V, went to Barcelona where he met with the Order of the Golden
Fleece in 1519. There he displayed as his device the columns of Hercules, but now with a different meaning.[6] Indeed, on the back of Charles's
seat in the choir at the cathedral there is a heraldic painting by Juan
de Borgoña with the columns of Hercules (Rosenthal 1971, 209).[7] From
that point on, Charles's emblem would use a banderole that beckoned
the traveller or adventurer: *Plus ultra* or *Plus oultre*, go beyond. After
all, the dangerous edge of the world had led to a New World filled with

wonders. In his new empire the sun never set and the golden apples of the Hesperides had been transformed into gold bullion that flowed back to Hispania in fleets that came to Cádiz and whose treasures were counted in Seville. The columns of Hercules thus became a symbol for one of the largest and wealthiest empires the world had ever known. As Marie Tanner affirms: 'Charles's emblem was to become Europe's most enduring symbol in the bid for universal theocratic monarchy' (1993, 155).[8] Even though the empire was divided at his death, funeral processions still embraced the notion of going beyond. At the Brussels commemoration, Spanish nobles led a riderless horse with the motto of the emperor, *Plus ultra*. Philip II would never abandon his father's idea of empire, wanting to become emperor of the Indies.[9] Indeed, his empire reached from Buenos Aires to what would be the southern United States: 'With the absorption of Portugal, Philip's authority now reached also into India, Indonesia, and China. The empire, so extensive as to stagger the imagination, was the biggest ever known in history' (Kamen 1997, 244). Although Philip reigned for about half a century, his final days were plagued with 'disaster and defeat' (1997, 312). Like his father, the glories of empire proved elusive in the end – his Quixotic quest, although in many ways triumphant, was a partial failure. It is no wonder that Cervantes penned his novel not long after Philip's demise. Twice had a Habsburg with a large deformed jaw led them to war and expansionism and twice, although untold lands were conquered, much was also lost.[10]

In his review of a book by José Ángel Ascunce Arrieta, Salvador J. Fajardo claims that linking Cervantes' novel to the Habsburgs is nothing new, although it makes sense to continue to invoke it since both Charles V and Philip II used chivalry to advance their agenda:

> In 1549, when the Emperor Charles introduced his son Philip to the courts of Europe as hereditary Prince, he did so as a 'Perfect Christian Knight,' and many of the triumphal entries and ceremonies featured the Prince as well as a 'Valiant Knight of Christendom.' Such pageantry was emblematic of the aspirations and grandiose fantasy that drove the politics of the Habsburgs, in the defense and propagation of Catholicism, through endless wars that exhausted the treasury and the country . . . (2002, 547)[11]

Although I also take up the Habsburgs, this book seeks to show that the geography of empire is implicated in the journeys of narrative. My point is that Cervantes, when he tracked the journey of Don Quixote, was carefully implementing Charles's motto, *Plus ultra*, a concept endorsed by his son Philip. Whenever the narrative comes to an impasse, due to genre conflict, the weight of parody, or exhaustion, to what I will call metaphorically the Pillars of Hercules, the knight is allowed to go beyond. One of the main reasons for this shifting of narrative has been pinpointed by Thomas Pavel. Since the work takes aim at books of chivalry, it cannot go on with this parody forever. Something has to give: 'Left as the only ingredient of a long-winded narrative, Quixote's eagerness to act as a knight-errant might soon have become tedious. And to keep Quixote's story at the size of a novella would have meant to miss a crucial element of chivalric novels, whose protagonists endlessly roam around the world' (Pavel, in press). Thus, the novel quickly moves into other genres, to give it a feeling of amplitude. The restricted geography of the novel is contrasted with the proliferation of conquered genres. A note of warning: there are so many territories of genre 'conquered' by the narrative that only some can be pinpointed. Of some of these territories I can only give a general inkling, while acknowledging that they are vast and complex.

Furthermore, these fields of genre, like the unknown lands beyond the Pillars, hide enigmas that the text seeks to both cover and unveil. As this book moves through the genres, a particular secret that is as connected to the knight as to the territories he encounters will begin to emerge. Indeed, the Pillars themselves embody the secret – only one of them is in Spain. The second is often located in the Atlas Mountains in North Africa. While Charles V was able to conquer Tunis, the African pillar stood defiant, as a sign of otherness in relation to Spain – for the novel goes beyond European and Western civilization. As Samuel P. Huntington states: 'Civilization is the broadest cultural entity . . . Civilizations have no clear-cut borders and no precise beginning and endings' (1996, 43). Although the concept of civilization as a broad cultural entity is a much debated one, and the very division of history into specific civilizations such as the Hindu and the Sinic or Chinese has often been questioned, it is still the case that historians can look at cultural entities that last a very long time, such as the ones mentioned above. When discussing civilizations Fernand Braudel states: 'The vocabulary of the social sciences, scarcely permits decisive definitions' (1994, 3). At the same time, humanists and social scientists must use the term while acknowledging its many historical connotations, starting with the debut in print of the term 'civilization' in 1756. While at first it was a term opposed to barbarism, in the nineteenth century it began to be used in the plural and assumed a very different meaning. So, to return to Samuel Huntington, while I do not agree with a number of his ideas, I do believe that the broad strokes with which he constructs different civilizations is a useful notion with the proviso that we acknowledge that we must not label individuals and groups on the basis of one or two distinctive character- istics.[12] Rather we must embrace the complexity of human identity and cultural interaction.

It is fascinating to note that both Christianity and Islam, although they emerged as religions, became the basis for two very different civi- lizations. As Braudel notes: 'As Christianity inherited from the Roman empire of which it was a prolongation, so Islam instantly took hold of the Near East, perhaps the world's oldest crossroads of civilized hu- manity. The consequences were immense. Muslim civilization made its own a series of ancient geographical obligations, urban patterns, institutions, habits, rituals and age-old approaches to faith and to life itself' (1994, 41). Thus, somewhere between the mythical creation of the columns of Hercules and the advent of the Spanish Habsburgs, a new civilization also came into being: 'Originating in the Arabian peninsula in the seventh century A.D., Islam rapidly spread across north Africa and the Iberian peninsula and also eastward into central Asia, the Subcontinent, and Southeast Asia' (Huntington 1996, 45). For Huntington, fourteen hundred years of history have demonstrated the continuing clashes between Islam and the West (1996, 209). It must, of course, be noted, that no civilization is homogeneous and static. Each is made up of different cultures and it is always changing and evolv- ing. The 'clash' of cultures that Huntington proposes ignores other in- teractions that were more complex, dynamic, sometimes cooperative, and more socially ambiguous than the dualistic oppositions encour- aged by his approach. It also sets aside the notion that a civilization that stands as an Other is often used to unite a people through sim- plistic slogans of enmity or what Lluís Basset, discussing our present circumstances, calls 'la apremiante necesidad de un enemigo de gran envargadura, capaz de polarizar y movilizar a las decaídas sociedades occidentales' [the urgent need to find a great enemy, capable of polar- izing and mobilizing the decaying western societies (2010, 130)]. While Huntington emphasizes the clash of civilizations, such confrontations are tempered in this book by underlining places and periods of coex- istence, mutuality, and even understanding. It is also buffered by the Jewish and *converso* presence in Golden Age Spain and in Cervantes' novel. How does this group fit within the clash of civilizations? While two civilizations seem to oppose each other, the Jews stand in the middle, their culture becoming an Other to both. Turning to the subject of this book, we may wonder, for example, why the Christian knight's preoccupations with the Moors and Saracens are at times shadowed by the Jewish question.

Given that Spain encompassed a strong Islamic component for over seven hundred years of its history (711–1492), and that Habsburg Spain became the centre for Western expansionism in the sixteenth century, it would make sense that the *plus ultra* which is being studied as a literary trope in this book is also 'contaminated' by clashes and conciliations with Islam. Cervantes was particularly aware of such moments since he was held captive in Algiers for five years. There he was faced with a society very different from his own, one that incarcerated him but one that was far more open. There he would have witnessed how renegades were able to quickly climb in society. This would contrast with his own experience at home where *moriscos* (converted Moors) were always suspect and were eventually expelled from Spain. In Algiers as well as in other North African ports, the language of trade (as well as that of lawless piracy) opened new spaces. It would be fitting to claim that Algiers in the sixteenth and seventeenth centuries was a much more cosmopolitan city than Madrid. Indeed, Cervantes' novel foregrounds the clash of civilizations as both a literary clash and a nuanced negotiation: the Arabic narrator seems to have very little esteem for his subject, a would-be Christian knight. At the same time, his image and his ideology fluctuate, as he appears at times to be writing as a Christian. This fluctuation may well echo the openness of Algiers, where Muslims, Christians, and renegades lived together. Indeed, renegades would often turn back to their former religion when returning home, thus increasing contamination over clash. And Algiers was not alone in its hybridity. As Maria Antonia Garces states: 'In the sixteenth and seventeenth centuries, the frontiers, although clearly demarcated, were fluid and permeable in every direction, especially so for those who had multiple identities such as the Jews, the Moriscos and the renegades from different points of the Mediterranean' (2002, 74). Cide Hamete represents both the clash of civilizations and the ability of different peoples to abide together in relative peace. He is both the enemy of the Christian knight and a figure that fuses and confuses cultures and civilizations. As will be seen later, Don Quixote can also be viewed in this manner, as a figure that can abide among the Other. But let us return for the moment to the knight's metaphorical conquests of genre.

Common wisdom has it that *Don Quixote* includes within its pages a number of different forms of prose narrative. Cervantes' interest in collecting different forms and genres may be due to the fact that collectionism was rising throughout Europe. The aristocracy would create cabinets of curiosities, or adorn their palaces with the best works of art. This was considered a mark of distinction. Cervantes, then, uses collectionism within one text: he displays Don Quixote's library and he also moves through a series of genres, combining and changing them. By transforming the objects displayed he comes up with something totally new. Such is Cervantes' metamorphic ability that today, even though books of chivalry are not read, his work remains one of the greatest classics of literature, not just in the West but throughout the world. Thus, chivalric texts are constantly collected in the novel, be it as books in the knight's library or as episodes throughout the novel. The novel serves as a parody of this genre, which many have asserted had almost disappeared by the time Cervantes penned it. This is actually not quite true – recent discoveries have shown that such novels continued to be written, albeit remaining in manuscript. Furthermore, they were used for courtly spectacles. Thus, in collecting the chivalric, Cervantes is being doubly fashionable (and not at all out of fashion as some would contend). His book appropriates both the collectionist propensity of the upper classes and the uses of chivalry as a playful mode to assert authority. By turning these into carnivalesque episodes, Cervantes' text both asserts and questions fashions and authority.

A second type of fiction that he utilized was the picaresque. In Cervantes' novel, the character of Ginés de Pasamonte embodies this genre. Ginés is writing an account of his picaresque deeds, claiming: 'Es tan bueno . . . que mal año para *Lazarillo de Tormes* y para todos cuanto de aquel género se han escrito o escribieren' [So good . . . that woe to Lazarillo de Tormes and to all that have written or shall write in that way] (1978, 1.22.271; 1998, 169). Although he points to the *Lazarillo,* his tale seems closer to the *Guzmán de Alfarache,* where the picaresque protagonist composes his tale as a galley slave much like Ginés. The many allusions to the picaresque in Cervantes' novel could well be the subject of a book – moving from the picaresque innkeeper who knights Don Quixote to the strange theft of Sancho's beast.[13] While the chivalric represents a longing for idealized chivalric-aristocratic values, thus looking at the past, the picaresque points to the present and the future. It reflects a society where traditional hierarchies are put under pressure with the rise of individualism and with the development of a bourgeoisie that did not have aristocratic privileges. As Richard Bjornson asserts: 'The situation was rendered more complex by the fact that the nascent bourgeoisie of fifteenth-and sixteenth-century Spain was largely composed of *conversos* (converts to Catholicism) with Jewish ancestors. Permanently alienated from the Jewish culture which they had abjured, as well as from the Christian one in which they had to live, these *conversos* could hardly escape an awareness of their own compromised identity, even if they succeeded in passing as Old Christians' (1977, 17–18). For Bjornson, the picaresque rises from this anxiety and many of its authors are *conversos* – and so are their protagonists. As such, the *pícaro* stands in contradistinction to the idealized knights of romances and even to the more impoverished but still noble *hidalgos*. But the picaresque, although it may have been born out of bourgeois and *converso* writers, also focuses on the poor and their plight. Anne J. Cruz clearly pinpoints and expands the subject of the picaresque: 'In a country where homogeneity was desired at any price such marginalized subalterns as the poor, criminals, *conversos, moriscos* and prostitutes shifted easily into the position of the Other, filling the void left by the leper' (1999, xvi). These novels, then, were written as a critique of social mores and as failed attempts at reform. They may not have been received as such: 'The authors' critical thrust is nevertheless thwarted when the public, in order to insulate itself against social change, converts the pícaro to the risible category of the clown . . . transformed into the liminal position of scapegoat through the symbolic unconscious of the new nation-state' (1999, xvi). From the start, then, Cervantes creates a clash of genres: the backwards looking and aristocratic chivalric vs the forward-gazing, critical, and polemical picaresque. This clash of genres reverberates with a clash of cultures and civilizations since the pure-blood Christian knight contrasts with the tainted *pícaro* whose ancestors may belong to a civilization that was warring with the West, Islam.

Some critics have seen traces of the sentimental novel in Cardenio's episode, where the crazed lover wonders among the crags and forests of Sierra Morena much as a savage, an allegory for Desire, roams the depths of Sierra Morena in Diego de San Pedro's *Cárcel de amor*.[14] Indeed, as Marina Brownlee reminds us, 'Grimalte, Panfilo and Arnalte become wild men as a result of their total alienation from society and its language' (1990, 211). In Cervantes, Don Quixote's penitence takes place in the kind of forbidding landscape common to the sentimental. For Brownlee, such places reflect 'the inability of the individual to control his environment through language' (1990, 212). We may consider whether Don Quixote, after the adventure with the galley slaves, has come to realize that he can no longer impose his verbal visions on the quotidian world. While the sentimental delights in wild and forbidding landscapes, the pastoral (thus its name) depicts idealized nature, the quintessence of perfection. The pastoral novel, a genre also taken up by Cervantes in *La Galatea*, pops up in many Cervantine narrative spaces, from the tale of Marcela and Grisóstomo to an imagined Arcadia. And yet, pastoral is often said to flourish at times when cultures are in crisis. Indeed, Don Quixote's pastoral will be imagined by an Arab, thus foregrounding that Spain was far from being a peaceful pleasance in this period. To these genres must be added the Byzantine or Greek novel, which may be gleaned, amid other genres, in the cluster of love stories that gather around Sierra Morena. And these tales that we might imagine as clustering into Greek novels, if seen individually recall the Italian *novella*. The reader can certainly find a foremost descendant of this form in the tale of the *Curioso impertinente*. There are many other genres through which the knight gallops. Celestinesque elements are foregrounded starting with the preliminary verses that claim that *Celestina* is a 'libro en mi opinión, divi[no] / si encubriera más lo huma[no]' [would be, in my opinion, a divine book if it would cover human (flaws)] (1978, 1.65). Some of its elements later reappear in one of the tales told by one of the galley slaves, etc. This book will foreground some of these genres, and introduce many others as well. While the novels of chivalry, the Italian romances, the Greek romances, the Italianate *novelle*, the imperial epic, the epic of the defeated, the pastoral novel, the sentimental novel, and other territories of genre will be traversed, others will remain outside the scope of this brief study. Theatre, farce, fables, and the rhetoric of speech-making may be named but will wait for others to further develop them.

Cervantes divides his novel into four parts, but I argue that it can be better divided into five segments and will thus point to four or even five moments when the 1605 *Don Quixote* reaches the end of a particular narrative thread; by changing course so as to be able to surmount the barrier, new discoveries are made as the narrative is allowed to go beyond its generic limits.[15] Perhaps it is this ability to surpass these blockages that allowed the modern novel to come into existence. And perhaps we can even see Cervantes' knight as a ghostly incarnation riding the horse that carried the motto *Plus ultra* at Charles V's funeral procession in Brussels.[16] Charles V, like Don Quixote, suffered a deep melancholy, a humour that attracted ghosts and visions. In Titian's paintings of the emperor, his yellowed constitution is often hidden with a golden light so as to preserve decorum. Don Quixote, on the other hand, is often referred to as having a yellow constitution, a mark of melancholy (De Armas 2006, 131–2). While some have claimed that Charles suffered from melancholy for many years (at least since 1545), Robert Burton prefers to view it as a mark of old age in people who 'had great employment' (1938, 183). When melancholy takes hold of such people, they abandon their worldly pursuits 'and leave off as Charles the Fifth did to King Philip, resign up all on a sudden. They are over-come with melancholy in an instant' (1938, 183). In other words, Burton marks the onslaught of melancholy to the time right before 1556, when Charles abdicated the crown and left for a secluded monastery at Yuste. It is at Yuste that the once-emperor became more and more ghostly: 'As his infirmities increased, his prayers grew longer, and his penances more severe . . . Restless and sleepless, ghost like, he would roam the corridors of the convent' (Stirling 1851, 533; Franklin 1961, 467). Don Quixote, then, resembles this ghostly emperor in his last days. Even more so since the knight rides long after Charles's demise and fills his travels with strange visions. Studying Herman Melville's *Benito Cereno*, H. Bruce Franklin compares the main character to Charles V and con-cludes that, like the emperor after he abdicates, he becomes 'the sym-bolic ghost of all power' (1961, 463). Like Cereno, Don Quixote is a ghost of power. But rather than retiring from the world, he enters the world and seeks power through melancholy visions. The emptiness of this pursuit, I argue, makes him into a ghost of all power. Charles's power is only a ghostly illusion in Cervantes' knight. He is a ghost haunted by visions which are trapped in a text – a text which, in turn, is supposed to have been written by an enchanter. The power does not belong to the knight. It belongs to the ghostly writer who sends him to conquer genres rather than lands.

Don Quixote's road, always interrupted by the excess, by the lim-its of parody or exhaustion of possibilities, may also recall the Roman *cursus publicus*, the Roman roads used to relay messages to all corners of the empire. Perhaps the roads taken by our imperious knight also send messages – messages of genre choices that can be deciphered. Some thirty years ago, Derrida seemed to announce the death of the study of genre through deconstruction: 'It is precisely a principle of contamination, a law of impurity, a parasitical economy' (1980, 59). But today, critics such as Ralph Cohen, Joseph Farrell, Alastair Fowler, and Thomas Pavel have taken up with new intensity the analysis of genre.[17]

Cohen explains that, while some features in a text strengthen the link to the genre, others are individualized and loosen it. Fowler adds that the new discoveries of the Renaissance and early modern periods brought back ancient genres and helped in the development of new ones.[18] But the fact that literary genres are unstable does not mean that they are not useful roadmaps. We need to accept that a text may follow the general *cursus* of a genre, but have its own aims. According to Pavel, we also need to accept that genres 'first and most obviously . . . change with time, as the comparison between Greek and Renaissance tragedy shows' (2003a, 201). And, as Farrell has shown, we need to recognize that theory often belies practice and that authors purposefully contaminate their work with other genres.[19] Thus Pavel's proposition is a practical one: 'To see genre as a set of good recipes, or good habits of the trade, oriented towards the achievement of definite artistic goals, makes the instability of generic categories less puzzling and less threatening. Genres . . . are unstable because the goals pursued by writers with their help vary' (2003a, 210). As we move ahead, we will see how Cervantes keeps changing strategies as the limits of a particular use of a genre or genres are reached or breached. But the goal of the narrative remains the same – to take the knight through impassable obstacles in an indomitable expansion of the *cursus* so as to conquer the diverse places of narrative and through this *cursus*, create a cohesive textual empire.

Empire and the novel seem to have little in common. It was thought that empire belonged to epic and epic fashioned a hero who represented and/or served to found a community. The novelistic genre, after all, was to deal with the particular rather than the great changes in history. Nor was the novel closely linked to the romances, rising from the rejection of these works, particularly the *Amadís de Gaula*, which enjoyed immense popularity in sixteenth-century Spain, France, and England. The *Amadís* fed upon the roots of Arthurian romance and delighted in quests, knights, and kings. The world of enchantment was always nearby, generating grand theatrical clashes between good and evil. The novel would eschew polarity while the romances often represented a clash of civilizations where pagans and infidels were often presented as monstrous. Their 'evil' nature was further unravelled as they refused to convert to Christianity.[20] Works like the *Las sergas de Esplandián*, the *Belianís de Grecia*, or the Italian verse romances such as the *Orlando furioso* focused on the battle between the Saracen infidel and the Christians, thus mirroring a continuing historical clash. At the same time, they lacked many of the characteristics that critics today ascribe to the novel: interesting and even idiosyncratic individual characters; a well-made plot; the representation of reality in a more accurate and nuanced manner; the presence of metafiction and its corollary, the ability to experiment with genre. More important, the early novel as it developed after Cervantes, was supposed to be about the individual, not the kingdom or empire in which he/she lived, although its mores and customs would be significant. These texts were to be written about private and domestic matters, such as romantic love, marriage, sibling rivalries, friendship, etc. Many other characteristics could be added such as the presence of an unreliable narrator and a playfulness that indicated textual awareness that histories often included fiction so that the opposite could also be true.

It has been argued that *Don Quixote* came about at a crucial time, when books of chivalry were beginning to be disdained (except as matter for courtly entertainments) and new models were being sought to fill this void. The picaresque, although it may have developed in part from native models, pointed to the classical authority of Apuleius's *The Golden Ass*, while more aristocratic forms imitated Heliodorus's *Aethiopica* as well as other Greek romances of the Hellenistic period. Indeed, among learned circles the *Aethiopica* came to be regarded as a new model for the epic poem, as the highest genre of antiquity failed to create lasting masterpieces in the early modern period. Cervantes' last work, *Los trabajos de Persiles y Sigismunda*, is considered by the author to be his best work since it is an imitation of Heliodorus. In the *Aethiopica*, as in Cervantes' last work, the main plot is about love, not war. And the knights and questing figures of old become princes and pilgrims of love. Thus we can see how *Don Quixote* parodies the old and incorporates the new. Cervantes' work is a parody of chivalric novels. To accomplish this task, Cervantes creates a pair of unforgettable characters, and places them in some of the most comic and endearing situations that we have in any form of literature. These two characters were remembered from the start, as they paraded in carnival processions and appeared in comic skits. Harold Bloom judges their irascible and loving, caring relationship: 'I cannot think of a fully comparable friendship anywhere else in western literature' (1994, 123). And a knight placed in quotidian reality is certainly a perfect situation for parody. Indeed it is a book that for Eric Auerbach has no rival in its representation of reality (1968, 334–58). Don Quixote's monomania, his fantastic desire to become a knight, and even an emperor, has led him to be placed by Ian Watt among the four great literary prototypes of Western individualism, along with Faust, Don Juan, and Robinson Crusoe. Indeed, as Bloom asserts: 'For me, the heart of the book is its revelation and celebration of heroic individuality both in the Don and in Sancho' (1994, 122).

While Cervantes' novel clearly stresses and problematizes individuality, it is not all about reality. After all, a world of knights, giants, and enchanters in the mind of Don Quixote exists in contiguity with the quotidian. Many consider the knight, in his determined and yet mad stance, a hero. Perhaps the text represents the highest qualities of the human being; perhaps it is a modern epic. To the dryness of the landscape, to the dryness of the knight's brain, to the dryness of the gentleman's disposition, to the dryness of Don Quixote's vigils over the idealized vision of Dulcinea, the text adds a number of oases: the laughter of friends, and the interpolated love stories that add humidity to the dryness of the narrative. In any case, the prologue asserts that the novel is dry, lacking all adornment; later we learn that Don Quixote's brain dried up from too much reading. Melancholy and choleric men were thought to share in the quality of dryness. Women, on the other hand, were known for the opposite quality, humidity. In this manner, many early modern thinkers such as Juan Huarte de San Juan criticized women's intellect. And yet, the feminine was needed in the world and in the world of texts since it added moistness to the environment thus allowing life to thrive. Genre and gender thus intermingle, as the dryness of male epic and chivalric tales contrasts with the humidity of the love stories. It also seems as if the male narratives are often linear, while the humidity of the love tales is more labyrinthine. It is as if Cervantes' novel were offering the reader an intimation of genres as being gendered.

These 'humid' amorous plots of the interpolations resemble those of the Italian *novelle*, short fiction that develops a comic or an amorous episode. The comic Boccaccio and the tragic Bandello come together here to add complexity of form. And by clustering these *novelle*, and narrating them in parts, leapfrogging from one to the other, Cervantes gives them the appearance of episodes in the Greek romances which were often presented through the technique of interlace.[21] Indeed, such interweaving was also common in the Italian romances such as the *Orlando furioso*. And to a much lesser extent, they could be found in the quests and adventures of the chivalric. Furthermore the interpolated stories in *Don Quixote*, as Dominick Finello observes, can themselves be linked to various genres: pastoral (Marcela and Grisóstomo), sentimental (Cardenio and Luscinda), *cortesana* (Don Fernando and

Dorotea), and exemplary (Anselmo and Camila) (1994, 120). That the use of *novelle* would lead to what is perhaps the first early modern novel is thus very fitting, since the earlier term, referring to news, is now transformed into a new genre.

The novel is indeed a novel genre, one that arises from experimentation with older forms,[22] and from the moving from one to the next, making detours through genres to arrive at yet another one. Indeed, this recalls what Ross Chambers has labelled as 'loiterature': 'Critical as it may well be behind its entertaining façade, loiterly writing disarms criticism of itself by presenting a moving target, shifting as its own divided attention often shifts' (1999, 9). Cervantes' novel, although proposing to satirize romances of chivalry, is always experimenting with genre, moving from one to the next almost without warning. While it criticizes chivalry, it seeks to avoid criticism by moving here and there and by forging a comic masterpiece that hides the many experiments. Cervantes goes even further, not restricting himself to known literary genres. He also imitates and parodies the Inquisitional indexes, volumes on hagiography, medical and mythological manuals, mnemonic guidebooks, scientific tracts, etc. Today we see *Don Quixote* as a mark of originality, as something totally new. As E.C. Riley asserts, beginning with the second half of the nineteenth century 'era poco menos una grosería por parte del crítico sugerir que el Quijote no era del todo original' [it became a gaffe for critics to assert that Quixote was not fully original] (1962, 98). Michel Foucault hails Cervantes' novel as the mark of a new episteme, 'the negative of the Renaissance world' (1970, 47); George Lukács sees it as the death-knell of a world permeated by belief, as the moment in which the hero is separated from the sacred. While the novel reflects alienation, fragmentation, and the lack of belief, the epic once portrayed a world that made sense and that could be comprehended in its totality (1971, 56–63). Anthony J. Cascardi has carried the notion of secularization further, explaining: 'We must regard this process not just as the result of a change in the patterns of religious belief but as a master-trope for the problem of authority as it is figures within literary history' (1997, 211). While ancient and Renaissance texts often used authorities from the past and welcomed authority, the novel questions such authorities, creating unreliable narrators and experimental forms that take us to the present. Nowadays the novel, in many cases, no longer seeks to approach reality. It should thus come as no surprise that the juxtaposition of Cervantes' novel and the postmodern world has yielded significant reevaluations, including Eric C. Graf's contention that Cervantes' turn toward women characters in opposition to epic adventures plays an important role in the evolution of modern feminist consciousness,[23] and Bruce R. Burningham's use of Cervantes to view contemporary texts and films and vice-versa.[24] And yet, in this book I would look back rather than forward and see how Cervantes' novel actually arises from a series of genres which he juxtaposes, parodies, or takes to extremes, some of which, as stated before, are not even considered as literary genres. As Cascardi states: 'The "invention" of the novel resulted from the re-fashioning of literary genres already in place, and Don Quixote stands in relation to the origin of the novel not as the invention of something radically new, but as the uncovering of new possibilities for the combination of elements that preexisted it' (2002, 59). Among the early elements and traditions we have both the epic and the books of chivalry, where kings and emperors play their roles. Following Virgil, then, Cervantes will introduce a new Augustus Caesar into his work – the emperor Charles V, albeit in a subtle and ambiguous manner. Cervantes' novel is not just about private concerns but also about questions of empire. And the novel, when viewed through the angle of genre, can also reveal that Foucault's insight is not fully applicable. It is not just the knight who lives in a world of magic and analogy. The narrative, as will be seen, although laughing at the theatrical magic of chivalric books, is complicit in magical thinking, utilizing both the revival of the magic of antiquity in the Renaissance and the heterodox magic of the Other.

But, are we deceived in looking for 'higher' genres in Cervantes' novel? Is it just a carnivalesque work or written in a humorous style? While the 'author' in the Prologue is portrayed as worrying that he is unable to write a prologue and that his book is too dry, a friend comes in and advises him on how to adorn his text with all the great authorities from antiquity and from Christianity. Having mocked through his advice how many writers clothe themselves in erudition by simply borrowing catch phrases in Latin or including abstruse names that can be footnoted, the friend ends up by telling the 'author' that he needs none of the above: 'Este vuestro libro no tiene necesidad de ninguna cosa de aquellas que vos decís que le falta, porque todo él es una invectiva contra los libros de caballerías, de quien nunca se acordó Aristóteles, ni dijo nada San Basilio ni alcanzó Cicerón' [This book of yours has no need of these ornaments you say it wants; for it is only an invective against the books of chivalry, which sort of books Aristotle never dreamed of, Saint Basil never mentioned, nor Cicero once heard of] (1978, 1.57; 1998,

19). Is the Prologue then mocking those who would look for authoritative genres where there are none? Or, is this Prologue a criticism of Lope de Vega's erudite strategies? Lope's *El Isidro* (1599), for example, contains a wealth of citations in the margins and a list of 267 authors cited, while *El peregrino en su patria*, an imitation of the Greek novel, has a table of more than 150 authors (Clemencín ed. 1833, 1.1.liv). Even though the friend's advice serves to satirize Lope de Vega's practices, *Don Quixote* incorporates at least some of the (fictional) friend's advice. The friend tells the author to include Cacus (1978, 1.56; 1998, 18) and later, the innkeeper is described as being thievish as Cacus (1978, 1.2.84; 1998, 29). Horace and Julius Caesar, Aristotle and Goliath are all figures from the Prologue that have significance in the novel. And, as Carolyn Nadeau has shown, the friend's advice to include references to Ovid's Medea, Virgil's Circe, and Homer's Calypso is carried out in the text of the novel. Dulcinea as a Circe-like enchantress and Maritornes as a Calypso figure show that 'Cervantes' treatment of female characters is a case of imitation and invention, in which he discovers the possibilities of artistic expression that lay dormant in earlier representations' (2002, 19). The question remains: how can Cervantes parody Lope's classical learning and yet turn to such stories himself in the construction of his novel?

Learning, as Don Quixote exemplifies, comes with intense study and is acquired at great peril. Cervantes portrays Lope as entranced by outer trappings, while *Don Quixote* exhibits an apparent simplicity and a textual integrity. While Lope commits the sin of 'pretentiousness,'[25] Cervantes carefully covers up his own learned subtexts, appearing to deauthorize imitation through the friend's advice. What he shows in the Prologue are two false forms of learning. The friend uses erudition to satisfy vanity and pretentiousness, while Don Quixote will use reading in such an extreme manner as to fail to distinguish between his own voice and perceptions and the worlds of the fictions he reads. Chivalric fictions are poisoning the knight's mind through this inability to distinguish the text of the world from fiction. While the knight mixes the quotidian and the fictive, Cervantes' novel, on the other hand, disallows the total identification between reader and text through a series of techniques that will distance the readers and allow them to see the mechanics of writing.[26] By calling upon active readers, the text also calls upon them to see how the mechanics of writing are inextricably linked to the process of imitation. Cervantes will then imitate other genres and take them to extremes, or contaminate them with other genres. In so doing, he creates new forms and new ways of perceiving. Thomas M. Greene has brilliantly demonstrated the range and scope of imitation of ancient authorities and genres during the Renaissance – a range that covered the sacramental imitation, where the pre-text could never be surpassed and was viewed as supreme, as well as the eclectic or exploitative imitation or contamination which 'treats all traditions as stockpiles to be drawn upon ostensibly at random,' thus creating a series of 'ahistorical citations' (1982, 38–9), and more complex and thoughtful forms, such as heuristic imitation where there is more of a conversation between the texts.

In many ways, Cervantes converses with readers, texts, and genres, always reaching for something new, for a new kind of inventiveness: 'el discreto se admire de la invención' [the judicious may admire the invention] (1978, 1.58; 1998, 20). He does so, first of all, by tackling books of chivalry and allowing the reader to understand how these books infect the mind of the would-be knight and, in so doing, make him view the world from the perspective of a type of fiction that delights in giants, monsters, dwarves, magicians, and a cosmic battle between good and evil with theatrical props and supernatural conflicts. The deranged character, then, foregrounds the excesses of a genre. In so doing, Cervantes' novel turns to a very ancient genre, that of parody. The term has a classical pedigree since it was used by Aristotle in the *Poetics* to refer to a writer, Hegemon, who wrote poems of grand epic style and structure while dealing with a much lighter subject. Only one ancient example of *parodia* is preserved: the *Batrachomymachi* (*Battle of the Frogs and Mice*). On the other hand, satyr plays (the origins of satire) often followed a tragic trilogy and placed grand mythological figures in a ridiculous situation.[27] Again, we have preserved but one in its entirety, Euripides' *Cyclops*. Although in ancient Greece parody and satire were different genres, today we seem to conflate them, as parody acquires a spectrum of meanings. For Linda Hutcheon, parody is very similar to the concept of imitation, as authors rewrite a well-known text in a more contemporary manner, while for Margaret Rose, parody is related to metafiction, as a text mirrors its fictional practices. There are some who view parody as a subversive genre, while others see it as conservative since it ridicules innovation. All four of these types of parody as well as the classical notions of *parodia* and satire are present in *Don Quixote*. We need only recall the hyperbolic language that the 'author' (only in the crazed knight's imagination) would use to tell of Don Quixote's exploits; or the famous battle between two armies of sheep, told by Don Quixote as if this was a confrontation between a Christian and a pagan army. Turning to satire, the knight often thinks of himself as a new Hercules, only to fail in all his labours in a foolhardy manner.

Turning to the four types of parody described above, we can ascertain that, throughout his novel, Cervantes imitates well-known texts, from epics to books of chivalry, thus following Hutcheon's strictures. Throughout the text, as Rose prescribes, fictional practices are foregrounded – such as the sudden appearance of a historian/magus who will tell the tale of the knight, Cide Hamete Benengeli. Indeed, in books of chivalry, many of the authors are from remote and even pagan areas. The device of the manuscript that is discovered and then translated is yet another of the many practices that are mirrored. As for the controversy concerning subversive versus conservative, we can say that Cervantes' text questions the hierarchical structures of the romances as well as the clear differentiation between good and evil. Throughout, Cervantes uses a series of genres not merely to imitate but also to innovate. The work also incorporates the conservative stance through Don Quixote's own outward behaviour. He rejects a series of modern technologies that threaten the survival of the medieval knights. At the same time, the work as a whole, in poking fun at the gentleman from La Mancha, destabilizes the conservative viewpoint. Of course, nothing is so simple in *Don Quixote*. The knight, while proclaiming himself a Christian knight, attacks clerics, and while envisioning empire, he rejects the justice of the king as in the case of the galley slaves. Parody, then, does not just critique one particular set of ideas. It critiques the notion of simple polarities.

Simon Dentith asserts that Don Quixote is considered the first European novel because it is a parody (2000, 56). As such, it predates a number of other works with a similar generic bent: 'Sheep are misrecognized as dauntless knights; laundry boxes will be mistaken for Gothic chests (*Northanger Abbey*); provincial seducers will be doted over as heroes of romance (*Madame Bovary*)' (2000, 58). In many ways, novels will parody different types of idealized or romance fiction, works that present a luminous aristocratic world where polarities of good and evil create tremendous clashes that impede the creation of complex characters or the problematization of moral dilemmas. As Robert Alter states: 'It is hardly a coincidence that a number of important novelists – Cervantes, Fielding, Jane Austen, Thackeray – started out writing parodies, for the sense of realism in the novel often depends upon a parodist's awareness of the awkward disparity between things as they really are and things as they are conventionally represented in literature' (1968, 101–2). Cervantes' novel can have its cake and eat it too: it parodies chivalry through the imaginings of the knight who sees ladies in distress, giants, and contending armies everywhere. On another level, the novel creates a sense of reality or at least of verisimilitude, through the careful description of characters and places in a forgotten part of Spain, La Mancha. Innkeepers, goatherds, prostitutes, picaresque figures, galley slaves, merchants, friars, judges, and even second sons of the nobility parade through a rustic landscape that has little to do with chivalry and much to do with the quotidian. But, as the everyday is transformed into ridiculous excess by the knight's imagination, the novel comes to life.[28]

Dentith explains that parody serves as trigger for the modern European novel: 'At the very center of this prototype is the integral use of parody, used often to indicate the delusive mentality of the protagonist or other characters, and as a weapon in the culture wars in which the novel is engaged' (2000, 59). Throughout *Don Quixote*, culture wars will indeed rage. The knight will seek to represent a glorious imperial past, while his actions will show that the mores of such a period could be questioned. Indeed, the knight, while in some ways parodying Charles V, also holds tight to a secret, to a mysterious cause that impels him to leave home and undertake his mission. This secret, I will argue, will eventually be glimpsed in chapters 45 and 46, through the subject the knight chooses to imitate when imagining a new adventure. Although derived from the Italian romances, the subject will be another. The mystery will serve to further unravel the culture wars within the text. Thus, although the terms 'parody' and 'imitation' will not be used extensively in this analysis, the study of genres from picaresque to epic and from chivalric to the Italian romances, will have these two terms as underpinnings. Parody is a type of imitation. It is far from being sacramental. Instead, Dentith defines it thus: 'Parody includes any cultural practice which provides a relatively polemical allusive imitation of another cultural production or practice' (2000, 9). In Cervantes, this polemic serves to question many of the assumptions proposed in the books of chivalry. Parody also extends to many other genres that, by clashing with each other, will expose some of their limits and presuppositions. Cervantes will use his crazed knight to gallop through a series of genres and conquer them through laughter and excess, through imitation and subversion, but most importantly, through invention and slight of hand. After all, readers who turn to the funny and humane adventures of knight and squire often feel that there is something hidden, something magical about the book that is just beyond their reach. The Romantic school of criticism delves deeply into hidden symbols. Perhaps esoteric theories concerning Cervantes' masterpiece do not reach the extent they have with Shakespeare but there are even those who go so far as to claim that the novel hides an abstruse allegory on religion. One critic, for example, asserts that when the knight dismounts from his horse or falls from it, it can signify the death of a pope or the sack of Rome (Camamis 1991, 1150–1); and when Sancho sleeps, a tragic fate awaits yet another pope through a strangely embedded calendar in the text.[29] Such excesses derive from the feeling that Cervantes' novel, very much like Henry James's stories, contains what Tzvetan Todorov labels as 'an essential secret, of something which is not named' (1977, 145). A novel as expansive as Cervantes' text goes well beyond one essential secret.[30] This book seeks to examine one key secret in the novel through an analysis of genre clashes and transformations, through an examination of the main character's actions and motivations, and through brief glimpses at the uncertainties created by a lack of an omniscient narrator.

Indeed, the Arabic narrator, Cide Hamete, conceals the secret, while propounding his animosity toward the gentleman from La Mancha. Only when the knight's actions begin to point to the secret will Cide Hamete become less adversarial. Indeed, in a narrative play, the text may want the reader to imagine how Cide Hamete fills the novel with words of Arabic origin. These have been recently detailed by Gamal Abdel-Karim, starting with *alcuza* and ending with *zalá* (2006, 46–55).[31] Cide Hamete is a complex figure. He is often praised in the text, although at one point we are told that he comes from a nation of liars. And his name Benengeli is polyvalent. Could it mean, as Sancho thinks, an eater of eggplant (*berenjena*)? Or is it something more complicated? Marcilly and Bencheneb propose that it serves to deny his Islamic religion, since *ben-engeli* means son of the Gospel and not of the Koran (1966, 97–116). Or, as Mahmud Ali Makki contends: 'Podría haber sido inspirado en el apellido de una ilustre familia hispanomusulmana, vecina de la ciudad de Denia cuyos miembros eran destacadas figuras en las ciudades de Levante entre los siglos XI y XIII' [His last name could have been inspired by that of an illustrious Hispano-Muslim family who lived in Denia and whose members were well-known figures in southern cities during the eleventh and twelfth centuries] (2006, 226). Thus, onomastics, the foundational principle so often used in the novel, yields a full range of possibilities. The name could be funny, thus parodying the great sages of the romances; it could simply highlight his Islamic faith; it could hide an anti-Islamic secret; or it could refer to a well-known Hispano-Muslim family. I would say that the name encompasses all of these meanings, concealing the mystery of diversity.

But Don Quixote's names and actions hide a much bigger secret.[32] Following Todorov, there is a double movement toward and away from the revelation. In the end, all that can be said is that the play of genre and narrative may point to a specific hidden mystery, one that deals with a clash of civilizations and the anxieties it causes the protagonist.[33] This secret both complements and contrasts with the vision of a knight as a ghostly Charles V. Don Quixote as a new Charles is deprived of all power except that of the imagination as he rides through the genres. He personifies an emperor who upon abdication has become 'the ghost of all power.' While the emperor repeatedly walks the halls of the monastery thinking of his past achievements and hollow present, the knight rides through an impoverished Spain, seeking the power that Charles discarded, only to find visions less substantial than his emaciated body. It may be that his haunting is there to warn those who sympathize with the knight that the imperial pursuits of the narrative are flawed, that the secret must be revealed. Indeed, the narrative is filled with ghosts that haunt the text and the knight. We may recall that Derrida has fostered the study of what he calls 'hauntology' (1994, 10). I will use the ghostly in a different manner, seeking to glimpse at the mysteries that hide between worlds and between genres. In a sense, this study comes closer to Todorov's view of the ghosts in Henry James, who are interpreted as part of the secret of narrative. While no one (except Sancho) really believes in Don Quixote's ghosts, he does, creating a kind of hesitation in the novel that points to Todorov's notion of the fantastic.[34] But the ghosts in the novel are there to point to an absence, to that which is missing and cannot be fully recaptured: 'the core of a story will often be an absence . . . and its quest will be the only possible presence' (1977, 184). Although we are delighted by the permutations of Don Quixote's quest, and we may even laugh at the ghostly appearances in the novel, there are secrets here that defy disclosure. As Todorov argues: 'In order for this ever-absent cause to become present, it *must* be a ghost' (1977, 154). Don Quixote is surrounded by the absent, by ghosts, as he unwittingly conceals the secrets of the narrative. But the novel makes his exploits even more mysterious. If Don Quixote stands for a ghostly Charles V, then what we have is a near impossibility – a ghost that is being haunted by other ghosts.

Ghosts are ever-present in sixteenth- and seventeenth-century literature. Elizabethan theatre is filled with hauntings. As Michael Hattaway
has shown, terrifying ghosts made for excellent theatre. They were such
a commonplace that their dreaded appearance was mocked in comic
plays: 'And tell us of the worrying of a cat / and a filthy whining ghost'
(2005, 112). In Thomas Kyd's *Cornelia*, for example the ghost of Pompey,
pale, gnashing teeth, and with scarce skin comes to her with a dire tale
(2005, 112). The Spanish stage was also filled with apparitions. Henryk
Ziomek points to 'Lope de Vega's fondness for presenting ghosts on
the stage' (1984, 66). But, to what purpose? Ghosts often serve to create
awe among the public, and to fill with dread scenes of tragedy. No one
can forget the shadow that warns Don Alonso of his coming doom in
El caballero de Olmedo [*The Knight of Olmedo*]. Ghosts also have another
important use: to whisper a secret from the past, an awful event that
returns them to a world now alien to them. Two examples will suffice:
Hamlet's ghost comes to warn the prince of a terrible secret. We may
read of a haunting similar to Shakespeare's in a play ascribed to Lope
de Vega, *Dineros son calidad*. These hollow beings impel the living to
action. And this is precisely what happens in *Don Quixote*, although
the ghosts' whispers are never heard. Throughout part 1, we hear in-
cessantly about ghosts. In chapter 17 the goings-on at the inn are attributes to Moorish ghosts; in chapter 19 a funeral procession in the night
seems like a ghostly apparition; and in chapter 20 a clanging of chains
make both Sancho and Don Quixote think they are in a ghost story.
These ghosts that haunt Don Quixote could well be visions created by
the excess of melancholy. Although this partially explains his imaginings, it says nothing of the secret they have come to reveal. This is the
mystery that will never be told, preserving the essential absence as key
to the text. At the same time, it is possible to build a theory overlaying
absence; it is possible to trace the figures on the carpet, the whispers of
the ghosts. These ghosts that pursue the ghostly knight are also ghosts
of a Christian empire that seeks to subject and exorcise the other.

The pages that follow, then, can be seen as a narrative that follows the
main narrative, focusing on clashes of genre, while revealing a deeper
clash and a more profound anxiety, one of civilizations. This metanarra-
tive, which seeks to follow the generic conflicts in the text, by no means
implies that Cervantes composed his text in a linear manner progress-
ing from certain challenges to others. He may have done so, but he
may also have worked in a much messier way than the final narrative
reveals. For example, Geoffrey Stagg attempts to prove that Cervantes

could have written the novel as a *novella*, and then, realizing the tale's potential, gone back and continued with the rest, revising previous chapters and adding others.[35] Stagg affirms that he is by far not the only critic to believe this: 'Muchos cervantistas comparten la opinión de que Cervantes, al empezar el *Quijote*, sólo pensó en escribir una novelita, y que luego cambió de plan' [Many Cervantistas share my opinion that Cervantes, when starting the *Quixote*, was only thinking of writing a novella, and then he changed his plan] (1964, 463). While some believe that the novella included the first six chapters, it can also be argued that it was to end with chapter 8. If this were so, Cervantes then took out the end of the battle with the Basque and began the second part of what now would be a lengthy work of prose fiction. He could have interpolated the Marcela and Grisóstomo tale even after he finished the first draft of the novel. Since we do not have manuscripts of the text, it is almost impossible to decide if he had the full narrative in mind when he set off to write his text or if he improvised as he went along.

My own view is that Cervantes probably had a general conception of what he was going to write and where this was going to lead him. He knew that he was going to deal with genre as a major question. He also knew some of the highlights of the plot: he was going to set his crazed knight on a quest where the obstacles were mainly in his mind. He was going to provide him with the basics he needed and send him out to prove himself both a fool and a visionary. And he was going to give him a lady, an imagined one. I also think that he foresaw that Dulcinea would be implicated in his failures. There is much, I think, that was planned. For example, Cervantes meant to have Don Quixote leave the road so that he and Sancho would go deeper into Sierra Morena. This would allow him to develop the notion of mystery and have the knight and Sancho start sleuthing around the Sierra, searching for the owner of a lost portmanteau and the meaning of a dead mule. Such sleuthing, with the repeated use of the word 'thread,' would beckon the active reader to delve deeper into the mysteries of Sierra Morena, both in terms of plot and genre. He meant to leave Don Quixote alone in Sierra Morena, in a *locus amoenus* with its spring, so that the topographical labyrinth that surrounded him would reflect the labyrinth of genres that would spring around him. And, the repeated imitation of the *Orlando furioso* was not just a way to deal with the Italian romances as one more genre. He chose the *Orlando*, not because it was particularly popular in Spain, but because it would allow him to reveal something very important about the knight. Thus, the discord at Agramante's camp would become the place where the genre would subtly reveal a major mystery and expose a most significant anxiety that plagued the gentleman from La Mancha. Let us look, then, at the ·proliferation, mutation, and clashes of genres; let us explore both the mystery of why Don Quixote set out on this mad mission and how the narrative would allow him to become a ghost of Charles V, conquering genres rather than territories. Let us ponder why the would-be Christian knight delights in abiding among the Saracens.[36]

The Novel's Structure and the Location of the Columns

Part 1:   A Pythagorean Parody of Chivalry. Chapters 1–8 (8 chapters)
Columns: The Knight and the Biscayan with Swords Upraised

Part 2:   An Arab's Audacious Pastoral. Chapters 9–14 (6 chapters)
Columns: Marcela's Celestial Hill and Grisóstomo's Grave

Part 3:   Magics of the Defeated. Chapters 15–22 (8 chapters)
Columns: Don Quixote and the Commissary

Part 4:   Greek Interlace. Chapters 23–46 (23 chapters)
Columns: Mambrino's Helmet and the Barber's Basin

1. Cardenio as Mystery
2. Clustered Mysteries
3. A Mysterious Constellation
4. The Mystery of the Saracens

Part 5:   The Quintessence. Chapters 47–52 (6 chapters)
Columns: *Plus ultra*

2 A Pythagorean Parody of Chivalry

I can't stop laughing . . . A lion skin over a yellow negligee! What's going
on? Why the high heel boots? Why the club?

– Aristophanes, *The Frogs*

The pillars of genre support and enclose the many narratives of *Don
Quixote*. By this I mean that Cervantes chooses a series of genres which
he would develop and transform in the course of a particular section of
the narrative. Within each segment, the genres provide both the stability of the known and the temptation of testing their boundaries. But
even while the narrative is transformed, it cannot go on indefinitely.
The rules that support it also keep it enclosed within certain boundaries. A point is reached where this particular path finds an ending,
where the *non plus ultra* looms with unknown and threatening possibilities. This will happen at least four times in the 1605 novel, so as to
create five narrative segments. Each time the narrative encounters an
impasse of such magnitude, the columns will appear in the novel in one
form or another. Something will represent them. They will signal the
end of that section of the novel. And indeed, in the 1615 novel, which
is beyond the scope of this book, the actual columns will be invoked to
move from one type of narrative to another.[1]

The first burst of narrative is comprised of the first eight chapters
of the 1605 novel.[2] These chapters form a kind of narrative unit based
on four key principles: the structure of the romances of chivalry; the
contamination of the chivalric with other genres; the disruption of the
knightly path through parody; and the use of Pythagorean numerology
so as to create cosmos. Obviously, having a hidalgo too old for chivalric

pursuits, who wishes to engage in a battle with imaginary enemies and speaks in hyperbole about his deeds as his adventures are held in ridicule, easily fits the third impetus for narrative, one that is centred on parody. In ancient times, Aristophanes parodied the serious drama of Aeschylus and Euripides in *The Frogs*. But he did more than that. In this antique comedy, Dionysus disguises himself as Heracles as he attempts to enter Hades in order to revive the ancient writers of tragedy. When his half-brother, Heracles, sees Dionysus dressed like him, sporting a club and covered with a lion skin, he cannot help but laugh. Indeed, as Dionysus and his slave exchange the Heracles costume back and forth depending on the occasion, laughter always ensues. In many ways, Dionysus as a parody of Heracles is very much like Don Quixote as a parody of Heracles/Hercules, a hero that the knight wants to emulate. In fact, at one point in the novel the Herculean hero imitates Dionysus thus recalling Aristophanes' comedy. Cervantes uses ancient parody, but also seeks a new context: Don Quixote as a parody of chivalric heroes. While Aristophanes parodies the tragedies of his time exclaiming: 'I need a poet that can really *write!*' (2007, 136), Cervantes parodies the romances of his period, pointing to their excesses – like the new poets of antiquity, these writers cannot write. Discussing 'the tradition within the modern novel from *Don Quixote* to *Vanity Fair* for which parody is an essential component' (2000, 21), Simon Dentith recognizes that the apparent destructiveness of parodic texts can create new fictions, from *Don Quixote* to *Tristram Shandy* (2000, 15).[3] Indeed, it may be that the clashes of genre that we are going to discuss have their origins in parody. But there is a thin line in Cervantes between parody and emulation. While the threat of contamination through laughter and mockery moves to undo the chivalric narrative, it is buttressed by the magic of Pythagorean numerology which creates a well-wrought text through cosmos.

The work, as we all know, both imitates and mocks the romances of chivalry. The formulaic structure of these books, so popular in Spain in the sixteenth century, gave comfort and pleasure to its readers. Generally, a hero is born of the highest nobility who, as prophesied, will overcome his enemies and fulfil his quest. He will overcome obstacles, defeating foes; prevail over the traps of evil enchanters so as to eventually gain the princess; and gain a kingdom or empire and become exceedingly famous. All this takes place in a faraway land, a place of wonder that recalls the newly conquered territories in Africa, Asia, America, and beyond. Cervantes follows this path, always undercutting his protagonist and turning the awe of adventure into a complex narrative where heroic dreams clash with a feeble but determined character that faces quotidian reality. The faraway land becomes a forgotten and sparsely populated corner of Spain, La Mancha. From the very beginning of the work, the narrative evokes chivalry but immediately swerves away from the traditional construction of a chivalric world. Works such as the *Amadís de Gaula* take the world of knights, evil enchanters, and epic contests as a given. In order to place the reader and the characters in this land, the *Amadís* and its progeny turn first of all to genealogy. Heroes must come from an exalted line. Explaining the originality of the opening of Cervantes' novel Juan Bautista Avalle-Arce contrasts it with the beginning of the *Amadís*, its acknowledged predecessor, and with the first lines of the *Lazarillo de Tormes*, the first Spanish picaresque novel, written, according to some, as a reaction to the romances of chivalry. The *Amadís* begins with a detailed genealogy of the chivalric hero. This foregrounds 'la plenitud de datos deterministas que se acumulan sobre Amadís de Gaula, y que lo disponen *a nativitate*, para su heroico sino' [the multitude of deterministic facts that accumulate upon Amadís de Gaula and dispose him from birth to his heroic destiny] (1975, 229). A similar determinism can be found in the *Lazarillo*, but it connotes the creation of an *antihéroe*, the antihero (Avalle-Arce 1975, 229). What is different in Cervantes' novel is that all such genealogical data is absent, thus giving a new type of freedom to the protagonist. His past does not appear to be important since the novel deals with his desired freedom to create his own future. This lack of genealogy has a double effect. First, it allows us to question Don Quixote's ancestry. Is his lineage so debased that he will not achieve greatness? If Amadís, found floating in a small barge on the waters, was the unacknowledged son of King Perión, then Don Quixote, abiding in an obscure region of Spain and in contemporary times, may well be related to kings and emperors of his recent past. The first pointer to a mystery within the text can be found in this comparison between books of chivalry and Cervantes' novel. What if the knight or the narrators are hiding a secret by not revealing the gentleman's past? What would his genealogy disclose? And why choose La Mancha as a place of origins? Is it to point to a stain (*mancha*) in the gentleman's ancestry? Yirmiyahu Yovel, for example, explains the anxieties of the Spanish *conversos* as related to stain: 'The syndrome of Jews (and Conversos) interiorizing the social stain attributed to their stock and feeling incredibly disgraced' (2009, 276). Don Quixote may be leaving home because of anxieties over a stain, be it in his ancestry and/or elsewhere. Discussing Henry James's stories, Todorov explains that such tales 'consist of the search for, the pursuit of, this initial cause, this primal essence' (1977, 145). A similar search for a cause can be encountered in Cervantes' novel. Todorov adds that the cause 'is often a character but sometimes, too, an event or an object. The effect of this cause is the narrative, the story we are told' (1977, 145). In Cervantes' novel, this cause seems to be what propels the main character. Thus we may ask: What is the cause of the knight's madness and of his adventures? We are never told explicitly. He will seek the magic of chivalry to alleviate his disquiet. Is Don Quixote, then, of lowly and tainted ancestry, or, as he hopes, of the lineage of emperors or would-be emperors? What is the knight's relationship to the emperor Charles V who proclaimed *plus ultra*?

This absence of chivalric markers is further punctuated by the total lack of the marvellous in daily life. Although Don Quixote blames his misfortunes on enchanters, they are nowhere to be found in La Mancha. Enchantments and prophecies become the building blocks of chivalry. Foretellings and good enchanters such as Urganda *la desconocida* [the unknown] guide the action. Evil enchanters such as Arcalaus and others, spawns of the devil, like the Endriago, place obstacles in the hero's path, only to further his glory. According to Barbara Traister, two basic types of magic are prevalent in literary texts of the period. The first is a literary magic that emerges from medieval romances and allows chivalric worlds to come to life through mighty opposites, through a cosmic battle of good versus evil. In this type, magic is used to arouse wonder and to move the plot (1984, 22–3). The second and less common form is the representation of a Renaissance magus, who searches for answers to the deepest questions of nature. These texts are more concerned with the theory of magic. But this second kind of magic is often adorned with medieval spectacular trappings so as to generate interest in a bookish, colourless, and theoretical representation.[4] I would add a third type of magic, the heterodox and forbidden magic practised by so-called witches, by *moriscos,* and other figures of alienation. This third type of magic will seep into Cervantes' text contaminating the first two, at times, pointing to a mystery that lurks beneath the surface. While the Cervantine text pokes fun at the literary magic of enchanters through Don Quixote's constant appeal to their ever-elusive presence, it allows for the infusion of Renaissance magic through astral magic and Pythagorean concepts. The first is used in these beginning chapters while the latter enters the novel at its inception through the planetary influences over the melancholy humour. This starry magic is foregrounded toward the end of the novel. Pythagoras enjoyed a revival among the Renaissance Platonists, and Marsilio Ficino incorporated many of his principles in his works.[5] Indeed, Ficino is responsible for the positive attitude toward melancholy and its planetary cause.

Discussing how Pythagoras 'invented' the word 'cosmos' with dominant motifs such as beauty, perfection, and reconciliation of opposites, S.K. Heninger asserts: 'During the Renaissance, as at most times in our intellectual history, the longing for order was so strong that the belief in cosmos persisted despite all evidence to the contrary . . . and with increasing insistence and ingenuity the dogma of cosmos was proclaimed' (1974, 147–8). The harmony of cosmos, as proclaimed by the Pythagoreans, was built on quaternity, which represented the physical emergence of cosmos from the mind of God. Thus, the world in which humanity abides is founded upon this number: 'In the world, all things are comprised in the quaternary, elements, numbers, seasons of the year, and ages of life. Neither can you name any thing which does not depend upon the quaternary as its root or foundation' (1974, 152). Cervantes, then, divides his 1605 novel into four parts as to abide by Pythagorean macrostructures. Instead of representing the magus, he will use the four-fold structure of cosmos as building blocks.[6] And yet, even here we have contamination from its main model, the *Amadís*. Let us recall that Rodríguez de Montalvo's text is divided into four books, much like Cervantes divides the 1605 novel into four parts, and part 1 ends with four knights, Amadís, Agrajes, Galaor, and Florestán, celebrating Briolanja's recovery of her crown. Thus, the number four, which will become a Pythagorean key to Cervantes, is already important in the *Amadís*. The chivalric book never points to is magic significance, although some of the continuations of the *Amadís*, and in particular the translation into French by Jacques Gohory, will foreground Renaissance magic.[7]

The principle of quaternity, then, serves to construct the emergence of cosmos or of the world of the novel. But, as will be seen, the *Quixote* can be viewed as having five discrete narrative paths – the four elements and the quintessence. Since the quintessence is related to the celestial, astral magic will seep into the text toward the end of the novel. In order to foreground the importance of the Pythagorean fourfold principle, the first chapter is divided into a series of quaternities. It starts by listing the four major objects which serve as the emblem for the hidalgo (a lance, a leather shield, a horse, and a hound); then it lists the four types of food eaten by this country gentleman. During the week he enjoys 'olla' and 'salpicón' [boiled meat]; Fridays he consumes 'lantejas' [lentils]; Saturday's feast is 'duelos y quebrantos' (which has a number of possible meanings – Jarvis translates it as an omelette); and the best meal, comes on Sundays, with 'algún palomino de añadidura' [and a small pigeon by way of addition] (1978, 1.1.69; 1998, 21) To call attention to the quaternities being discussed, the narrator tells how this food takes up three fourths of the knight's income. The last fourth is given over to clothing and again, four types are mentioned. The novel, then, begins by presenting four sets of four: possessions, food, income, and clothing.

Once the structure is set up, the narrative finds different ways to apply and depart from quaternity. It continues to establish cosmos by showing four members of the household, four tasks for which the *mozo* is responsible, and four names for the hidalgo. The gentleman is said to engage in two occupations while neglecting two others, thus creating another quaternity. And, turning to books of chivalry, the reader discovers that the two friends of the gentleman from La Mancha argue over who is the best chivalric hero. As expected, four fictional characters are discussed.[8] However, the novel departs from quaternity when, surprisingly, the future knight picks only two chivalric texts as those closest to his image. We would expect him to pick *Amadís de Gaula* as one of them, since this work, as noted, is the main chivalric example in the Cervantine text. But the knight singles out instead *Don Belianís de Grecia* and the works of Feliciano de Silva, a continuator of the *Amadís*. In this perfectly structured world, duality shows the first crack in the harmony. These works become important since they represent what is wrong with the hidalgo. He claims to enjoy Silva because his writings are replete with 'entricadas razones' [intricacy of his style] which he sees as pearls of wisdom (1978, 1.1.72; 1998, 22). These obscure and witty concepts evoke the excess in reading, writing, and conceptualization which is the central characteristic of the melancholy person. The *Belianís*, on the other hand, exhibits an excess of violence emblematized by the many scars that crisscross the protagonist's body.[9] Indeed, from the start of the *Belianís*, violence and the maiming of the body are foregrounded. Serious wounds are everywhere, and not just on Belianís's body: 'se partieron tan malheridos qual podéis pensar, ca al que menos heridas lleuaua tenía más de veynte muy peligrosas, principalmente la que Arsileo lleuaua en el muslo y las puñaladas de don Belianís que hasta las entrañas parecían llegarle' [they left so severely wounded, as you might think, so that the one who had the least amount of cuts had twenty dangerous gashes; mainly the cut that Arsileo had in his thigh and the stabbings that Don Belianís had, which seemed to reach his entrails] (1997, 1.43). In order to provide a clue of how these two books would affect the future of Don Quixote, the text explains that his brain dried up from too much reading. Now, the tetrad or quaternity, according to the Renaissance, has four basic features: 'All things are born from hot, cold, moist and dry' (Heninger 1974, 160). These qualities are the basic composition of the four elements of the material world (earth, water, air, and fire) since each of the elements share two of the qualities. The elements, often pictured in a circle, act in ways contrary to each other and are thus at war, disrupting the system of the cosmos they are meant to create. But an opposite movement holds them together without allowing them to fully merge into each other: 'By sharing qualities, however, the elements build up a force for stasis around the circumference of the figure – what Empedocles described as primordial love' (Heninger 1974, 163).

The macrocosm of the novel formed by a series of quaternities, including the four elements, is replicated in the microcosm of Don Quixote's physiology through the four humours. As Heninger explains: 'Just as the four basic qualities interact to produce the four elements that comprise the world's body, they make him a microcosm' (1974, 168). The four bodily humours (blood, choler, melancholy, and phlegm) not only led to the establishment of four body types but also served to categorize the many forms of behaviour of an individual from classical times to the early modern era. The humours were also key to medical examination and practice. As Daniel L. Heiple states: 'The Western theory of medicine began, possibly in the sixth century B.C. with the Greek philosopher Alcmaeon of Crotona, and certainly with Hippocrates . . . This medical theory was quite simple. It postulated that the body is healthy if its chemical composition is in balance and unhealthy if one of its humors . . . predominates over the others' (1979, 65). The dryness that affects the gentleman from La Mancha is a quality that is shared by the melancholy and the choleric humours. The knight is out of balance since he reads violent works exacerbating the choleric humour and relishes reading tomes with intricate language overworking his mind and thus increasing his melancholy. Once these two humours are radically out of balance, Don Quixote loses his wits through an excess of dryness: 'se le secó el cerebro' [his mind dried up] (1978, 1.1.73).[10] The knight's physiology in many ways reflects the geography of La Mancha, where dryness and heat predominate. Thus, a perfectly ordered cosmos has a figure that breaks the harmony therein, and lives in an area that reinforces his imbalance. And this is as it should be since the gentleman from La Mancha will serve as a vehicle of parody. He also breaks the quaternity by engaging in chivalry at the wrong time in his life. The four ages of a human being are related to the four seasons and he is much too old to engage in activities reserved for the springtime or even the summer of life. Once again, this element parodies the books of chivalry, not only by having an older man, but by the fact that he is really unable to do appropriate chivalric deeds in spite of his determination. He is as vigorous and agile as his horse, Rocinante. These traits reverse what Feliciano de Silva had done in his own novels. Propelled by the popularity of Amadís, he must keep him alive while his progeny engage in new deeds, and he must keep him fighting foes. As Daniel Eisenberg asserts: 'Silva se sintió obligado a explicar en casi cada uno de sus libros, y con matices diversos, la capacidad de un caballero de setenta, ochenta y hasta cien años para acometer aventuras como si fuera un mozo' [Silva felt obliged to explain in almost all of his books, and with diverging methods, the capacity of a knight who was sixty, eighty and almost a hundred years old to engage in adventures as if he were a young man] (2000, 59). Cervantes, in turn, does not explain; he just parodies Silva so as to create humorous and astounding situations.

Having said all this, we must also recall that excessive reading, the life of the mind, which is connected to melancholy, leads back to Renaissance Platonism and the idea of the magus. Marsilio Ficino, worried that his philosophizing was exacerbating his own melancholy humour, wrote a medical and magical treatise on how to contain melancholy. His language in many ways reflects that of Cervantes. In the fourth chapter of part 1, he tells us that agitation of the mind dries the brain and makes it cold, thus making it prone to melancholy. While Cervantes foregrounds the dryness of melancholy, Ficino points to its coldness. For Ficino, the life of a scholar exacerbates the melancholy humour and is thus placed under Saturn. The Renaissance philosopher does not view Saturn as a mere malefic. However, it should be approached cautiously as if we were taking a poison. In spite of its noxious qualities, it is also the planet of philosophers. Since it is the highest of all Ptolemaic planets, it rewards the person under its influence with the highest wisdom. It is the planet of contemplation (1989, 365). At the same time, this notion of contemplation can be considered as malefic since it takes the human being away from this world. Depending on its placement, the planet can also be a marker of incarceration, illness, and death.[11] Thus, Ficino sought to use the powers of Saturn to further his wisdom, while tempering it with the graces – the three benefic planets, Jupiter, Venus, and the sun. He also explained how a number of foods, hymns, gems, and talismans could be used to bring life to the melancholic, balancing his character while still harnessing the best of the saturnine person, wisdom. In a sense, then, Don Quixote is under Saturn. He becomes melancholy through excessive reading, which dries his brain and increases the prevalence of this fluid in his body. The text, then, is once again evoking Renaissance magic. Rather than follow Ficino's advice, the gentleman from La Mancha eats the wrong foods (such as lentils, which are drying), exacerbates the melancholy humour through lack of sleep (sleep would humidify his constitution), and in his vigil he reads, further compounding his imbalance.[12] Melancholy characters are said to be visionaries. They can see realms beyond. They may also have bizarre visions based on their imbalance. Don Quixote, then, has waking imaginings or quasi-visions of elements from his readings. If we were to follow the theorists of the period, some would say that his visions have a touch of wisdom; others would claim that they had a touch of madness. Indeed, the melancholy humour is often called *balneum diaboli*, the bath of the devil, since demons could insinuate themselves into one's physiology and impart false knowledge (Burton 1938, 174). Citing Jason Pratensis, Robert Burton concludes 'that the Devil, being a slender incomprehensible spirit, can easily insinuate and wind himself into human bodies, and cunningly couched in our bowels, vitiate our healths, terrify our souls with fearful dreams' (1938, 174). And invoking Agrippa he also claims that 'melancholy persons are most subject to diabolical temptations and illusions, and most apt to entertain them' (1938, 175). In a sense, then, Don Quixote approximates the Renaissance magus and may have glimpses of a higher or saturnine truth. But, his visions are forever suspect since he does not study the higher arts such as philosophy and theology that would turn his thoughts upwards; nor does he take the necessary remedies to balance his constitution, becoming prone to devilish visions. At the same time, there is enough wisdom in him to become a quasi-creator. Like the author of his 'history' he knows how to establish new worlds. They are tempting worlds that seduce with their fictions.

Foundations are not only built through number with their four elements and humours. The would-be knight comes to realize that the creation of a new world requires naming. In fact, idealistic theories of language hold the belief that words spoken in certain languages or at certain moments are true in that they impel creation. As Hermann

Iventosch has pointed out, the first chapter of the novel is onomastic in nature, dealing with the Platonic vision of the creation of a new world through naming (1963–4, 60). In other words, antique magical thinking linked name and form.[13] In order to create a new world for himself, the future knight must be careful to choose the appropriate name for all, since names provide the foundational frame for future action. In chapter 1, Don Quixote names his horse, himself, and his lady, only neglecting to name his weapons. The time he takes to ponder these names must also conform to the foundational frame. He takes four days to name his horse and twice as long to name himself. This doubling of four reflects the fact that his name is a compound one. Having called himself Don Quixote he needs to complete the name in the way Amadís de Gaula had done by using place. He decides on Don Quixote de la Mancha. When we finally discover this fourth and last name of the gentleman, his future chivalric name, we recall that he is first named 'Quijada.' This name means 'jaw,' thus underscoring the deformed jaw of the Habsburgs, including that of Charles V. The emperor was never happy with the way portrait artists depicted him. Harold Wethey explains: 'We know that the ruler's extremely deformed jaw did not permit the upper and lower teeth to meet or the mouth to close' (1971, 19). Titian solved this and other problems to the emperor's satisfaction, stressing decorum instead of relying on imitation. He transformed a deformed jaw into a jaw of determination.[14]

This suspicion that Don Quixote is related in some manner to the emperor can lead the reader to look back, to recall that one of the knight's favourite books was the *Belianís de Grecia*, its first and second part having been published in 1545. It should come as no surprise, then, that this chivalric novel was also one of Charles V's favourite works. Its author, Jerónimo Fernández, was a lawyer in Charles's court. The emperor's enthusiasm led him to start a third part which was finished by his brother Andrés after the author's demise. The work carefully inserts Spanish interests since Belianís is said to be the son of the queen of Spain and fights against a Persian knight for the love of Florisbella de Babilonia. The chivalric book focuses on the battles between Christians and infidels, an element that recalls the battles between Charles V and later Philip II against the Ottoman Empire. However, the author does not denigrate the Other, but shows the grandeur of the East, although their warriors are repeatedly defeated. In the climax of the work, Achilles is brought back in order to fight for the Christians and is amazed to see that many of his enemies are those of olden times: 'y al príncipe Achiles le pareció que nuevamente se le representasen las passadas batallas, auqnue les parecía cosa de sueño, que aquellos caualleros auiendo tanto tiempo que eran muertos, tornassen agora a hazer batalla' [and it seemed to Prince Achilles that the witnessing of old battles was a thing of dreams since these knights who had died long ago were once again waging battles] (1997, 2.388). The Greeks and Christians (including Belianís) are facing the Trojans, led by Hector, who is also revivified. The battle, then, becomes something more. Ancient heroes come back so that a chivalric romance can embrace the epic stories of antiquity transformed through the centuries into the chivalric matter of Troy. By reviving the ancients, Jerón imo Fernández seeks to even surpass them with his imaginative tale and violent telling. As Howard Mancing explains: 'The four modern Christians survive, while all the ancient heroes die in combat; Christians defeat pagans and moderns defeat ancients at the same time' (2001, 113). The work, then, lauds itself as being a text that can revivify and surpass the ancient epic. It also takes the side of the Greeks as representatives of the West, while the Trojans are consigned to paganism even though the Habsburgs often exalted them due to Aeneas's mythic lineage that went as far as Charles V, according to the emperor's laudatory chronicles. Published ten years after the famous conquest of Tunis by Charles V, Jerónimo Fernández's chivalric text is a not so subtle praise of the emperor's wars against the Turks, wars that led to a series of imperial triumphs where Charles was often seen as going beyond. We need only recall the emperor's entry into Naples in 1535 where he was depicted as 'Atlas sustaining the world, Hercules with the imperial columns, Mars, Fame and Faith. Here for the first time, the emperor's Turkish victories were acclaimed in a series of canvases decorating a triumphal arch' (Strong 1984, 83). The entry into Florence was particularly grandiose: 'At the Porta di San Piero Gattolini there was an arch consisting of the imperial column device with PLVS VLTRA above it . . . As he turnedout of that street, a silver statue of Hercules made the inevitable comparison with the emperor who had likewise banished the hydra' (Strong 1984, 84).

In Cervantes' novel the gentleman named 'jaw' can be viewed as a ghostly emperor, haunted by his deeds and riding the world again. As a powerless ghost of power he can achieve nothing but melancholy visions. And we can observe him riding a pale and wan horse, Rocinante. The riderless steed at the Brussels funeral procession is now emaciated and carrying forth the ghost of empire – a ghost that as we shall see hides secrets from the past, a ghost that is haunted by anxieties. By naming the ghost we begin to exorcise his madness. Indeed, there are those who believe that the knight's madness is a devilish one, that he must undergo a series of purgations, of exorcisms, to be healed. Michael Hasbrouck was one of the first, if not the first critic to show the many allusions to exorcism in the novel and to follow the knight from possession to cure (1992, 117–26). For Hasbrouck, the knight is possessed throughout the 1605 novel and only begins to change in part 2: 'En la primera parte se delinea, pues, una asociación entre don Quijote y las fuerzas diabólicas, ya que muestra muchas señales de estar poseído por el demonio. El caballero andante carece de control sobre sus propias facultades y hasta ataca a figuras religiosas' [In the first part the association between Don Quixote and the diabolical forces is delineated, since he shows many signs of being possessed by the devil. The knight lacks control over his own faculties and even attacks religious figures] (1992, 122). These attacks, I would argue, arise from his anxieties, from the ghosts that haunt him. On the one hand, Don Quixote wishes to be the perfect Christian knight, fighting pagans; on the other, he resents his own fears, which impel him to adopt this persona, and thus attacks those who symbolically represent control over his ideas and those of his land. Expanding on Hasbrouck's essay, and mirroring some of Henry Sullivan's theories regarding Don Quixote's stay at the duke and the duchess's palace as a kind of grotesque purgatory, Hilaire Kallendorf, explains how the knight is cured of his madness through a series of self-exorcisms that conclude with his becoming Alonso Quijano *el Bueno* at the end of the 1615 novel. Citing a treatise by Gómez Lodosa on self-exorcism, Kallendorf asks if Cervantes could have known it and thus structured the knight's quest for freedom. Regardless, she believes this is a tool used by the knight to liberate himself (2003, 180). Furthermore, she associates this self-exorcism with the rise of the novel: 'Self-exorcism is paradigmatic of the autonomous action of a novelistic character' (2003, 157). I would echo Hasbrouck, Sullivan, and Kallendorf's theories, arguing that self-exorcism and purgation are used in the novel to take Don Quixote out of the other-worldly sphere of influence of an emperor whose deathly melancholy has invaded the knight. But I would add that the other ghosts that gather around the knight are anxieties that cannot be resolved through exorcism, since they demand his recognition of heterodox practices and beliefs as a way of healing his fractured psyche as well as the clashes of culture and civilizations that besiege his land.

So far we have only dealt with one of the gentleman's names, the one associated with the emperor. We must now move to the heterodox. His original name fluctuates through the text, from *Quijada*, to *Quesada* and *Quejana*; his genealogy is missing. What is hidden in the family? Is this ghostly past hiding a more terrifying haunting? As Dominick Finello states, the trinomial used to name the gentleman from La Mancha could point to his otherness: 'One for example could interpret the portrait of the country hidalgo as a play on cryptic surnames . . . These initial words in the novel, still a mystery, playfully suggest New Christian attempts to protect their identities' (1998, 26). Josep Solá-Solé, goes even further showing that the name *Quejana* refers to a lament of having been born in obscurity, the lament of being *converso* (1981, 717–22). It is easy to intuit, then, why the knight rejects his real name. But why does he adopt the name of Don Quixote? The most common interpretation is that it refers to a thigh-guard, thus associating the name with the knight's sexual anxieties. Dominique Aubier, on the other hand, relates the name to two Jewish words: *Keshot* (truth) and *Kishott* (plant) (1966, 249). Carroll Johnson has recently added one more element. *Quezote* is a garment worn by *moriscos*. He goes on to discover that the *quezote* was also called *quixote* in Spanish treatises of the period. Furthermore, this Moorish type of garment was adopted by Christian nobility on festive occasions (2004, 13). Johnson perceptively concludes: 'Cervantes gives us a character whose name, and presumably therefore his identity is simultaneously derived from the identical-sounding names of two very different articles of clothing . . . We all know the story of *quixote* as thigh-guard, a garment that remits to the Christian, European, feudal-chivalric world and which defines its bearer in terms of that cultural paradigm. At the same time, the same name contains another *quixote*, a lightweight, festive outer garment that remits to the Arab-Islamic cultural orbit, the Other in opposition to which the officially approved Spanish identity was to be constructed' (2004, 17). This whole semantic play has created a new world for the gentleman from La Mancha, one that both hides and reveals the mystery of his ancestry and the anxieties of his quest.

While quaternities have created cosmos, the knight has fashioned his new persona through naming, and the names he uses and those he is called are latent with mysteries to be deciphered. His new name alone cannot make him into a true knight. First of all, he needs to discover that his lineage is of high nobility, even perhaps royal. Works like the *Amadís de Gaula*, as noted, begin with a detailed genealogy of the chivalric hero. This chivalric book sees nobility as a prerequisite for greatness. It places human beings in a predetermined social class. When we turn to Cervantes' novel, we find no such prehistory, either at the beginning or later in the work. The only information given is that he is a poor hidalgo, the lowest form of nobility, who spends more than he can afford on books. Any expectation that a greater lineage will be discovered is constantly dashed. Even while Don Quixote defends those who are of lowly birth and rise to greatness, he still hopes that the sage historian that writes about him will discover royal blood in his veins: 'y podría ser que el sabio que escribiese mi historia deslindase de tal manera mi parentela y decendencia, que me hallase quinto o sesto nieto de rey' [and perhaps the sage, who writes my history, may so brighten up my kindred and genealogy, that I may be found the fifth or sixth in descent from a king] (1978, 1.21.262; 1998, 161). None of this ever happens, and we are left to guess as to who may have been Don Quixote's ancestors. Although some critics praise Cervantes' novel pointing out that the unknown ancestry produces a new kind of hero, one with greater freedom to create his own future, I would argue that this is part of the parodic elements of the text. While chivalric heroes descend from the upper classes, picaresque protagonists, during this period, usually come from families that have Jewish or Moorish ancestry. Thus, their lack of limpieza de sangre [purity of blood] is a pointer to their roguishness. In Cervantes' times, many would hide their 'impure' blood so as not to be subject to Inquisitional oversight or other forms of discrimination. Perhaps the 'historian' is hiding Don Quixote's ancestry for this very reason. A chivalric hero of dubious parentage certainly fits the polemic nature of parody.[15]

Don Quixote has thus created an onomastic cosmos and an imagined ancestry so as to become a knight. However, to become a 'true' knight, he must also be marked by the heavens as the one who is to engage in a quest. In the novels of chivalry, the hero is often marked from the start. Amadís de Gaula is set on a raft soon after he is born and left to whatever fate the waters will bring him. Much like Moses, he survives this trial. He is taken in by royalty and his mysterious birth is acclaimed through his new name, the Donzel del Mar, the Youth from the Waters. In Belianís de Grecia, a similar marker can be found. While still very young, Belianís is faced with a major adventure – a magical cave that contains a lion, a bear, and a prophetic wall (Fernández 1997, 1.4–12). While some of his elders fail to even enter the magical abode, Belianís vanquishes his mysterious foes and becomes the subject of the prophecy. Don Quixote, as stated, is already almost fifty years old when he seeks adventure. There is no flashback that narrates a special moment that has marked him as a great and future knight. In order to overcome this lack, he decides to imitate countless chivalric heroes, and sets out at dawn to seek adventure. What he has is an unbounded optimism backed by imagination. The narrator mocks him for it: 'Imaginábase el pobre ya Coronado por el valor de su brazo, por lo menos, del imperio de Trapisonda' [The poor gentleman already imagined himself at least crowned emperor of Trapisonda by the valour of his arm] (1978, 1.1.75; 1998, 23). In a clear parody of the romances of chivalry, he invokes the empire of Trapisonda or Trebizond, claiming that he will become its ruler like so many other characters in these books. Indeed, the narrator refers to him as 'el pobre' [the poor man], a term that serves to ironically commiserate with this mad gentleman and also to show the gap in rank, income, and ability between him and what he wants to become. Toward the end of the 1605 novel, the canon of Toledo once again pokes fun at this commonplace: 'Y ¿cómo es posible que haya entendimiento humano que se dé a entender que ha habido en el mundo aquella infinidad de Amadises, y aquella turbamulta de tanto famoso caballero, tanto emperador de Trapisonda ... tantas sierpes, tantos endriagos, tantos gigantes ...?' [How is it possible any human understanding can persuade itself there ever was in the world, that infinity of Amadises, that rabble of famous knights, so many emperors of Trapisonda . . . so many serpents, so many dragons, so many giants?] (1978, 1.49.577–8; 1998, 436). The canon thus equates the many generations of Amadís that have appeared in the romances with the many emperors of Trebizond that people such novels. Feliciano de Silva, for example, takes the reader over and over again to the faraway land of Trebizond. The *Lisuarte de Grecia* (the seventh part of the *Amadís*) tells how Lisuarte and Perión fall in love with the two daughters of the emperor of Trebizond, Onoloria and Gricileria.[16] In the *Amadís de Grecia* (the ninth part of the *Amadís*) Silva tells of the *Caballero de la Ardiente de Espada* (Knight of the Burning Sword), Amadís de Grecia, who is the son of Lisuarte de Grecia and Onoloria of Trebizond, thus following up on the couple described in the *Lisuarte*. In addition *Belianís de Grecia* by Jerónimo de Fernández, another one of Don Quixote's favourite authors, shows the emperor of Trebizond together with Belianís helping in the siege of Babylon (Cervantes 1833, 14–15). The name even appears in the title of a chivalric romance, *Claris de Trapisonda*, which is preserved in manuscript. Indeed, many books of chivalry were never printed, but were shared in manuscript form.[17]

Citing the many emperors of Trapisonda/Trebizond which appear in the romances, works such as *Esferamundi, Lindadelo,* and the *Caballero del Febo,* Clemencín compares the uses of Trebizond to those of Constantinople: 'Todavía se repite más en la biblioteca caballeresca la mención de Emperadores de Constantinopla . . . Los autores de muchos libros caballerescos hablaron de ambos imperios como coexistentes, por lo cual aparece que quisieron referir sus historias al tiempo que medió entre la fundación de Trapisonda que fue por los anos de 1220, hasta el de 1453 en que se perdió Constantinopla' [The mention of emperors of Constantinople is repeated even more in the chivalric library . . . The authors of many chivalric books talked about both empires as coexistent, from which it appears that they wanted to refer their stories to the time between the foundation of Trebizond around the 1220s until 1453, when Constantinople was lost] (Cervantes 1833, 2.429–30).

Don Quixote specifically wants to be the emperor of Trebizond. Why this specific empire? Trebizond was one of the three new empires that arose when Constantinople was conquered in 1204 (Miller 1969, 14). The best known of the three, the Byzantine Empire was restored in 1261 at Constantinople. The empire of Trebizond (Trapisonda), whose capital was on the Black Sea, remained in Christian hands from its inception until 1461. It survived the fall of Constantinople and thus the conquest of the Byzantine Empire by the Ottoman Turks by eight years. As the last surviving Christian bastion in Asia, Trebizond became the subject of a longing for the survival of Christian empires in the east, an element of nostalgia tapped by the romances of chivalry. They also became lands that were 'closed' to Christians, and thus the object of fantasy. This is not to say that Christians never visited Trebizond after it fell to the Ottomans. When Charles V consolidated the Holy Roman Empire into the largest Western empire to date, he had to deal with the other 'superpower' of the times, the Ottoman Empire. Their rulers had not stopped at Constantinople but were even threatening the gates of Vienna. In becoming a knight, Don Quixote expresses a triple longing: the return of an age of chivalry, the return of Trebizond as a Christian empire, and the return of Charles V's Holy Roman Empire, with the predictions that he would become a *Dominus mundi.* The fact that Trebizond fell and Charles's empire was divided at his death made it even more urgent for Don Quixote to engage in his quest. While he leaves home out of anxieties concerning his ancestry and doubts as to his beloved's lineage, he goes on the road to bring back a past where things were simple (or so they appeared in the romances); where there was a clear opposition between Christians and their pagan opponents. In the Spain of Don Quixote's time, such oppositions were blurred by the many who had converted: *conversos* and *moriscos*. For many in this period, they were far from being the pillars of a Christian civilization. These recent converts were watched carefully by the Inquisition in case they slipped into any of the old practices. They were also accused of having impure blood, and barred on that account from public office and many social distinctions. It is almost as if the first chapter of Cervantes' novel is constructing pillars that should not be erected. It is as if the text is telling us that the mystery should remain hidden, warning the reader: *non plus ultra*. The novel, then, begins with an imitation of the romances of chivalry and the geography of ancient sites. It buttresses the structure with Pythagorean quaternities and onomastics, and then parodies what is presented through a crazed knight who hides a terrifying secret, one that sets him on his quest. The question remains. Can the Other be a part of the fabric of empire? Or has the clash of civilizations become so intense that the Other must be banished from Christian lands? The secret of the novel balances itself between these two pillars: the Christian Gibraltar and the African Atlas. Don Quixote must pass between, hiding his secret, riding away from his ghosts.

3 Questioning Quaternities

The number four stands much admired, not only in the quaternity of the elements, which are the principles of bodies, but in the letters of the Name of God which in the *Greek, Arabian, Persian, Hebrew* and *Egyptian* consisted of that number; and was so venerable among the Pythagoreans that they swore by the number four.

– Sir Thomas Brown, *Pseudoxia epidemica*

If Don Quixote is to become emperor of Trebizond or, more likely, a ghostly recollection of Charles V, he must find a way to connect with the heroes of the past even though he has no ancestry. Thus he seeks the mantle of Hercules, whose twelve labours were emblematic of valour, fortitude, and the ability to conquer the most terrifying of foes. Hercules' twelve labours were associated with the twelve signs of the zodiac, the twelve constellations that the chariot of the sun crosses through the year. Hercules is then akin to the sun, and the twelve constellations represent the twelve labours. Don Quixote wants to be seen as a solar and Herculean hero. After all, Spanish kings were said to descend from Hercules. The knight may even want to surpass Hercules, to go beyond the Pillars, assuming the role of a new Charles V. His jaw of determination will lead him forth. He also wishes to be a new Apollo, ruling earth as the sun rules the heavens.[1] In fact, he envisions the telling of his own tale as beginning with a reference to Apollo/Sol: 'Apenas había el rubicundo Apolo tendido por la faz de la ancha y espaciosa tierra las doradas hebras de su hermosos cabellos . . . cuando el famoso caballero don Quijote de la Mancha, dejando las ociosas plumas, subió sobre su famoso caballo Rocinante, y comenzó a caminar por el antiguo y conocido campo de

Montiel' [Scarcely had the ruddy Phoebus spread the golden tresses of his beauteous hair over the face of the wide and spacious earth . . . when the renowned Don Quixote de la Mancha, abandoning the lazy down, mounted his famous courser Rosinante and began to travel through the ancient and noted field of Montiel] (1978, 1.2.80; 1998, 27). In his first sally, then, Don Quixote evokes quaternity through the number four since the sun is the fourth of the Ptolemaic planets. And yet, this turns out to be a disnarrated moment, what Gerald Prince defines as 'all the events that do not happen but, nonetheless, are referred to (in a negative or hypothetical mode) by the narrative text' (1988, 2). The disnarrated shows a crossover between the Pythagorean narrative and Don Quixote's desires. After all, Iamblichus tells us that Pythagoras 'was sent down to men from Apollo's train' (Celenza 1999, 672–3). The melancholy knight may be a sage of old. Regardless of this tantalizing possibility, what actually happens must be placed in the field of parody. Don Quixote's hyperbolic language and view of himself is immediately deflated. He sets out on his journey in the month of July, the hottest month of the year, thus aggravating his humoral imbalance. As the text explains: 'Con esto caminaba tan despacio, y el sol entraba tan apriesa y con tanto ardor, que fuera bastante a derretirle los sesos, si algunos tuviera' [He travelled on so leisurely, and the sun advanced so fast, and with such intense heat, that it was sufficient to have melted his brains, if he had had any] (1978, 1.2.81; 1998, 27). It is this kind of satire that led the eighteenth century to canonize Cervantes' work. In the first deluxe edition of the text in England, John Vanderbank includes as a frontispiece the figure of Cervantes, now in the guise of a new Hercules or Apollo, setting out to protect the Muses. Far off, on Mount Parnassus, the monstrous forms of chivalry have taken over. Cervantes accepts the mask of satire and the club of Hercules as he sets out to restore Parnassus to the Muses. Cervantes' narrative, then, may present the knight as a false Hercules and a mock-Apollo, but Vanderbank believes that these links can be extended to the narrative itself, which sets out to defeat and conquer the monstrous narratives of chivalry. Indeed, the text sets out to conquer not only chivalry but many other forms, and thus seeks to become something new, something novel that will go beyond the known world of genres.

Don Quixote finds that, in addition to the time of his sally, there are three other problems to be solved, thus creating another quaternity that must be dealt with on his road to victory. He must have a mythic marker; he must be knighted in order to move forward; and he must have a device on his shield even though he has not triumphed over any foes. Marker and shield may well go together. Here Don Quixote's solution evinces once again his ability to use language to create his imagined world. Since his shield is white or plain he thinks that he will clean it quite carefully so as to make it look as white as an ermine (1978, 1.2.80; 1998, 26). Although he is not allowed to carry a marked shield, the very whiteness of it, he believes, will evoke the ermine which was a common heraldic device. Once again, Don Quixote is intent on naming and has chosen a very telling device. The ermine, when encircled in mud, 'would prefer to be captured rather than to sully itself while trying to escape' (Rowland 1973, 74). The ermine's story was to be found in emblems and dictionaries of the Renaissance and Golden Age (Covarrubias 1987, 146). This legendary behaviour made this small animal a symbol of chastity or 'of the wearer's personal integrity' (Rowland 1973, 74). From Ferdinand I of Naples to Elizabeth I of England, the ermine became a prized symbol of royalty, decorating robes of princes and prelates and appearing in heraldic devices, emblems, and paintings. Charles V was no stranger to this prized animal. Even after renouncing the empire and retiring to Yuste, he kept 'no less than sixteen robes of silk and velvet, lined with ermine or eider down' (Prescott and Kirk 1882, 273).

But let us return to the cosmic quaternities that impel the imperial narrative. This first part of the novel is composed of eight chapters, two sets of four that mirror each other with the one difference that in the first four chapters the knight travels solo, while in the last four he has a squire. And each set reaches its crescendo in its last or fourth chapter. In fact, to emphasize quaternity in the fourth chapter the author tells us that he 'llegó a un camino que en cuatro se dividía' [he came to the centre of four roads] (1978, 1.4.99; 1998, 41). Allowing Rocinante to choose one of the paths, the knight is faced with adventure. There are two adventures in each of the fourth and the eighth chapters, thus creating a quaternity of adventures. These and other methods, such as naming, have created a fictional cosmos of perfect balance and stability. Each chapter takes up its numerological principle. Thus, chapter 1 deals with beginnings with the self, and with the worlds created by the narrator and by the knight through quaternities, cosmos, and naming. Chapter 2 represents duality. Here the knight is faced with the world. As he sets out to face others he must account for his plain shield that tells of his lack of adventures. Thus he must find someone to knight him. Chapter 3 takes up mediation between inner and outer perceptions. Thus he encounters the innkeeper or castle-keeper who counsels

him – one of his counsels is to get a squire. And chapter 4 takes us to
the initial fulfilment of the quixotic quest, engaging in adventures. As
stated, two adventures will crown chapter 4 and chapter 8. Indeed, the
number eight, which represents the number of chapters in this section,
was the number of justice for the Pythagoreans (Agrippa 1987, 206).
Although the gentleman from La Mancha is in search of justice, the discordant elements in this segment are his humoral imbalance and many
of the resulting 'chivalric' actions.

In spite of his verbal abilities, his prowess in naming self, horse, lady,
and shield insignia, the key discordant element in these chapters is the
knight himself. Unable to see the world as it is, he envisions images that
derive from his reading. These visions are the result of his dryness and
his melancholy. The world is metamorphosed in front of him as he is
deluded in thinking he has a princess for a lady and a royal insignia on
his shield. The delusion reaches its peak when, after deciding that he
will ask the first person he encounters to knight him, he sees in the distance an inn which he takes to be a castle with drawbridge and a moat.
But there is one element lacking, one that casts doubts on his vision. He
stops his horse, Rocinante, waiting: 'que algún enano se pusiera entre
las almenas a dar señal con alguna trompeta de que llegaba caballero
al Castillo' [expecting some dwarf to appear on the battlements, and
give notice, by sound of trumpet, of the arrival of a knight at the castle]
(1978, 1.2.78; 1998, 28). Sure enough, after waiting for some time, he
hears a sound of a horn. No matter that the dwarf sounding the horn is
a swineherd. The sound gives him confidence and he approaches the
castle. He 'sees' that it has four towers. As a foundational number, it
confirms to Don Quixote that this place will grant him a knighthood
and thus become the foundation for his future adventures. Don Quixote requests to have the castle-keeper or innkeeper arm him as a knight.
Not only is the innkeeper not a knight nor a gentleman but, instead
of reflecting chivalric qualities, his previous life-adventures evince his
picaresque leanings. Thus, he comes to represent the genre that stands
in opposition to the chivalric. By arming Don Quixote as a knight he
subverts the whole hierarchical conception of knighthood and imparts
in Don Quixote the spirit of plebeian humour and picaresque carnival.[2]
Indeed, the innkeeper is described as 'no menos ladrón que Caco' [as
arrant a thief as Cacus] (1978, 1.2.84; 1998, 29). The reader of this passage could simply understand Cacus as a word for thief, one that is
even used in contemporary Spain. For example, even to this day children play at 'polis y cacos' or cops and robbers. But, this simple term

hides a mythological referent. Cacus was a giant and a thief who stole Hercules' cattle. The ancient hero is able to recover his cows after he defeats the giant in battle. When faced with such a character, one would expect that Don Quixote would be reminded of Hercules and immediately do battle with his foe. Don Quixote should have taken the role of Hercules. But the knight sinks to the ground instead, kneeling before this modern Cacus, and requests that the 'giant' innkeeper arm him as a *caballero* (1978, 1.3.87). This is one of Don Quixote's greatest transgressions in the novel. In his desire to be knighted he fails to perform his first Herculean task. The gentleman from La Mancha not only succumbs to the giant but becomes his vassal. In fact, he accepts the castle-keeper's advice, returning home to search for clothes, money, medicine, and a squire. These four items are again foundational, as they form the nucleus of Don Quixote's needed possessions in his second sally. And yet these foundations stand on very shaky grounds. As he sets out to become a new solar hero, a new Hercules that will conquer the cosmos, he has as his mentor a picaresque character. How will he rival the antique hero or ever achieve the *plus ultra* of Charles V? The pillars of genre have become destabilized in the world of the knight. He stands in a liminal space between a knight and a *pícaro*. No matter how much he manipulates language or transforms the world through vision, the father of his quest remains a picaresque innkeeper.

And there is a hidden problem here. Picaresque narratives delight in presenting the genealogy of their protagonists. Yirmahayu Yovel asserts: 'The picaro often speaks with the voice of the Converso, especially when recounting his origins' (2009, 265–6). I would add that this type of character often hides and reveals a lineage that contains *conversos* or even *moriscos*. In *Lazarillo de Tormes*, for example, Lazaro's father is a thief; this recalls the allusion in Cervantes to the innkeeper as a new thief Cacus. Arrested, he 'confesó y no negó' [confessed and did not deny] (1976, 101). The phrase, although a parody of the Bible, may also point out that he is a *converso*, someone who has converted to Christianity. Sent to war, the father becomes an *acemilero*, an occupation often practised by those of Muslim origin. To further emphasize otherness, the narrative then shows Lázaro with a stepfather who is named Zaide – a black man of Moorish origins (1976, 104). Picaresque characters, then, are the reverse of Old Christians and knights. As Yovel contends: 'The picaro is the anti-hidalgo' (2009, 263).[3] Don Quixote is being knighted by his opposite, and yet this action may also indicate that the gentleman from La Mancha shares the *pícaro*'s ancestry. But we can only surmise this. We have a clue, but no proof. As we move further into the text, new clues will present themselves that can take us this way or that, searching for that absence, for that secret of which Todorov speaks. For this reason, what Yovel says of the picaresque is particularly important for readers of Cervantes: 'The picaresque mask of irony is clear but not transparent: we know it exists but must decipher its particular instances which often elude the alert reader too. Readers must become amateur detectives' (2009, 265). What Cervantes will do in his novel is to make it clear that the reader must become a detective. As will be shown in chapter 6, the novel does this by presenting us with a 'case' that must be solved. For now, all that can be said is that the failures of Don Quixote can be linked to the failures in establishing a proper tetradic foundation for the construction of himself as a knight. And the failure in construction derives from his own anxieties, from the ghosts of a past that haunts him, and from the phantoms of a mind that will replace the tensions of his society with the simpler ways of the knight as represented in books of chivalry. His heterodox visions turn the world upside down as a blank shield acquires the royal qualities of the ermine, an inn becomes a castle, and prostitutes are viewed as great ladies. Don Quixote must think that perhaps he too descends from an emperor or will become one.

While his inner world stands on shaky foundations, those of the narrative pulsate with possibilities. To the three major genres of this first segment – chivalry, parody, and Pythagorean philosophy – a fourth has been added to enliven the mix, that of the picaresque novel. And to further test the boundaries of genre, the picaresque innkeeper is called a new Cacus, a giant who is evoked in Virgil's canonical epic. In Book 8 of the *Aeneid*, as King Evander performs rites in honour of Hercules, Aeneas sails up the Tiber to meet him. In the place where Rome would stand one day, Evander tells Aeneas the tale of Hercules and Cacus. The story, then, has a direct bearing on the founding of Rome. But Rome became an empire through war and conquest, in other words, through thieving. The resulting booty of conquest was seen as 'the outward sign of the inner glory which is the heart of *Romanitas* and its destiny' (W.R. Johnson 1984, 5). The problematics of Cacus reflects the ambiguities of the narrative and in turn leads to a consideration of the ethics of chivalric conquest and imperial expansionism. Are emperors, even modern ones, heroic figures who seek to gain what is beyond, the *plus ultra*? Or are they thieving picaresque figures who just care for booty – the gold of America, the spices of Asia, or the slaves of Africa? Is Cervantes' text a parody of novels of chivalry or of the desire for conquest? The mixing of genres has enriched the texture of the text and problematized its meanings.

Knight and narrative, struggling with difficult and dangerous questions, move on to chapter 4 where the first two adventures take place. Proud to have been knighted, Don Quixote searches for adventure. And sure enough, the narrative obliges. He hears 'voces delicadas como de una persona que se quejaba' [a weak voice, as of a person complaining] (1978, 1.4.95; 1998, 37). He realizes that these cries are from someone needing his assistance. Following the cries into the woods, Don Quixote comes upon a young man, tied to a tree, naked to the waist, who is being flogged by a farmer. Don Quixote does not listen to the farmer's reasons for punishing the boy. He does not care to hear that the boy had not tended well to his master's flock of sheep, losing one every day. While Don Quixote pretends to be a knight believing firmly in his made-up world of chivalric visions, Andrés, the boy, will also fashion himself so as to allay all suspicions of thievery and call upon the knight's charity for the victimized. When Don Quixote tells Andrés to go back home with the farmer now that he has intervened to solve the problem, the youth refuses to do so since he fully believes that his master will skin him alive, '¿porque en viéndose solo me desuelle como a un San Bartolomé? [for when he has me alone, he will flay me like any saint Bartholomew] (1978, 1.4.97; 1998, 39). The narrative now invites one more genre to intrude into this masquerade. St Bartholomew is part of hagiography. Agustin Redondo has already pointed to the importance of this allusion, pointing out that both flogging and flaying were involved in this saint's martyrdom.[4] But the manipulation of language to come up with new realities is not at an end. When the farmer explains to Don Quixote that Andrés owes him for three pairs of shoes and two bloodlettings, the knight replies: 'quédense los zapatos y las sangrías por los azotes que sin culpa le habéis dado; que si él rompió el cuero de los zapatos que vos pagastes, vos le habéis rompido el de su cuerpo; y si le sacó el barbero sangre estando enfermo, vos en sanidad se la habéis sacado' [set the shoes and the blood-lettings against the stripes you have given him undeservedly: for if he tore the leather of the shoes you paid for, you have torn his skin; and if the barber-surgeon drew blood from him when he was sick, you have drawn blood from him when he was well] (1978, 1.4.96–7; 1998, 38–9). The broken leather of the shoes comes to represent torn human flesh, while the bloodletting recalls the blood that issues from the flogged or flayed skin of the would-be martyr. At the same time, St Bartholomew is the patron saint of all trades which deal with skin. Cervantes' playful text shows Haldudo and Don Quixote haggling over leather and skin as merchants, as traders in skin.

The evocation of merchandise leads smoothly to the second adventure in chapter 4. When Don Quixote sees merchants from Toledo going to Murcia to buy silk, he imagines a new adventure. Don Quixote's reaction is well-founded. Commerce was often at odds with the enmities created by traditional (warlike) empires. And Toledo has become 'the city of business,' as clearly seen in *Lazarillo de Tormes* (Maiorino 2003, 6). Furthermore, the production of silk was one of the 'crafts and skills of the Islamic nations' (Jardine 1996, 63). More to the point, Carroll Johnson explains that although Granada was once the primary source for silk, 'following an epidemic that decimated the mulberry and the expatriation of most of the *morisco* labor force to Castile following the unsuccessful revolt in the Alpujarra in 1568, Grenadine production suffered an abrupt decline and the Toledo merchants had to find another source. Special permission was given for the establishment of a silk industry in the hands of the *moriscos* in Murcia' (2000, 7). Not only were *moriscos* engaged in the production of silk in this city, but Murcia was often associated during Cervantes' time with 'judaising *conversos*' (Kamen 1997, 84). Indeed, the very fact that the troop is made up of merchants creates, in a society intent on purity of blood, a suspicion of Jewishness. Don Quixote as an 'Old Christian' hidalgo must oppose the mercantile. The tripling of Otherness (Islamic silks, Murcian Jewishness, and Toledan picaresque materialism) combines with the 'noxious' presence of the mercantile craft to trigger in Don Quixote a 'Catholic' reaction. He orders the merchants to 'confess' that Dulcinea is the most beautiful woman in the world. When the merchants state that they need to see at least a portrait of the lady, Don Quixote claims: 'La importancia está en que sin verla lo habéis de creer' [The business is, that, without seeing her, you believe, confess, affirm, swear and maintain it] (1978, 1.4.100; 1998, 41). This totalizing faith is what the knight requires of the multicultural and tolerant mercantile profession. They must confess their 'Christian' belief or be destroyed. Of course, the irony of the situation is that in establishing Dulcinea as the goddess, Don Quixote becomes the proponent of a kind of paganism opposed to the Christianity he ostensibly supports. Furthermore, Dulcinea is from Toboso, a town known for its *morisco* inhabitants (Castro 1966, 81; Carrasco Urgoiti 2006, 126; Graf 2007, 37). Finally, the beginning of the novel, leaving out the gentleman's ancestry, casts doubts as to his 'Old Christian' background.

Is his Catholic response one that is too prompt and extreme, one that points at the knight's own anxieties over his past or that of his (imaginary) lady? Chapter 4, then, the height of cosmos, has little to do with Pythagorean philosophies. Instead, it brings together hagiography and pagan mythologies; the chivalric and the picaresque; parody and epic. They are fused in such a seamless manner that a reader can lightly enjoy the narrative road, even though it carries a heavy load of contaminated genres and thorny questions. The polemical nature of parody, as outlined by Dentith, lends the chapter part of its complex humour, polyvalent tonality, social range, and ideological spark.

The next four chapters repeat the pattern of the first four. Chapter 5 is once again about new beginnings. Don Quixote has been left mangled and hurt on the road. Picked up by a peasant neighbour, Pedro Alonso, he is taken home. In his quasi-delirium, Don Quixote affirms his imagined world. First, he tells the bewildered peasant that he is Valdovinos, a character from the ballads, which in turn comes from a legend based on the Charlemagne cycle. The times of Charlemagne will be evoked over and over again in the novel, from the balsam of Fierabrás to the climactic discord at Agramante's camp as the Saracens besiege Paris. But in chapter 5 the text focuses its allusions to the Spanish ballads on the subject. According to the story, Valdovinos is led to the forest by Carloto, son of Charlemagne. There, the emperor's son plots to murder him so that he can marry his beautiful wife and soon-to-be-widow, Sebilla. The Marqués de Mantua, hunting in the area, hears the cries of his nephew, the wounded Valdovinos. He arrives in time to hear of the treachery and to swear to avenge his nephew. Don Quixote, mangled and lying on the ground uses the ballads to first call upon his wife and then to his uncle: '!Oh noble marqués de Mantua, / mi tío y señor carnal!' [Oh noble Marquess of Mantua, my uncle and lord by blood] (1978, 1.5.103; 1998, 44).[5] In so doing, he places himself in the entourage of one of the most famous of emperors. Having done this, he quickly reverses the situation. Don Quixote is so confused by the beatings that he received that, helped home by Pedro Alonso, he now turns to a different story to make sense of his plight: 'porque en aquel punto, olvidándose de Valdovinos, se acordó del moro Abindarráez, cuando el alcaide de Antequera, Rodrigo de Narváez, le prendió y llevó cautivo a su alcaldía' [for at that instant, forgetting Valdovinos, he bethought himself of the Moor Abindarraez, at the time when the governor of Antequera, Rodrigo de Narvaez, had taken him prisoner, and conveyed him to his castle] (1978, 1.5.105; 1998, 44). The narrator tells us exactly where Don Quixote had perused this second story. He did not read it as a text standing on its own but as it appears as an interpolation in Jorge de Montemayor's pastoral novel, *La Diana* (1559).[6] No matter where he read it, it is important to note that this is a key text from the mid-sixteenth century that seeks to 'imagine chivalry as a conduit for generous relationships towards Moors' (Fuchs 2009, 36). This is the first instance of such an imaginative practice on the part of the 'Christian' knight, Don Quixote. Although most critics have pointed to Don Quixote's increasing madness and confusion by becoming two figures rather than one from legend, what has been missed, I think, is a link that begins here and explodes in chapter 45, the link between the Charlemagne stories and the positive vision of the Moors or Saracens. Here, Don Quixote is first Valdovinos, who is attacked by a son of the emperor and then becomes the good Moor who is given permission by the Spaniard who captures him to go see his beloved, on condition that he return and give himself up after seeing her (a promise he fulfils). One of the great difficulties encountered in Spanish chronicles and ballads is that Charlemagne, although fighting against the Saracens and consolidating his Christian empire, is not always viewed in a positive light. He had designs on Spanish territories. Thus, Spaniards (together with Saracens/Moors) would just as soon join him as fight him.

The notion of the good Muslim who fought alongside the Christian is a very difficult concept to understand at the time that Cervantes was writing his novel. With the fall of Granada in 1492, many believed that Moorish religion and culture had been wiped out of the country. Many of the clauses in the edict, or *Capitulaciones de Santa Fe*, allowing for Moorish culture to survive, were ignored. But, as Barbara Fuchs states: 'Yet a culture profoundly marked by Andalusi forms survived in sixteenth-century Spain, long after the fall of Granada, and stood as an often unacknowledged challenge to the official narrative of suppression' (2009, 11). In spite of a growing maurophilia used in ceremonial acts such as the *juegos de cañas* and in literary texts, maurophilia failed to deflect the growing animosity between the Spanish Crown and its *morisco* inhabitants. The results were quite predictable by 1605.[7] In fact, Israel Burshatin believes that this maurophilia as reflected in the Abindarráez's tale is actually 'a self-flattering depiction of Christian control over the Moor and his world' (1984, 196–7). Others, such as Kathleen Bollard are more nuanced. This critic argues that 'the *novela morisca*, while offering a much more positive portrayal of Muslim men, is not consistent in characterizing the Moorish hero, and that the *Abencerraje,* in particular, by emphasizing the emotionalism characteristic of the hero of romance or the sentimental novel, undercuts Abindarráez's masculinity through the implicit comparison to Narváez's epic stature' (2003, 299). However we may interpret this story, the fact remains that the *moriscos* would be expelled from Spain four years after the publication of Cervantes' evocation of Abindarráez. Don Quixote's double-vision in this chapter is then an acknowledgment that alliances can shift; that Christians can just as easily turn against other Christians; that Spanish history shows heroic moments where Moors and Christians banded together against a common enemy; and that the Moor could have as strict a code of honour as a Christian. Don Quixote, in this moment of confusion, is expressing the confusion that may have been felt by many at this time. Should the Muslims who had converted to Christianity and formed such an integral part of the economy and culture of the peninsula be summarily dismissed as enemies? Should their culture as a whole be denigrated, their language prohibited, their customs found suspect? What of ancient times when the clash of civilizations found a kind of buffer in Iberia?

This, then, is the general thrust of chapter 5. There is also a more specific theme. It is Don Quixote who, considering himself a great future Christian knight, becomes both the victim of Charlemagne and the figure of an idealized Moor. Perhaps this sudden shattering of his persona reveals something of his inner conflict – of the secret that impels the narrative. Does he somehow sympathize with the 'enemy'? While this conflict could be framed in terms of justice and fairness, Don Quixote is seldom in favour of the Moor. He follows the romances of chivalry where Saracens are the enemy. So, what is it within his being that suddenly reveals a new facet? What is the mystery he is hiding and that comes out in moments such as these? Is Otherness something he is fleeing because it is an integral part of his being? Or is it all due to the lineage of his beloved Aldonza/Dulcinea? Is it her Otherness that drives him from home? Are his actions meant to adorn her with chivalric feats so that Aldonza/Dulcinea's 'real' ancestry would not be revealed? Whatever the answer, we must recall that in the Pythagorean scheme, we are back to oneness, to a foundational chapter. We have seen how onomastics were a key to chapter 1. Naming is once again of great importance. Don Quixote, albeit briefly, can be known by two other fictive names: Valdovinos, the victim of Charlemagne's son, and Abindarráez, the idealized Moor. While the name Don Quixote will continue to prevail, these others will be swept under the weaves of the tapestry of narrative so as to conceal a mystery.[8]

Chapter 6, representing the number two, should move from the single-mindedness of the chivalric self to duality. The only problem is that the perfect set of quaternities has been questioned in the fifth chapter. Onomastics have revealed the knight's shattered inner self. However, the narrative does not pause to consider the implications. It moves to duality with a vengeance. This time the knight is not faced with the world. Instead, the world tries to destroy the basis for his imaginings. Most of his library is burnt. The works here can be divided into three or four sections: chivalric, pastoral, epic, and miscellaneous. The first division points once again to the importance of quaternity, while the second recalls that six (the number of the chapter in which this appears) was considered the first perfect number by Pythagoras since it comes out of the sum of one, two and three (Bulatkin 1972, 35). Books of chivalry reinforce the melancholy of reading and the choleric aspect of knightly endeavours. Thus, most of them are consigned to the fire by the priest and the barber. The presence of pastoral books is quite significant. *La Diana* is saved from the flames even though passages dealing with Felicia the magician and the enchanted waters should be deleted. Nothing is said, on the other hand, of the interpolated tale of Abindarráez. Does the priest who is saving the novel not recall this episode? Does the edition that Don Quixote has include the tale? Does the priest approve of the figure of the idealized Moor? Whatever the answer, pastoral also points to the second segment or part of the novel, where this genre will emerge and revolve around a rather heterodox figure, Grisóstomo. In order to fully authorize the inquisition of books, a trilogy of epics is saved: *La Araucana, La Austríada*, and *El Monserrate* (1978, 1.6.121). These are meant to show the prowess of Christian Spain. After all, the first deals with the battles in America; the second with Flanders and the Mediterranean; and the third with the founding of the Monastery of Montserrat. *La Austríada* stands at the centre of this epic trilogy, and here the Ottoman Empire is depicted as the enemy while the battle of Lepanto represents the great Christian triumph. Don Juan de Austria, the hero of this poem and illegitimate son of Charles V, also fought the *moriscos* at Granada. This book, found by the priest and the barber, then, reasserts the negative role of the *moriscos* and their threats to Spain, something that Don Quixote's vision has briefly placed in doubt. In this scrutiny of the knight's library, epics that favour conquest of the Amerindians and the Muslims are praised, together with religious epics that bring back pious legends.

The priestly inspection of Don Quixote's library, the selection of books to be kept or to be censored, not only sensitizes the reader to clashes in cultures, but also points to the appearance of Inquisitional indexes of prohibited books, the *Index librorum expurgatorum*, such as the ones published in Madrid in 1584 and 1612. As José Pardo Tomás states: 'los índices dibujan perfectamente los contornos de la cultura en letra impresa que se consideraba debía quedar fuera del alcance del lector hispano. Son, pues, el marco de la censura, su punto de referencia más general y sistemático' [these Indexes clearly delineate the shape of print culture that was considered outside the reach of the Spanish reader. These Indexes, then, serve to frame censorship, becoming their main and most systematic point of reference] (1991, 49). While the chapter becomes a mock-Index, censoring mainly chivalric romances, its presence at this point calls to mind that Cervantes had used as one of his main treatises on the humoral psychology of Don Quixote, the work of Juan Huarte de San Juan, *Examen de ingenio para las ciencias*. This work, which had enjoyed great popularity, although not on the list of censored books of 1583, did appear the following year on the list of books to be expurgated. Huarte de San Juan worked until his death in 1588 to revise the treatise so that an acceptable version would be republished. It came out six years after his death, in 1594. Thus, Cervantes, while mocking chivalry, seems to be pointing to, among others, a book which he used, which had been expurgated (Pardo Tomás 1991, 214–15; Iriarte 1948, 87–8). The imitation of genres in Cervantes' work, then, is not restricted to the well-known literary types. The text also plays with hagiographic texts, Inquisitional indexes, medical manuals, mythographies, scientific tracts, and many others types of works.

Chapter 7, reflecting the third chapter, deals with mediation. Don Quixote finds Sancho and makes him his squire. Sancho will help him to deal with the world. Finally, chapter 8, the Pythagorean number for justice, leads to a new fulfilment of cosmos. Don Quixote will engage in two more adventures, thus having a total of four adventures in this first part. The first of the last two adventures is the most famous of all, that of the windmills. Although there is much to say about it, we must soon continue the narrative road. But if we pause briefly to gaze at this adventure, we find a few elements that are of particular concern. First of all, we are faced with the amazing metamorphosis of windmills into giants. This is one of Don Quixote's greatest imaginative feats, one which rivals scenes in Ovid's *Metamorphoses*. Ovid most often uses metamorphosis as part of the natural world. His metamorphoses move from a higher to a lower order of being.[9] Cervantes' novel most often follows the example set by Ovid as beings are transformed into other beings, except that he moves from lower to higher beings – prostitutes into ladies, herds of sheep into armies, etc. Cervantes' inanimate objects are often changed into other inanimate objects (inns to castles). Very seldom does Ovid or Cervantes go from animate to inanimate. Just as we remember vividly how Pygmalion's statue is given life, so we remember how windmills, in the knight's mind, also become alive – turning into threatening giants rather than into a beautiful woman. The episode also combines the mythological with the epic. It only takes one word, thus pointing to the allusive economy of the narrative. The knight calls one of the giants Briareus, recalling manuals of mythography where he is described as a hundred-armed creature from the beginnings of time. It also calls to mind Dante's *Divine Comedy*, a Christian 'epic,' where the giant is described in an ekphrasis in Dante's *Purgatorio* and inhabits the deepest pit of hell in the *Inferno*. Although on the one hand we can visualize Don Quixote battling beings from the nether regions, on the other hand he may be battling Christianity itself. Windmills of old were made of four sails, thus representing a cross that whirled with the wind, a concept that has not escaped the scrutiny of critics such as Maldonado de Guevara (1954, 77–100). What is curious about the narrative of the windmills is that such a brief episode has turned into an emblem of the whole novel. We are amazed at the sails of the mill becoming the arms of a devilish giant or a whirling cross. We are amazed as the sails of the mill turn faster and faster as the wind picks up; we are amazed at the quickness of a narrative that causes awe by its rapidity, and its ability to paint the scene with such few words. Indeed, the windmills themselves are not described, just named. When it is Sancho's turn to describe them, and try to reason with the knight that he is not facing giants, the squire points to their technology: 'y lo que en ellos parecen brazos son las aspas, que, volteadas del viento, hacen andar la piedra del molino' [and what seems to be arms are the sails, which, whirled about by the wind, make the millstone go] (1978, 1.8.129; 1998, 59).

The episode, then, recalls the first chapter with its emphasis on naming. Genres need only be alluded to in order to come into existence. But the episode also describes the technology of windmills, thus adding mechanical treatises to the list of genres. This also creates a subtle link with imperial pursuits. As has been noted repeatedly, Don Quixote seems to imitate Charles V, and become a *Dominus mundi* who espouses the ideals of chivalry. But Charles was very interested in technology. The knight's opposition to certain advances may seem to establish a tension between the two figures. But, let us reconsider. Charles V so much admired the inventions and machines of Juanelo Turriano, the Italian engineer, that upon the emperor's abdication, he invited Juanelo to join him at Yuste. The *Veintiún libros de los ingenios y máquinas de Juanelo Turriano*, attributed to this technician from Cremona, describes the various types of mills in the eleventh book. Juanelo devotes a great deal of attention to water mills, but also describes those run by animals, by humans, by weights, etc.[10] A careful reading of Turriano's chapter on mills shows that Juanelo, like Don Quixote, disliked windmills. Turriano complains that windmills 'no sirven en España y menos en Italia por causa que los vientos no son ordinarios' [they are useless in Spain and even more in Italy because the winds there are not ordinary] (1983, 342). Don Quixote assails these inventions as 'vile creatures' since they do not belong in the Spanish landscape. Turriano explains that windmills are suited to Germany, Flanders, and France since the winds in these countries are moderate. In Spain, however, windmills are useless because of the great fury of the winds: 'no se pueden conservar por causa del gradissimo furor que llevaría que todo lo rompería' [they cannot be preserved because the great furor of the winds would tear them apart] (1983, 342). Following Turriano, then, Don Quixote is right in extirpating such giants/windmills from Spain. But as he gallops forth and attacks the mill, he is defeated precisely by that element Turriano warns against: 'La volvió el viento con tanta furia que hizo la lanza pedazos' [the wind whirled it with so much violence that it broke the lance to shivers] (1978, 1.8.130; 1998, 60). Thus, the furious wind that is supposed to make the windmills useless in Spain becomes the wind that defeats Don Quixote. In this example, the knight's attack is not against technology but against what Juanelo deems to be inventions that are inappropriate for Spain. In this sense, there is no tension between the chivalric and inventive Charles V and the crazed knight from La Mancha. No matter. To explain his defeat, Don Quixote claims that Fristón the enchanter has changed the giants into windmills, thus taking us back to the *Belianís de Grecia*. The genre clashes astound: Christian epic, mythology, technological manuals; but what astounds most is a vision that can combine technology and chivalry, Christianity and paganism, the cross and the nether regions.

The last adventure is triggered when Don Quixote views a woman travelling in a carriage and immediately deduces that this must be an abducted princess. I would argue that, just as the harmony of beginnings is altered by the allusion to the *Belianís*, the ending of this narrative segment is also signalled by this work. At the end of the second part of *Belianís de Grecia* an aerial chariot, led by twenty dragons with deformed figures in command, appears in order to abduct not only Belianís's beloved Florisbella, but also a number of other princesses and ladies as well as Queen Aurora.[11] As the knights watch in confusion, the sage Belona prophecies that the women are now enchanted and must be released within two years or be lost forever. As the knights sail to Assyria to answer this call to adventure, the second part ends. Readers would have to wait thirty-two years to read the *Tercera y cuarta parte del invencible príncipe don Belianís de Grecia,* now published by the author's brother, since Jerónimo Fernández had died. Cervantes imitates and parodies this moment in chapter 8. Here the 'princess,' who is a travelling lady, has to witness the battle between Don Quixote and her coachman, a battle that is broken off in the middle since no more text is said to remain. This first part of Don Quixote ends with a promise to search for the manuscript. The structure that slowly emerges in Cervantes' novel also recalls the *Amadís* where each book resolves a problem, but creates at the very end a new situation that will be developed in the following book.[12] It all leads to the great war in Book 4 were everything is resolved. The suspenseful climax that ends each book is thus replicated by the ending of the second part of the Belianís and by Cervantes' abrupt ending of chapter 8. But while Rodríguez de Montalvo and Jerónimo Fernández use it just as a narrative device, Cervantes will appropriate it for a double purpose. First, the mock-heroic battle between the coachman and the would-be knight, even though arousing suspense, parodies the astounding and hyperbolic clashes in the books of chivalry as well as the suspense in the battles between good and evil. Second, this climax serves as a signal for the change in genre.

While on one level, the ending of the eighth chapter recalls the climactic pauses in books of chivalry, the structure of this first part itself calls for an ending. The two adventures in chapter 4 mirror those in chapter 8, creating a quaternity and thus signalling a 'perfect' text, one which the knight keeps dismembering with his crazed adventures. And yet, both knight and narrative strive to uphold quaternity, the first in an eccentric manner, the second attempting to keep the character within the bounds of the world that is being created. It is also a world built on onomastics. The gentleman from La Mancha uses numerous identities and names to advance his quest. He is a new Hercules befriending rather than killing the thief Cacus; he is an Armenian defending St Bartholomew against martyrdom; he is a member of Charlemagne's court, victim of treason; he is a chivalrous Moor from Granada; he is Jupiter flinging his thunderbolts at Briareus and other giants; he is a pagan attacking the Christian cross or a heretic challenging the hounds of God from the Benedictine order. He is a Christian knight suspicious of heretical merchants; and a figure of empire who seeks to challenge the peripheral Basque.[13] He takes so many names: Abindarráez, Hercules, Valdovinos, and Don Quixote. He does so because naming is at the heart of creation, a creation that stems from a God whose name, many thought, consisted of four letters in many languages or religions, be it the Christian, Muslim, Jewish, or classical paganism. Although the tetragrammaton is never invoked, it inspires these chapters. It becomes a heterodox image, a symbol of the unity of religions, of the quaternity that brings about creation according to many cultures.

Having put together a double set of four chapters that mirror each other, it would be very easy to create two more sets of quaternities. But how would that contribute to the development of the work? In order to signal the dangers of a world beyond this tightly conceived cosmos, one where only replicas or new forms (or monsters) can be found, the narrative subtly points to the Pillars of Hercules. In this case, the columns are constructed of knight and Basque as they stand poised to do battle and hold their swords up high. If Don Quixote, as an embodiment of Hispania, stands for Gibraltar, then the Biscayan must be the other – the African heights. This positioning also points to a mystery in the narrative, the opposition between Catholic and Other, and the suspicion that even those who claim knighthood may belong to the other side. Whether they maim each other or not, what needs to be sundered is the obstacle that stands in the way of creating a new path to narrative. And to signal that we have reached the limits of the known world, the limits of narrative, the narrator actually informs the reader: 'en este punto y término deja pendiente el autor desta historia esta batalla, disculpándose que no hallo más escrito' [in this very crisis, leaves the combat unfinished, excusing himself that he could find no more written] (1978, 1.8.137; 1998, 66). There is nothing beyond. The narrative is lost, and the contestants must remain forever with their swords on high at the gates that warn of *non plus ultra*.

4 An Arab's Audacious Pastoral

Escaping the obviousness of things pastoral, and escaping the 'genre' in the Western sense, the Arabic poet's self-view becomes instead a projection onto a personified firmament. The nightly sky of his loneliness is his pasture, the scattered constellations, his herd.

– Jaroslav Stetkevych, *The Zephyrs of Najd*

The well-wrought urn with the crazed knight as its only crack had to be circumvented, made more brittle and more resistant at the same time.[1] It had to change even though it was buttressed by Pythagorean doctrine. After all, Pythagoras also announced that everything is in a state of flux, as time flows like a river, never reversing course. Ovid revelled in recounting Pythagoras's many examples of the rise and fall of rivers, cities, and empires.[2] And perhaps it is these examples that led Cervantes to envision the constant transformation of reality through quixotic visions and the many mutations of narrative genres. Cervantes' novel must open a new path for his narrative, one which will go beyond the impasse. First, the new path must endanger the work of art even further. This is accomplished by a master stroke. A sword must come down on the perfectly symmetrical narrative, a sword that is envisioned as cutting a human body as if it were a pomegranate. This break and the passage beyond are accomplished by the discovery of a manuscript at the market in Toledo. As Eric Graf explains: 'When Cervantes evokes the pomegranate at the precise moment in which he freezes the action of the battle between the Castilian knight and his Basque adversary, only to then introduce us to it again by way of a text discovered in a town famous for its ancient Jewish population, a text written in Arabic by Cide Hamete and then translated into Spanish by a Morisco, he has created a linguistic, cultural, and geopolitical emblem of the entire history of Spain' (2007, 112). Toledo, as Graf has noted, is an ideal cross-cultural site. This city is also the perfect place to find a *morisco* boy who can translate the Arabic manuscript. Toledo points to a time when the city prospered under Muslim rule, when it prospered as a centre of learning and *convivencia* as Jews, Muslims, and Christians undertook to translate key works from the past; as a site of empire under Charles V; and as a place where Philip II presided over the clarification and implementation of the Edicts of Trent as part of the Catholic Counter-Reformation. Thus, the manuscript reflects the tensions within Spanish culture. It points to Christian zeal, the yearning for universal empire, and the riches of other civilizations that are no longer allowed to coexist in Spain. It will not be long before the *moriscos*, viewed with great suspicion and accused of collaborating with the Ottoman Empire, are expelled. A second fissure emerges as Cide Hamete Benengeli, an Arabic historian or enchanter, an enemy of Christianity, is said to be the author of the manuscript. His presence seems to trigger a rivalry with the knight, a representative of a totalizing imperial view. Cide Hamete will tell stories that should not be told; and he will take Don Quixote places where the gentleman from La Mancha should not go. Just as dangerous, or so the text claims, is the propensity of Arabs to lie. And yet, the narrative is so slippery that it suggests there could be more to the relationship between 'author' and character. There could be a secret that will slowly unravel through the battle over genres.

The perfect narrative with its Pythagorean structure has been breached. The knight had imagined his own narrative in the first part, as one where he is led by Apollo, in his quest to become a solar hero or even a Pythagorean sage (1978, 1.2.80; 1998, 27).[3] But, as noted before, this is an instance of what Gerald Prince calls the disnarrated, of what does not happen.[4] The empire where the sun never sets does not fully belong to the knight, even though he will shatter a number of barriers. The columns that held the Biscayan and Don Quixote with swords on high are now replicated. There are two new contenders: the knight and the Arabic narrator. Their contest will continue to the very end of the work (or so it would appear). Together they will forge a new path that can no longer embrace Pythagorean perfection nor can it discard it. Instead of the Pythagorean, the now fragmented and unreliable narrative will be reinforced through contamination with the pastoral, an ideal form to conjoin to the chivalric. After all, some of the earliest Spanish pastoral narratives were fragments within chivalric romances. Not only that, they were thus interpolated by one of Don Quixote's two favoured authors, Feliciano de Silva.[5]

This second part has a double prologue that complicates the 'simplicity' of pastoral. First, the narrative becomes contaminated with the rather confusing narrative of the knight and the Biscayan, which, as Michael Gerli reminds us, is 'retold, however, from a different perspective, and a different tone, four times in less than five printed pages' (1995, 65). Gerli relates the 'gaps, incongruities and disjunctures' found here to the heterotopia, that is, the rejection of textual utopias (1995, 63). Second, a meeting with some goatherds leads to Don Quixote's speech on how he will reestablish a Golden Age. While the goatherds contrast with pastoral idealization, the speech on the Golden Age seems consonant with pastoral, since, as Thomas G. Rosenmeyer asserts: 'The two concepts are the two sides of the same coin' and were thus used by Virgil in his *Eclogues* (1969, 235). At the same time, pastoral seems to be in opposition to chivalric endeavours. At least, this is what William Empson once stated. It is the 'process of putting the complex into the simple' (1974, 22). The complexities of war were thus transformed into pastoral laments.

Under the veneer of apparent pastoral simplicity that lulls the reader into forgetting the fissures caused by Toledo, the finding of the manuscript, and the presence of an Arabic narrator, the text shows that there is nothing simple about pastoral. First, this segment of the novel contrasts the life of ordinary goatherds with the false Arcadia created when Marcela and Grisóstomo dress up as shepherds and begin to imitate a form of fiction in their lives. Second, we are left to ponder if Don Quixote's speech on the Golden Age reflects the episode in any way. The 'amorosa pestilencia' [amorous pestilence] (1978, 1.11.157; 1998, 78), which is absent from the mythical age, seems to cause havoc in a modern Arcadia. And, to take pastoral as far from utopia as possible, Cervantes begins by telling of the death of Grisóstomo – a death supposedly resulting from his unrequited love for Marcela – the paradoxical topos of *et in Arcadia ego*.[6] In his discussion of Pythagoras's philosophy, Ovid reminds us that youth leads to old age and death, much like the ages of humankind are always changing. The Golden Age will eventually yield to its opposite, the Age of Iron, where warfare predominates. Although no longer buttressed by Pythagoras, the pastoral episode has not forgotten his claims.

Although Don Quixote enters pastoral out of curiosity, the narrative reasons do not seem to be his own: genre and politics. The highest and most respected of the European genres in the Renaissance and early modern period was the epic. In order to ease into this form, Cervantes' text paradoxically turns to the pastoral and takes the knight to the funeral of Grisóstomo who has ostensibly died of love for his Marcela, a woman who donned the shepherdess attire to get away from the young men of the region who accosted her with amorous proposals. Grisóstomo was one of them. Becoming a shepherd he would write poems to his lady. But she would spurn all. He thus set his mind to die of love and thus be revenged on this cruel mistress. Or perhaps he shifted course and decided to perish for fame. As he lay dying he ordered that his poetry be burned in the manner of the ancient Mantuan poet.

Of course, this gesture became the gist of the scene, the perfectly artful way for a poet to be remembered. During the Renaissance a whole series of writers wanted to imitate the literary career of the most famous authority from antiquity. Studying the poet laureates of the English Renaissance, Richard Helgerson concludes that these poets did not just want to write great works, but to become the voice of their times. The work of these poets begins not with a text but with an ambition. Spenser, Jonson, and Milton are 'three poets whose ambition preceded and determined their work, three poets who strove to achieve a major literary career and said so' (1983, 1–2). In other words, these poets announce their career before engaging in it. Thus, a number of writers from the Renaissance link their career announcement with an allusion to Virgil. In this way, they are 'planning ahead,' and this plan does not focus on one work, but goes far beyond it: 'One must be able to think in terms of decades, perhaps generations . . . The master plan, like scaffolding, holds everything in place' (Lipking 1981, 79–80). And of course, Virgil was the ur-architect of the literary edifice. Ever since Ernst Curtius, critics have noted that many authors imitated his sequence of genres. The spurious first four lines of the *Aeneid* explained Virgil's career moves. In youth, one must write eclogues, poems of pastoral life using a low style. As one matures, works about tilling of the fields, about the relations between calendar, agriculture, and civilization must be developed and presented in a middle style. And as proof of the mature poet, the high style must be used in the epic. This highest form must sing of a hero's foundational deeds, his making of a culture or empire. Virgil's *Aeneid* was to be a work in praise of Augustus Caesar, detailing the hero's journey from Troy to Italy, where he would become the ancestor of the founders of Rome. Thus the famous Virgilian wheel represents the moves from eclogues to georgics to epic (*Aeneid*), and from low to high style. There were appropriate trees, animals, and instruments for each genre. The Renaissance revelled in this *cursus*. William Kennedy, for example, has explained how Petrarch's works, in spite of its changes in focus, tend to imitate the Virgilian wheel.[7] Patrick Cheney has discovered Spenser's imitation of the Virgilian *cursus*, while Anne Lake Prescott has studied the poetry of Clement Marot and Du Bartas as an imitation through the sacred of a profane career.[8] To make matters easier, Renaissance poets sometimes shortened the moves. It was enough to begin with pastoral and end in epic.

   Cervantes utilizes this myth of the poet's career to fashion himself – but instead of writing poems, he will do so through his fiction. He signalled the beginning of his career in the Prologue to his pastoral novel *La Galatea* (1585). This work announces the type of career Cervantes wants to follow – that of Virgil. It is not my intention here to study in detail this literary career, since I have done so elsewhere (De Armas 2002). I will simply present a brief synopsis so as to be able to continue the study of genre in Cervantes' novel. Recalling that, according to Helgerson, paratexts such as prologues are places in which the writer represents himself, let us look there.[9] In the prologue to *La Galatea*, Cervantes immediately establishes a direct link between pastoral novel and Virgilian eclogue. Eclogue belongs to youth, although the Cervantes of this Prologue confesses that he has started late (due to his sojourns abroad and his captivity in Algiers). Nevertheless he affirms that he can still write this type of work: 'habiendo apenas salido de los límites de la juventud' [having barely gone beyond the limits of youth] (1995, 156). Referring to the three Virgilian styles he describes how a writer must begin with the lowest ones since these are enriched in this manner. These forms also help the author 'para empresas más altas y de mayor importancia' [for higher and more important matters] (1995, 156). Following Virgil, Cervantes explains to the reader that the eclogue is a way to learn not only the humble style but also to start ascending and start comprehending higher forms, including the epic. Eclogue or pastoral can hide the highest of genres. For this reason, the Virgilian eclogues and even the georgics have been labelled as audacious genres by Virgil (Coolidge 1965, 12). Cervantes uses almost the same phrase to describe his writing in *La Galatea*: 'he dado muestras de atrevido' [I have shown signs of daring] (1995, 157).

   This is not the time to describe the audacity of *La Galatea*, how it rises in style and themes. What is important is that the Virgilian daring points toward epic, and this epic would be, for Cervantes, his last book, *Los trabajos de Persiles y Sigismunda.* Cervantes' career, thus, seems to be a canonical one. He wants to be the Spanish Virgil, while writing in prose. In this sense, Cervantes follows what Thomas M. Greene calls a heuristic imitation, which involves producing texts that 'come to us advertising their derivation from the subtexts they carry with them, but having done that, they proceed to distance themselves from the sub-texts and force us to recognize the poetic distance traversed' (1982, 40). A number of critics have noted the parallels between the *Persiles* and the *Aethiopica* of Heliodorus, a Greek romance that many during the early modern period considered to be a new model for the epic. Recently, Michael Armstrong-Roche has modified this perception. He believes that Cervantes' last work has much to do with classical epic and with Virgil. For example, while Aeneas has to abandon Dido to follow his martial impulses, 'the challenge that Cervantes set himself for his prose epic is itself epic: how to make a hero credibly heroic – and, notably, fit to govern a Kingdom – whose first priority is love' (2009, 169). In this sense, we can come to understand the daring and audaciousness of this work which has almost been forgotten: 'we can renew our appreciation of Persiles' freshness, complexity and daring by looking back to epic' (2009, 8). In a similar manner, I think that we can also look back to epic to understand some of the daring elements of Cervantes' *Don Quixote,* a book that is at the very centre of his literary career, between pastoral and epic.

In this first pastoral episode in *Don Quixote,* daring is first exhibited by asking the question: What would happen if a poet who announced an epic career died young? And, is suicide an appropriate move in the life of a poet who wants to attain renown? These are the dilemmas posed by Cervantes through Grisóstomo. The response to the first problem is to be found in Virgil. As noted, lower genres were supposed to hide higher genres within their texts. For this reason, eclogues and georgics may seem audacious (*audacibus*), a term that the Roman poet uses more than once. Epic questions may be muted, hidden, or shaded in the pastoral so as to hint at future career moves. Aware of his ability to point upwards, Grisóstomo models himself after Virgil. His pronouncement that his poems must be burned was a gamble but one that could pay off with eternal fame, since this was precisely what Virgil had ordered should be done with his *Aeneid.* And sure enough, some of Grisóstomo's papers are saved from the fire. The narrative is clearly manipulated so that the 'Canción desesperada,' the 'Song of Despair,' is one of the poems to survive. A masterpiece, it combines the registers of eclogue and epic. The poem explains that it is written in 'nuevos modos' [new modes] (1978, 1.14.181).[10] The poem is a testament to pastoral's amorous despair, but it is also a work deeply contaminated by epic. Grisóstomo chooses to imitate the sixth book of Virgil's *Aeneid* in order to rival Aeneas's *catabasis*. The poet-shepherd retells Aeneas's journey to the underworld as a way to visualize the torments that the dying lover expects to encounter. As in Virgil, we find images of the three-headed Cerberus, of Tityus, Egion, and Sisyphus. In answer to the second question, Grisóstomo switches the historical moment. He is now a poet under the patronage of Nero rather than Augustus Caesar. Lucan was said to have written poems critical of the emperor, raging against a tyrant who set fire to Rome. In addition, the last books of the *Bello civili*, better known as the *Pharsalia*, contained anti-imperial and pro-Republic sentiment. These writings and the fact that he may have joined a conspiracy against the emperor sealed his fate. The cruel and angry emperor ordered his death. That is, he ordered that Lucan commit suicide. The poet was only twenty-five years old. In a burst of contamination and parody typical of Cervantes, the epic images of Grisóstomo's poem also imitate Lucan's *Pharsalia*, thus presenting two historical moments and two very different lives. Revelling in the fact that the *Pharsalia* is an epic that counters many of Virgil's notions, style, and structure, Grisóstomo begins with Lucan and ends with Virgil. This swerve from a republican to an imperial poet reverses history and makes this a curious feat, one where the poet does indeed die young and commits suicide. While in life Lucan died at the hands of a cruel emperor, in Cervantes, Grisóstomo ends his life because of a 'cruel' woman. In this sense, the second problem is also solved. The poet can commit suicide following Lucan. Grisóstomo thus fashions himself as an epic poet who has mastered techniques of two very different epic poems, one that sings of imperial triumph and another one that signals defeat. The shrill language of Lucan contrasts with the more lofty ideals of Virgil so as to produce truly a new way of writing.[11]

These opposing epics point to clashing political visions. And they are placed within pastoral because, as Annabel Patterson and Benjamin J. Nelson have argued, pastoral, even in its beginning with Theocritus and Virgil, is not a move away from the world. It is anything but a shift toward simplicity: 'Thus, writers throughout history would return to Virgil's *Eclogues* to comment on either their personal state of crisis or their country or region's sociopolitical turmoil' (Patterson 1987, 44–5; Nelson 2007, 40–1).[12] Has Don Quixote been brought to pastoral to face the temptation of Virgilian fame? Or is he here to be moved by Lucan's laments? The two famous epics can also coexist in the same poem so as to contrast two moments of Roman history which then comment on Spanish rulers. It has often been remarked that Cervantes was much less fond of Philip, particularly toward the end of his reign. While Augustus Caesar, for whom Virgil wrote his praises, stands for the revered Charles V, Nero, who had Lucan murdered, could be a reflection of Charles's son Philip II. Nero is said to have ordered the death of his own mother, while Philip was rumoured to have imprisoned his own son, Don Carlos, and then had him murdered. Philip sealed himself in the famous Escorial Palace and Monastery which he had built, while Nero was infamous for the construction of the *Domus Aurea*, an immense palace. There was a kind of inclusiveness to Charles V, under whose reign the works of Erasmus and other humanists were considered and tolerated; Philip II enforced the strictures of the Counter-Reformation and even prevented students from studying at foreign universities. His policies culminated in the expulsion of the *moriscos* from Spain under his successor Philip III. As the tensions rose between Christians and converted Moors, some literary forms sought to present an idealized vision of the Moor, one who was an idealized lover. Lope de Vega, as Alan Trueblood reminds us, developed the Moorish ballad together with the pastoral romances in the years he was lamenting the loss of Elena Osorio (1973, 48–85).

It may not be a coincidence that Cervantes introduces the Arabic narrator in the same segment as he gives us his vision of pastoral. Grisóstomo shares with the Moorish lover an interest in astrology. During the Middle Ages and the Renaissance the West considered that Arabs were particularly knowledgeable on the lore of stars. Indeed, we shall see how Arabic star images will be hidden at the very end of part 1 of Don Quixote. At this point, Grisóstomo shares with Arabic culture an interest in the stars. Indeed, it was said that Arabic poetry transferred pastoral to the stars, where the self became a herdsman accompanied in his loneliness by the planets and constellations (Stetkevych 147).[13] Grisóstomo, in some ways, is precisely such a herdsman since he pursues Marcela, and she, fleeing to the forests, recalls the constellation Virgo, the goddess Astraea, who fled to empty spaces, then to the mountains, and finally to the stars. But this is not all. Grisóstomo's laments for the beloved reveal what some consider to be the melancholy of the Other. As he gets ready to die and tells others how to behave in mourning, he exhibits a non-Christian attitude: 'Y también mandó otras cosas, tales, que los abades del pueblo dicen que no se han de cuplir ni es bien que se cumplan, porque parecen de gentiles' [He ordered also other things so extravagant that the clergy say they must not be performed; nor is it fit they should, for they seem to be heathenish] (1978, 1.12.162; 1998, 82). Recalling Lope's use of pastoral and Moorish ballads in his love laments, Cervantes, perhaps inadvertently, exhibits the Arabic pastoral set in the sky. He also turns this double confluence into questions of culture and politics. Cervantes' pastoral hides conflict and heterodoxy, pointing to the Spain of the Habsburgs where the Other must remained hidden or be banished.

But there may be one more hidden element in this pastoral interlude. A discerning reader may want to ask: Why is it that immediately after the 'author' of the text is revealed as an Arab, this Cide Hamete Benengeli decides to continue his tale by sending Don Quixote into a pastoral space where a heterodox figure imitates Virgil's foundational epic as well as Lucan's epic of the defeated? The first clue to an answer had come in chapter 5. Here, the tale of the idealized Moor Abindarráez is located as an interpolation in the first Spanish pastoral novel, *La Diana*. Thus, pastoral is not only contaminated by epic, but also by Moorish culture. In Grisóstomo's tale, the would-be shepherd acts in non-Christian ways. The Arabic narrator may be attempting to connect not only ballads but also the pastoral novel to the remnants of Moorish culture in Spain. By taking Don Quixote to this land, he would have him recall his previous 'delusion' where he could be both the Christian Valdovinos and the Moor Abindarráez. But Cide Hamete may also be attempting to show that his work, that is *Don Quixote*, is an epic text whose hero truly embodies the culture of his time, a culture that was becoming fragmented through a clash of civilizations. The knight is a conflicted character who propounds Christian knighthood, but is constantly returning to heterodox practices, to contemplations and visions of the Other, whether Muslim, Jew, or convert. Cide Hamete may have us consider that his text is an epic of the defeated, an epic of the Other, one where Muslims and Jews, *conversos* and *moriscos* may view the hero with benevolence. After all, Don Quixote is both constantly defeated and constantly envisioning a different world. For Cide Hamete, this pastoral moment of reflection could be a mirror of the melancholy *converso* and *morisco*, a pastoral that hides the epic of the defeated. In spite of loss, the pastoral also envisions Virgil because he dealt with foundations. The Arab may be pointing to the foundations of a new Spain, one soon to be deprived of diversity. If Grisóstomo represents the Other, then who is Marcela? She certainly is a very human character, someone who can counter Grisóstomo's objections and attain a kind of agency and freedom. But Cervantes' text often encodes many meanings. The fact that she defends her freedom does not mean that Cide Hamete could not have conceived elements of the symbolic in presenting her to the reader. If Grisóstomo is the heterodox figure of the Other then his desire is for the land in which he abides, his beloved Spain. Kingdoms and continents were constantly represented during this period as allegorized women. In this case, Marcela will walk away from Grisósomo, will walk away from the Other who wishes to abide in her lands. She prefers to be alone, to be self-sufficient as a Christian land without the taint of Otherness. The Grisóstomo-Marcela episode can reflect the plaint of the Other (Grisóstomo) as he is barred from the land he loves. It reflects the expulsion of the Jews and prefigures the forced exile of the *moriscos*. It is no coincidence, then, that Cide Hamete appears in the narrative right before pastoral. He wishes to point to the text as belonging to him and show that the pastoral lament is part of his legacy.

So far, we have discussed Grisóstomo's literary career and the poem that was read after his death, the 'Canción desesperada.' The conflict between two epics and the uses of pastoral, as we have seen, may point to conflicts on Spanish soil, to the foundations of a new culture through a clash of civilizations. But Cervantes is not finished with questions of imitation and genre confusion. While discoursing on the relations between pastoral and epic, Cervantes also imitates Ariosto's *Orlando furioso*, which was written as a playful imitation of Virgil. Thomas Hart asserts: 'The first stanza establishes Ariosto's proud claim that his poem belongs to the tradition of Virgilian epic. The claim – not wholly serious, of course, but not just a joke either – is embodied both in the words he uses and in the way they are joined together' (1989, 58). Cervantes' novel also refers once and again to Virgil. The difference is that the playfulness here is mediated by the *Orlando furioso*. Thus, the work is doubly playful while pointing to Virgil and laughing with Ariosto. Indeed, the Marcela episode serves to combine Virgil and Ariosto, genre with gender. Let us turn then from Marcela as allegory to the Marcela of flesh and blood. Marcela belongs to the category of the *mujer esquiva*, so often presented in the theatre of the period. The *esquiva*, for the seventeenth century, was a woman who acted against nature, rejecting the love of men due to vanity or pride. In the works of Lope de Vega and other playwrights, she is humbled in the end, acknowledging love and the need to have a man in her life. In spite of a concerted effort by the men in the play to label her as cruel and misguided, she never gives in and in the end retires to the forest in imitation of the goddess Diana. Melveena McKendrick asserts that 'none of the playwrights of the Golden Age sympathizes with his *esquivas* in the way that Cervantes sympathizes with his Marcela' (1974, 145). But Cervantes is not only alluding to the theatre of his period. As Hart asserts, he may also be pointing to the figure of Angelica in Ariosto's Italian romance, *Orlando furioso* (1989, 78). Angelica, daughter of the emperor of Cathay, is sent to Charlemagne's court in order to distract the warriors from their battle against the Saracen invaders. She is thus able to captivate Orlando, Rinaldo, Ferrau, Maugis, and even some of the Saracens such as Ruggiero.[14] Differing from Marcela, she does succumb to love in the end, falling for an African soldier and fleeing with him to Spain and beyond. Like Cervantes' novel, Ariosto's poem includes pastoral. It surfaces when Orlando, pursuing Mandricard, comes upon an idealized countryside: 'He came to a stream which looked like crystal; a pleasant meadow bloomed on its banks, picked out with lovely pure colours and adorned with many beautiful trees. A welcome breeze tempered the noontide for the rugged flock and naked shepherd, and Orlando felt no discomfort, for all that he was wearing breastplate, helmet and shield' (Ariosto 1983, 278). As in Cervantes' novel, the trees are covered with inscriptions of love. In Cervantes, Grisóstomo and numerous other 'shepherds' write of their love for Marcela. Here, the vegetation only displays words that point to the passion between Angelica and Medoro. Pastoral is where Orlando discovers that his beloved has run off with a Moorish soldier. Orlando, however, does not want to accept such a discovery. Clorinda Donato asserts: 'Orlando desists from acknowledging the truth, surmising that a rival, smitten with his lady, has written those inscriptions to defame her and make him jealous. Thus, Orlando reads objective reality subjectively . . . There is no doubt that such a scene foreshadows don Quijote's encounters with windmills and armies' (1986, 16). Even in the preliminary poems in Cervantes' novel we encounter a reference to the madness of Orlando and how it parallels that of Don Quixote. The verses also speak of how the imagined Dulcinea is somewhat like Angelica (1978, 1.66). The Marcela episode is a variation on this theme. Like Don Quixote, who invents Dulcinea, Grisóstomo is in love with his vision of Marcela. Both prefer their subjective emotions to objective reality. Their madness, then, imitates that of the hero of the *Orlando furioso*. To further that comparison, the Grisóstomo-Marcela episode evokes pastoral, which is the locale where Orlando does his best to reject his discovery of Angelica's new love. Like Angelica, who creates competition and rivalry among the men, Marcela triggers numerous laments. But there is a difference. Angelica is bemused by men's passions and in the end falls for Medoro, thus atoning for her *equivez*, as was common in the period. Marcela, on the other hand, tells the assembled male shepherds that rivalry is not her fault and triumphs over men's desire by turning her back on them and turning to Diana's forest.

However, the pastoral episode in Cervantes is more concerned with epic. Moving away from the Italian romance, Marcela assumes a new genre role. Marcela, the supposed cruel woman who was said by men to be the cause of Grisóstomo's death, appears at his funeral. In so doing, she uses an important technique from epic, appropriating the male song of power, war, and foundations for herself. Marcela appears upon a hill as she looks down on the funeral of Grisóstomo, a moment that recalls an epic teichoskopia. The term teichoskopia or 'view from the wall,' is, as Norman Austin asserts, 'the *locus classicus* for the traditional Helen portrait' (1994, 17). It derives from the famous passage in the third book of the *Iliad* where Helen comes to the walls of Troy to view the deadly contest between her abductor and lover Paris and her husband Menalaus. Virgil follows suit. In the *Aeneid* we find Dido in her tower, viewing Aeneas's departure and contemplating her own suicide. While Helen speaks to the elders at the wall and is viewed and judged by them but not by those below, Dido curses Aeneas and his people as they depart, her words carrying her despair across the waves. In spite of the differences, both epic poems showcase a woman who looks down from above.[15] Cervantes imitates the gendering of teichoskopia, recalling Helen in the *Iliad*, Dido in the *Aeneid*, Antigone in the *Phoenissiae*, and Juno in the *Odes*. Although closely imitating the classical device of a woman who looks down from a wall at the assembled men, there is something missing – there is no wall, just a hill upon which Marcela stands. This leaves Marcela wide open to attack, and that is precisely what happens. Ambrosio lashes out against her. He certainly has the upper hand – he has the *evidentia*. Quintilian observes: 'Suppose I am complaining that someone has been murdered. Am I not to have before my eyes all the circumstances which one can believe to have happened during the event? . . . Will not the blood, the pallor, the groans, the last gasp of the dying be imprinted on my mind?' (2001, 6.2.31; 3.61). In this case, Cervantes presents the visual through narrative, so Ambrosio need not bring it to the mind's eye. After all, the body of Grisóstomo is just below the hill where Marcela is standing. As Roberto González Echevarría has explained, this scene as well as the whole episode, resembles a trial.[16] Ambrosio, as prosecutor, asks: 'si con tu presencia vierten sangre las heridas deste miserable a quien tu crueldad quitó la vida' [to discover whether the wounds of this wretch, whom thy cruelty has deprived of life, will bleed afresh at thy appearance?] (1978, 1.14.185; 1998, 99). What he does not realize is that through his question he is actually proving her innocence, since the corpse does not start bleeding, as was thought it should do in the presence of the killer.

Deceived in thinking that he has the body of evidence, that he has autopsy, what Ambrosio must now do is to use further techniques to blame Marcela.[17] In order to arouse negative emotions in the spectators, Ambrosio becomes indignant that she would dare come to the burial. He accusingly inquires of her: '¿O vienes a ufanarte en las crueles hazañas de tu condición, o a ver desde esa altura como otro despiadado Nero, el incendio de su abrasada Roma?' [or comest thou to triumph in the cruel exploits of thy inhuman disposition? or to behold from that eminence, like another pitiless Nero, the flames of burning Rome?] (1978, 1.14.185; 1998, 99–100). The anecdote of Nero, who was rumoured to have set fire to Rome in order to rebuild it, and who watches the destruction from above, had become a commonplace in the early modern period, appearing in the *Celestina*, and even in the 1615 *Quijote*. In both texts it is used as an analogy for the fires of love, which ravage the lovers (Calisto and Altisidora).[18] Ambrosio's question, then, includes a double analogy and a double condemnation. First, Marcela is like Nero since they each observe with glee a lamentable event – the destruction of ancient Rome and the death of Grisóstomo. Second, the burning fires of Rome are analogous to the flames of passion experienced by Grisóstomo and to the actual flames burning his papers at the funeral. Again, like Nero, Marcela watches with satisfaction the destructive results of the flames of passion.

The Nero analogy seems to emphasize not only cruelty and destruction, but also the fact that teichoskopia has lost its walls; the term no longer conforms to its original meaning. The hill upon which Nero was said to be standing was, according to one legend, the Tarpeian rock. Both Fernando de Rojas and Cervantes in part 2 of his novel allude to a Spanish romance in which Nero stands upon this particular hill to watch the fire. This rock was highly charged with meaning, since it was here that Tarpeia betrayed the city to the Sabines, either for love of gold or for love of the enemy general. It was subsequently used to hurl traitors and murderers to their death. Indeed, when Nero fled Rome after Galba's rebellion, he was terrified of what they would do to him: 'he would be led naked through the streets with his neck in a yoke; he would be beaten with rods until he died, and his body would be thrown from the Tarpeian Rock' (Champlin 2003, 5). These possibilities led him to commit suicide. Thus, the hill upon which Nero stands evokes murder, betrayal, and destruction, as well as visions of the emperor's own demise for his crimes to Rome. And this confirms Ambrosio's negative intent in his depiction of Marcela – she has betrayed and killed Grisóstomo.

But Ambrosio's argument is about to crumble. First, he makes a rhetorical mistake by not mentioning the location from where Nero viewed the fire. Perhaps he has done this for the sake of brevity or lucidity. But unfortunately for him, this ellipsis, the withholding of place, opens up a new possibility. There were more canonical locations for Nero's viewing of the fire, and there was one in particular that stood out. Pedro Mexía in his *Silva de varia lección*, a book often consulted by Cervantes, states: 'assí ardió siete días y noches la ciudad, gozando él [Nero] deste hermoso espectáculo desde una torre' [and thus the city burned for seven days and seven nights as Nero enjoyed this lovely spectacle from his tower] (Mexía 1989, 1.34; 1.474). Nero's tower is actually pinpointed by Suetonius: 'Nero watched the fire from the tower of Maecenas, delighted with what he termed "the beauty of the flames" and, dressed in his stage attire, he sang of "the Fall of Troy"' (2000, 217). This alternate site provides Marcela with the walls that accompany the view from above in a full teichoskopia. Furthermore, the fact that Nero sings of the fall of Troy while watching the burning of Rome brings together the two key ancient epics with their respective teichoskopia: the *Iliad* with its battle for Troy and the *Aeneid*, which has as subtext the founding of Rome. In his biography of Nero, Edward Champlin makes it clear that the negative vision of this emperor was not shared by all, and that many viewed him in a positive light. Indeed, his histrionics may only reveal his own sense of tragedy, 'comparing current evils with ancient disasters' (Champlin 2003, 49). Marcela, like Nero, may be pointing to current evils, the fact that men will not allow her to live in peace. And like Nero she is truly bemoaning the fall of Troy in the sense that it had become a common metaphor for the conquest of a woman's body (as in *El burlador de Sevilla*, for example).[19]

The power of Marcela's speech is further reinforced by yet another place: the tower where Nero stood belonged to Maecenas, the quintessential patron of the arts, who provided for the poets of the Augustan Age. It inspires Nero to sing of the 'fall of Troy' and Marcela to respond to her accusers. Maecenas was Virgil's patron – a poet who sang of the *pax romana* and the Golden Age established by the emperor Augustus. Indeed, this age was said to have been turned upside down by Nero's cruelty in the latter years of his rule. Now Virgil, as noted, was the poetic model for Grisóstomo. While Grisostomo's poems may emphasize Marcela's cruelty, she chooses a teichoskopic location to look down upon the men and give her reply. She is not silent and racked with guilt like Helen, but comes closer to the Virgilian Dido who curses her lover. She is 'unwittingly' aided by Ambrosio's ellipsis,[20] since she can claim that she stands not upon the Tarpeian rock but upon Maecenas's hill and tower, a place that was in many ways consecrated to Augustan poets such as Virgil. Thus, she takes her place as the figure that competes with Grisóstomo to become a new – a female – Virgil.

In Virgil's poem, Aeneas is the trigger for a teichoskopia. Ordered by the gods not to remain in Carthage and to give up amorous pursuits for epic-imperial ones, he abandons Dido. His hasty departure is viewed by lovesick Dido from the top of a tower, in the form of a teichoskopia.[21] This cruel separation will lead her to curse the hero who is abandoning her and driving her to suicide. Arturo Marasso, one of the few critics who have noted Cervantes' imitation of the Dido episode in Virgil states: 'Dido murió por Eneas; Grisóstomo por Marcela. Una misma crueldad y una idéntica desventura arrastran al suicidio a los dos enamorados' [Dido died for Aeneas; Grisostomo for Marcela. A parallel cruelty and an identical misadventure lead the two enamoured men to suicide] (1954, 85). Thus, Cervantes' scene reverses the gender roles. While Aeneas was the cruel one, here Marcela is said to share this fault; and while Aeneas departs to become an epic hero, Marcela turns away to become a goddess of the forests, both embodying their own genre (epic and pastoral). If we look at the Cervantine episode as a mere reversal of Virgil's, I think we are missing the main point. We must keep in mind that Marcela's alleged cruelty is part of Grisóstomo's epic plan. He defames her in order to gain fame and fulfil his poetic career. But his poetry does not sing of a new empire, unless it is the territory of Marcela's body, which is denied to him. He is as cursed (and famous) as Aeneas. Marcela stands upon the hill of Maecenas where she also sings her song. Without her words, the episode would not be as memorable. After all, she is the woman on top. The teichoskopic women of classical literature often suffer and often are unable to act – but they see the full picture, they see the scene below where men battle out of both desire and hatred. In this subtle imitation of the classics, Cervantes takes up teichoskopia in order to imitate and surpass the ancients. He shows Marcela as Helen, as Dido, as Nero,[22] but also as part of the song, as a key component of epic and pastoral, of a new and novel genre. Although it is true that Dido curses Aeneas, her actual words do not reach him or his crew. They move upwards to the realm of the gods. Marcela also goes beyond witnessing in her teichoskopia. Her words are not for the gods. They are for the men who accuse her, and her exalted language is used to move and convince her audience. Although some may claim that her words only carry the histrionic cruelty of Nero, I would argue that her tone brings to fulfilment the epic majesty and exalted location of the teichoskopic women who emerge from an ancient past.

It should also be noted that fortified walls were also the domain of men, and that some chose to speak from above. In the sixth book of Lucan's *Pharsalia*, Caesar constructs an immense wall in an attempt to contain Pompey. Charles Saylor explains: 'In this construction, natural turf is ignored by Caesar and houses of natives are used indiscriminately along with parts of city walls. The vast wall shuts in rivers, forests and wild animals . . . Lucan calls it *bellis . . . spes inproba*, and states that Caesar works against nature' (1978, 146). His work and his hubris are compared to that of Xerxes, who yoked the Hellespont against the will of the gods. In contrast, Pompey uses the city of Dyrrachium whose very location supports the walls and vice versa. He even scatters his men over the hills around the city. Thus, he works in harmony with nature, using 'natural topographical defenses' (Saylor 1978, 145). Given this situation of the natural versus the wall against nature, it should come as no surprise that eventually, Caesar becomes trapped by his own hubristic walls and Pompey can break free. But not before Scaeva, an agent of Caesar, tries to become a part of the wall itself: 'the violation of human limits is played out point by point in the spectacular account of his disfigurement . . . each disfiguring cut not only makes Scaeva more difficult to recognize but measures his spiritual regression away from being human until he ends as a wall, a completely unfeeling, inhuman entity' (Saylor 1978, 251). While Scaeva's cries from the wall become more and more inhuman, Pompey's speech, the one before the battle at Pharsalus, is a true teichoskopia in which he exhorts his men to think of these walls as those of Rome and fight for the city (Saylor 1978, 254). In this epic of the defeated, Pompey asks his soldiers to envision a republican Rome, and follow the pleas of the suffering mothers of the city and of the disheveled senators. His triumph is not to be, but as he falls we may recall Scaeva's inhuman teichoskopia. There are, I think, distinct parallels between this double teichoskopia and the Marcela-Grisóstomo episode. He may stand for Caesar, who walls in Marcela, attempting to trap her with his songs, with his epic, and with his death. He can be seen as the hubristic inhuman epic wall that, even in death, leaves an accusatory epitaph upon the stones of his tomb. Marcela, on the other hand, stands upon the hill, a natural promontory from where she can defend herself. She recalls Pompey's belief in using nature's topography to advantage. But she also stands with Pompey at the walls of Pharsalus. She knows that in spite of a brilliant speech she will lose the war. Like Pompey, she will eventually retreat. He will go to Egypt to meet his death, while she will enter the forest, proclaiming the death of her bond with the pastoral landscape. Like Diana and Astraea she seeks the deepest woods where she can abide in defeat but in freedom.

In conclusion, the tale of Marcela and Grisóstomo may appear at first as a mere retreat into pastoral, a land that is removed from the *negotium* of literary careers, of politics and empire. But Cervantes hides within the pastoral a number of crucial elements. First, he subtly describes Grisóstomo's literary career as one akin to Virgil's. However, Grisóstomo dies too young to fulfil his ambition and one of his poems, rescued from the flames, is not just a pastoral lament but a work contaminated by epic. A closer look shows that the text melds two opposing types of epic, Virgil's epic of empire and Lucan's epic of the defeated. This last element calls for a consideration of what Cervantes' novel represents in terms of empire. It also reminds us that Lucan died young, committing suicide like Grisóstomo. While Lucan did it at Nero's command, Grisóstomo does it out of amorous passion (and/or ambition). The clash of epics is not over at his death. Marcela comes into the scene and surveys it as in an epic teichoskopia. She takes it upon herself to reverse the Aeneas-Dido scene, where the view from the wall signalled his departure to carry out his epic destiny and her suicide. Here, instead, Marcela comes to defend herself, to argue that she is not a new Nero, the cruel killer of Lucan/Grisóstomo. In evoking Nero, she also points to the emperor's poet and signals contamination with Lucan's use of the teichoskopia. She will be part of the epic of the defeated, while maintaining her liberty. But it is the female teichoskopia that is most important. While most women on top can view the epic battle but cannot affect what happens, Marcela's speech seeks to do just that. Cervantes, then, takes an epic device from classical antiquity and carries it to a new level, giving woman a voice and a degree of agency. Marcela becomes an epic figure, impacted by both Virgil and Lucan. Cervantes also sprinkles subtle allusions to the Italian romance. Since Ariosto's *Orlando furioso* contains playful imitations of Virgil, Cervantes' text can be seen to contain this same playfulness now to the second degree, mediated by the Italian. In this new version there are curious parallels: Orlando, Don Quixote, and Grisóstomo, who believe in subjective imaginings over objective reality; and Angelica, Dulcinea, and Marcela, who are different forms of the imagined beloved. Only Marcela becomes a woman who can truly defend herself against the male imagination.

The novelty of Cervantes' novel then, can be found in the gaps and fissures, in the battle of genres, in the struggle for voice. In this second section of the work, we begin with a city that encapsulates many worlds – Toledo with its pomegranate. Then, the chivalric world turns to pastoral, in what may appear to be a typical contrast between the false court and the virtues of the countryside. And yet, we come to understand that pastoral is not only false, as it describes figures that are disguised as shepherds, but it is also a subterfuge for epic. Looking deeper, we see the clash of epics not only in Grisóstomo's poem but also in Marcela's teichoskopia. All of these clashes have come shortly after Cide Hamete Benengeli has emerged as 'author' of the text. Why should an Arab turn to pastoral? It may be that the clashes of epic hide clashes of civilization. In the midst of pastoral the reader is invited to consider the foundations of the new Spanish empire, one where the Other is defeated and vanished. The Arabic narrator may envision Grisóstomo as a heterodox hero who wishes to abide in the land configured as Marcela. But she has her own Christian epic to develop. Grisóstomo, in spite of espousing the Virgilian career, paradoxically follows the epic of the defeated, the epic of the *converso* and the *morisco*. Now the knight has been able to glimpse the highest genre, one that is far above chivalry, and once he has caught a glimpse of clashing epics and civilizations in the land of pastoral, it is time to move on. The limits of pastoral have been strained. The passage has become truly audacious, with many signs of epic ventures and mysteries of Otherness. This enclosed world, about to burst, must yield an opening into a new world. As it is, the pastoral seems like an island surrounded by a forest, difficult to escape, a *non plus ultra*. Searching for the pillars that lead out of pastoral, the reader discovers that Marcela's teichoskopic position may be viewed as one of the pillars that allow us to go beyond. She appears upon a hill as a marvellous vision. This place's natural topography foregrounds her link to nature (or her superiority to the Other). While a number of critics view this apparition as a theophany and Marcela as a goddess,[23] I would add that it can be taken as a greater wonder. Marcela has become a figure of epic, one that has agency. Thus, the hill upon which she stands is one of the pillars, one that seemingly leads to the highest genre or even to the heavens. The second is much more modest in appearance. It is made of the raised earth from Grisóstomo's grave. Rising even higher is the stone with his epitaph that marks his burial place. This stone still speaks through its epitaph, forming a type of teichoskopia which tells us that Marcela is forever cursed. In reality, it is Grisóstomo who may be condemned for his suicidal plot and his will that contains elements that the priests would not allow 'por ser cosas de gentiles' [for they seem to be heathenish] (1978, 1.12.162; 1998, 82). Or is it the other way around? Marcela/Spain may be cursed for expelling the Other, while Grisóstomo curses her for not allowing a broader vision of the land. For the Pythagoreans, the number six is the Scale of the World, while for Christian numerologists it recalled that God had created this world in six days (Agrippa 1987, 191). Thus, the celestial, terrestrial, and infernal realms come together in this number, the number of chapters in this segment. Once Marcela leaves and Grisóstomo lies below, the epic battles subside long enough for Don Quixote to find a way out. The knight must traverse the space between the heavenly realms and the abode of the dead in order to depart pastoral. After all, this genre partakes of the Golden Age, a time when the gods mingled with the human race; it is also, paradoxically a genre that welcomes death as a respite for the suffering lover, and one that some considered to be too pagan, even heathenish. It is a genre hopelessly contaminated by epic and by Moorish tales. Once the myth of Arcadia is disrupted and the opposing epics sing of victory and defeat, it is time for the chivalric pair to be on the road. Passing between the pillars, they come upon a new narrative landscape.

5 Magics of the Defeated

Anxiety. The anguish and constriction of the heart.
— Covarrubias, *Tesoro de la lengua*

Anxiety is the reaction to danger.
— Freud, *Inhibitions, Symptoms and Anxiety*

The third part of the text returns us to the beginning. Once again we have eight chapters (chapters 15 through 22), the Pythagorean number for justice; and again we encounter chivalric adventures that are parodied. But the perfectly wrought chapters of the first segment give way to an episodic structure where adventures take place one after the other, each trying to surpass the one before with new twists and surprises. The adventures, seven in all (if we count the haunting at the inn), are told by a rival to the knight's ideals, one that delights in his unreliability. This third part begins with a highly humorous parody that at times becomes farcical. But once the knight drinks of the magic potion, the balsam of Fierabrás, the flavour of the epic-chivalric reenters the narrative.[1] After all, the balsam first appears in a *chanson de geste*, part of the Carolingian cycle. Once the balsam is ingested, Don Quixote participates in four epic/chivalric adventures: the two armies, the corpse, the fulling mill, and Mambrino's helmet. This glittering object, derived from Boiardo's *Orlando inamorato* and Ariosto's *Orlando furioso*, brings down the knight through hubris. Chapter 22 leads to the collapse of the epic-chivalric through contamination with the picaresque and opens up again the Pillars of Hercules. Thus, two objects, potion and helmet, punctuate this section. The novelist has prepared the reader for their conjunction since

LE BAUME DE FIER-À-BRAS

(Don Quichotte, part. I, ch. 17)

5.1 Don Quixote brewing Balsam of Fierabras. Paris 1884. Illustrator: Jules Worms. Courtesy of the Cervantes Collection, Cushing Memorial Library, Texas A&M University Libraries.

both are alluded to in chapter 10, where the ending of the adventure between the knight and the Biscayan coachman is told. While French *geste* and Italian romance vie for importance, exhibiting its suspect magic, epic also reinforces the structure of this third segment. Even though Virgil is repeatedly invoked, the knight's many defeats point to Lucan's epic of the defeated.[2] And yet, as we seek for signs of the *Pharsalia*, its presence seems evanescent. The clash of genres continues in this segment, including the Virgilian epic, the epic of the defeated, the Italian romances, and the French Carolingian verses, with its pious tale of the triumph against the Saracens. Even medical manuals, ghostly folk tales, and erotic tales become a part of curious contaminations, weaving generic uncertainties into the text.

Don Quixote and Sancho have a hard time escaping pastoral since the genre is enclosed by a forest wall. As a figure akin to the goddess Diana and Astraea, Marcela seeks those recondite places in the forest, away from the company of men. Thus, the episode is a buffer between pastoral and the quotidian; it is a bridge between the last section and segment three. Indeed, it should not come as a surprise that, before leaving the forest the chivalric pair find themselves in a site akin to a *locus amoenus:* a break in the forest with a pleasant field with a stream, a perfect place for a nap. Sancho's beast and Rocinante are set free to graze. However, the restful delight of the place is disrupted by devils, enchanters, or by a trickster Arabic author who bring into the scene some muleteers who are also leading their Galician beasts to pasture. The usually sedate Rocinante decides he wants to frolic with the lady beasts, but they are not at all amused, rejecting him forcefully. The subtext of the episode, according to Chad Leahy, deals with 'la yegua gallega como mujer esquiva y el de la mujer gallega como moza lasciva' [the Galician mare as *a mujer esquiva* and the Galician woman as a lustful maiden] (2008, 90). While the *esquiva* (a woman who will not marry due to vanity or pride) points back to what Marcela's motivation might be according to the moralists of the time, the *lasciva* points forward to Maritornes. As for Rocinante, he acts like a bestial Grisóstomo. The muleteers try to disengage Don Quixote's horse from their mares, but Rocinante is showing unusual passion. On seeing how his great horse is treated by the female beasts and their Galician handlers, the knight takes his sword and enters the fray, followed by Sancho. Needless to say, they lose the battle as they are overpowered and beaten with sticks. Don Quixote moans with a 'con el mismo tono afeminado y doliente que Sancho' [in the same feeble and lamentable tone (as Sancho)] (1978, 1.15.196; 1998, 165). While Rocinante shows male desire while chasing the mares, Don Quixote becomes 'feeble,' or as the Spanish text asserts, 'effeminate.' It is as if master and horse have reversed roles. Furthermore, the episode is a polemic and humorous parody of pastoral. Men are like Rocinante, lusting after Marcela/the Galician mares.

And the site also parodies mythological tales: in Diana's forest, men cannot succeed in their amorous intents. Those who try to fight become effeminate.

Attempting to rise above his defeat, Don Quixote decides that this has been a punishment from Mars: 'en pena de haber pasado las leyes de caballerías, ha permitido el dios de las batallas que se me diese este castigo' [I believe the God of battles has permitted this chastisement to fall upon me as a punishment for having transgressed the laws of chivalry] (1978, 1.15.193; 1998, 106). Don Quixote thus turns away from the feminine and places himself under the rule of Mars, accepting punishment for attacking those who are far inferior to a knight. The mythological allusions do not end here. The knight is in such bad shape that he must be carried by Sancho's ass. Don Quixote tries to stem any further breach of decorum recalling how Silenus, the tutor of Bacchus, had ridden on an ass as he entered Thebes (1978, 1.15.196; 1998, 109). Unfortunately, the knight seems more like a creature of Bacchus, god of laughter, than the wise (and often drunk) Silenus. And the image of Silenus recalls Bellini's *Feast of the Gods* where Bacchus is dispensing wine, as Silenus's donkey betrays Priappus as he sets out to seduce a nymph. Ovid's *Fasti*, the source of the painting, tells how the ass's indiscretion led to his being sacrificed. Perhaps this episode prefigures the theft of Sancho's beast a few chapters later. The beast may be innocent, but it has become a vehicle for a knight, a breach in decorum for which it must atone. In spite of the many myths hidden in this episode, Leahy reminds us, this comic adventure serves as a buffer between pastoral and the everyday world (2008, 89); and I would add that it also serves as a bridge between myth and reality. As in the second segment, Cide Hamete presides over the debacle that brings about a new narrative. While in chapter 10 he spoke about the Biscayan, now he speaks about the Galicians. Spain's periphery seems to want to do violence to the knight who represents Castile, the centre, the site of dominance. And yet, Don Quixote, although he wants to represent an imperial centre, is running through the fields, accosted by visions and beatings, a ghostly emperor, filled with anxieties.

Given the thrashing they have received, the chivalric pair's only recourse is to go to the nearest inn or castle and perhaps concoct the famous balsam of Fierabrás. Once there, they are greeted by Maritornes, among others. Although she is from Asturias, her lust, as stated, has been prefigured by the Galician mares of the previous episode. This lustful woman's name, as Augustin Redondo reminds us, inverts the

name of the Virgin Mary: Mari/tornes (1998, 159). Thus, she is far from
virginal. Although as Henry Mendeloff asserts, a bedroom farce is enacted, with Don Quixote as protagonist, it can be added that epic is not
far away. The hero's inner struggle as to whether to respond to the amorous intents of Maritornes, whom he views as the princess of the castle,
recalls the famous episode of Dido and Aeneas, albeit highly debased.
While Aeneas sails away after having enjoyed the favours of the queen
of Carthage, Don Quixote retains Maritornes in his bed while telling
her that he must not succumb to temptation. The Arabic historian actually delights in saying things he should not, in breaking with decorum.
While Don Quixote had previously engaged in the disnarrated as he
imagined how his story would be told, Cide Hamete engages in the
non-narratable. The text actually comments on his tendencies to narrate what he should not: 'pues las que quedan referidas, con ser tan
mínimas y tan rateras, no las quiso pasar en silencio' [which, however
seemingly minute and trivial, he would not pass over in silence] (1978,
1.16.201; 1998, 113). The English translation actually fails to provide the
full meaning of the Spanish in this case, rendering 'rateras' as trivial.
But the term derives from 'rata' or rat. Sebastián de Covarrubias defines 'ratero' as 'el hombre de baxos pensamientos' [the man with base
thoughts] (1987, 896). The historian, like Don Quixote, engages in the
base and the anti-heroic.

But the knight will not accept this role. The balsam of Fierabrás restores hierarchy and Don Quixote's authority. After all, it works for him
and not for Sancho, a sign that he is indeed a great knight who can
imbibe the heroic potion, while a squire can never taste such subtle
and dangerous draughts. After Don Quixote is purged from drinking
it, his health seems restored, but when Sancho takes it, it is as if he
had taken poison. The balsam, an invention that became part of pious
Christian tales, was made from the liquid that served to embalm Christ.
In the earliest poem on this legend, dated around 1170, the Saracens
have taken a series of relics from Rome: 'the holy crown, the nails from
the cross and the lance that pierced Christ's side' (Morrissey 2003,
68). The mission to retrieve these items and obtain the balsam is not
as clear-cut and knightly as might appear. As Robert Morrissey states,
there are a number of unheroic acts: Charlemagne shows excessive
anger, Roland tries to avoid the assignment, and Ganelon also serves
his own interests (2003, 69–71). Depending on the version, the balsam
was stolen from either Rome (as in the 1170 *chanson*) or Jerusalem by
the giant Fierabrás. It was restored to Charlemagne by Oliveros after

a mighty battle.[3] In Cervantes' novel, however, Don Quixote does not need to fight a Saracen giant in order to obtain the balsam. He brews it with oil, wine, salt, and rosemary (1978, 1.17.209; 1998, 120). Healed, he can now partake of the epic/chivalric. The first problem in this parody of the pious text is that Don Quixote cannot possibly brew the liquid in which Christ was embalmed. No matter what ingredients he may use, the balsam lacks the once present body of Christ. So, Don Quixote is at least guilty of mislabelling his product. More important, as he brews it he prays and makes signs: 'Pidió luego una redoma para echallo, y como no la hubo en la venta, se resolvió de ponello en una alcuza o aceitera de hoja de lata de quien el ventero le hizo grata donación. Y luego dijo sobre la alcuza más de ochenta paternosters y otras tantas avemarías, salves y credos, y a cada palabra acompañaba una cruz, a modo de bendición' [Then he asked for a phial to put it in: and there being no such thing in the inn, he resolved to put it in a cruse or oil-flask of tin which the host made him a present of. And immediately he said over the cruse above four-score Paternosters and as many Ave-Marias, Salves and Credos, and every word was accompanied with the cross, by way of benediction] (1978, 1.17.210; 1998, 120). What he has done is to fashion an *ensalmo,* a potion and prayer used to cure the sick in a way that was forbidden by the church. In his 1538 treatise, Pedro Ciruelo, writing against all superstitions, divides them into four types: necromancy, divination, *ensalmos,* and the use of talismans (1978, 47). He also dedicates a whole chapter to the *ensalmadores* who perform these cures. He exhorts those who have suffered wounds and other physical traumas to go to doctors and pharmacists and to pray to God. At no point is the wounded to resort to *ensalmos,* which are of two kinds: of words alone and of words and substances (1978, 80). Such words incur the sin of blasphemy since they obtain their power from the devil. As for the substances used by these healers, they have no power in themselves. They are endowed with power by the devil. One may argue that the words intoned by Don Quixote as he prepares the balsam are Christian prayers. Even so, these are sinful according to Ciruelo. If a sick man wants to pray to God asking for healing, this is perfectly licit. But when the prayers are said as part of an *ensalmo,* they are used in a superstitious manner. These words cure 'por astucia secreta del diablo' [by a secret cleverness of the devil] (1978, 82).

Ciruelo was not alone in condemning this practice. Given the prevalence of *ensalmos* in Golden Age Spain, many religious authors spoke up against them. And yet, this practice spread to America, where, as

Araceli Campos Moreno finds, these and other magical texts pervaded the viceroyalty of New Spain: 'Los textos se transmitieron oralmente o mediante hojas manuscritas que corrían de mano en mano. Varios de esos textos se pueden hallar en las denuncias y procesos que el Santo Oficio emprendió' [The texts were transmitted orally or through sheets in manuscript that were disseminated from person to person. A number of these texts can be found in the accusations and trials of the Holy Inquisition] (2001, 70). This historian has collected fifteen prayers, seventeen *ensalmos,* and forty-six *conjuros* examined by the Inquisition between 1603 and 1630. As they proliferated in America, the *ensalmos* continued to be condemned in Spain. Perhaps the most important treatise on these ceremonies was written some years after Cervantes' novel by Manuel do Valle de Moura, an Inquisitor from Portugal. Armando Maggi, who has carefully studied *De incantantioniibus seu ensalmis* (1620), provides and translates De Moura's definition: '*Ensalmi* are benedictions or evil invocations (*imprecationes*) composed of a certain formula of words, primarily holy ones, and sometimes also of some material things like wine or cloth . . . Many individuals, first of all, Spaniards, make use of these [*ensalmi*] to heal wounds and different diseases and to remove various forms of injuries . . .' (Maggi 2001, 55–6). This is precisely what Don Quixote does in the text. De Moura's treatise also highlights an element neglected by Ciruelo – the use of gestures or ceremonies. They are used to 'affect reality' (Maggi 2001, 51). And we note that for Don Quixote 'a cada palabra acompañaba una cruz' [every word was accompanied by the cross] (1978, 1.17.210; 1998, 120). The knight thus seems to know quite well how to perform an *ensalmo.* For De Moura, the words can potentially be addressed to two different listeners, God and the devil, and even when addressed to God 'a human speaker may be unaware that his or her first addressee, and thus primary benefactor, is not God, but the devil' (Maggi 2001, 67). Even though he is using Christian prayers, by not stating directly that the addressee is the Christian God, Don Quixote is already diverting his pious words to the devil. Furthermore, those who suffer from melancholy have a 'borderline identity, which, because of the nature of its mental disease, lends itself to the Enemy's attack, since the devil primarily attempts to undermine the natural course of our thoughts' (Maggi 2001, 76). We have seen that Don Quixote, from the very beginning of the novel, suffers from this humoral imbalance. There is no question, then, that Don Quixote is committing a mortal sin and a blasphemy, not only by the standards of Ciruelo, but also by those of De Moura. He never calls on God for help, although he uses Christian prayer; he uses Christian signs to produce magical effects; he utilizes substances that by themselves would not cure but are endowed with 'miraculous' and devilish power through the ceremony; and he is a melancholy figure, afflicted with a sickness that calls upon the devil.

I believe that Don Quixote's transgressions are also part of the mystery which is hidden in the text, an anxiety that leads him to pretend that he is a Christian knight. As Sigmund Freud once stated: 'Anxiety is the reaction to danger' (1959, 82). However, Don Quixote is always seeking danger. The danger he embraces is that of the adventure of the Christian knight. This real or imagined danger allows him to forget the anxiety about an 'unknown danger . . . Neurotic danger is thus a danger that has still to be discovered' (1959, 100). Stephen Greenblatt has argued that Freud is not particularly applicable to the early modern period: 'The subject in Freud is most often encountered in states of extreme alienation. Driven by compulsions over which it has little or no control, haunted by repressed desires . . . Yet the intensity of Freud's vision of alienation would seem, in much of his writing, to depend upon the dream of authentic possession' (1986, 213). While in Freud there is an 'irreducible identity,' in the Renaissance and early modern periods the self is configured through 'a collection of attributes' (1986, 216). For Greenblatt, this identity 'may not originate in . . . the fixity, the certainty, of our own body . . . Shakespeare's characters are frequently haunted by the sense that their own identity has been lost or stolen' (1986, 218–19); and this is because it is perceived only in the mask, 'something constructed and assumed' (1986, 222). Although there is much of the theatrical mask in Don Quixote, there is also a deep sense of a haunted identity, of a subterranean and almost unfathomable self that is in conflict, thus leading to profound anxieties. In terms of Christian seventeenth-century Spain, Don Quixote is avoiding the heretical or sinful stain that pollutes his soul; he refuses to listen to the conflict hidden within. Through apparently crazed action, he is attempting to lighten the weight that engulfs him, or, in Sebastián de Covarrubias's words, the 'congoxa y el apretamiento del corazón' [the anguish and constriction of the heart] (1987, 124), which is his definition for anxiety. The knight must move away from himself and constantly produce new images, new adventures, so that the outer danger will obscure his psychic malaise, the demons or ghosts that torment him. This danger is the secret of the text, one that is carried by the knight from adventure to adventure. Only at times will Don Quixote's actions point to the trauma hidden within himself. If Don Quixote acknowledged such a situation, then his reaction would simply be fear. But he hides it, only to produce · some of its 'symptoms' in revelatory moments, such as in the *ensalmo*.

These ceremonies, De Moura tells us, were often performed by a convert to Christianity, who may appear to embrace the 'true' religion but actually preserves some of his older beliefs (Maggi 2001, 65). Not only is Don Quixote committing a mortal sin and engaging in hetero-dox practices, but he is engaged in one that is often related to *conversos* and *moriscos*.[4] There are many examples of this. According to Julio Caro Baroja, ca. 1530s, a notorious *conversa* named *la beata*, Leonor Barzana de Toledo, whose father was burned for 'Judaizing,' was condemned for her incantatory use of formulaic Christian prayers, using them for a number of different heterodox purposes, and with herbs and candles (1967, 2:75–94). In addition, Isaac Jack Lévy and Rosemary Lévy Zum-walt have documented many such prayers and incantations that were used by some Sephardic Jews who left Spain – performances that are still remembered by their descendents.[5] There *ensalmos* were presum-ably also used by the *conversos* who remained in Spain after the ex-pulsion. These two critics claim, for example, that the term *prekante* 'connoted a ritual curing through prayer that was conducted by the *prekantadora*, who was a specialist and a healer of bounteous good will' (2002, 152). In addition to prayers, motion was important. Instead of the sign of the cross used by Don Quixote, some *conversos* would use the *pasar la mano*, passing the hand or making circles with the hand over parts of the body (2002, 155). In contradistinction to this particular practice, Don Quixote uses the signs over the herbs rather than over the body. But there is no question that he knows what he is doing. In using salt, he recalls that the *prekante* used this ingredient for purification in the rituals (2002, 156). Indeed, rosemary was another key ingredient used perhaps due to its pungent odour, and because it averted the evil eye (2002, 94, 104, 105, 131).[6] As for the wine, it appears mostly in cures where the water of the night dew is also used (2002, 135). Oil, of course, was a prevalent remedy. Thus, Don Quixote follows much of what we know of the ancient Jewish curative practices: motions over the body, prayers, and the four ingredients: salt, rosemary, wine, and oil.

While those who sought to cure viewed their trade as positive, many Christians equated them with sorcery. In Cervantes' *Persiles y Segismunda*, for example, Rutilio marries a mysterious woman who frees him from prison and who cures with herbs and words. She turns out to be a witch with demonic powers. Shortly thereafter, Cenotia, a *morisca* from Granada, boasts of her powers (Díez Fernández and Fernández Aguirre de Carcer 1992, 33–67). Cervantes, then, foregrounds the curative yet devilish powers of the Other. Indeed, the *moriscos*, like the *conversos*, had available to them manuscripts containing *ensalmos* such as the *Misceláneo de Salomón* (Martínez Ruiz 1985, 217–22). It was said that the Saracens, descendants of Shem via Ishmael, were not only ferocious warriors, but also magicians (Tolan 2002, 10, 20). When the Saracens of old became transformed into the Moorish enemies of Spain, they preserved these characteristics. They would undoubtedly practise *ensalmos*. Cervantes spent five years as a captive in Algiers, a place described by María Antonia Garcés as a 'freewheeling society, distinguished by its cultural crossbreeding and its hybrid lingua franca, which was a mixture of all Mediterranean languages' (2002, 88). Thus, Cervantes may have learned from this multicultural site many different ways of performing these heterodox rituals, which would have been much in demand given that a number of the captives were tortured. Don Quixote's *ensalmo*, then, may have an African provenance. Since the balsam of Fierabrás is such an important motif in the novel, the question must be asked as to why Don Quixote points to a Christian balsam which was snatched from the Saracens and brought back to Charlemagne, while he actually concocts a heterodox *ensalmo*, which may be part of the *converso*, the *morisco*, or the Algerian curative repertoire. Cervantes, then, transforms the Carolingian cycle and the chivalric romances in the polemical manner which Dentith finds key to parody (2000, 59).

Equally curious is why the chivalric pair believes that the inn is haunted by Moors. While Don Quixote searches for the 'moro encantado' [enchanted Moor] who beat him in this enchanted castle, Sancho asserts that he was beaten not by one, but by four hundred Moors (1978, 17.208; 1998, 118). These hauntings take place precisely when the whole question of heterodox practices (and origins) is foregrounded. Let us recall that in *Hamlet* the ghost comes because something is rotten in the state of Denmark. It is true that the old king has come to see his son, but the ghost comes to tell him that he must avenge the evil that has been perpetrated. Jacques Derrida would say that 'this being-with specters would also be, not only but also, a politics of memory, of inheritance, and of generations' (1994, 19). This critic says of a spectre: '*It is* something that one does not know, precisely, and one does not know if precisely it is, if it exists, if it responds to a name and corresponds to an essence. One does not know: not out of ignorance, but because this non-object, this non-present present, this being-there of an absent or departed one no longer belongs to knowledge. At least no longer to what one thinks one knows by the name of knowledge' (1994, 6). This is precisely what is happening at the inn. Don Quixote, by recalling a long-forgotten recipe of an *ensalmo,* has a kind of knowledge that he can no longer name, that is no longer his. The spectre may be that of a past he has erased in order to search for a most Christian and glorious future. Although he cannot name what haunts the inn, the answer lies in forgotten and heterodox knowledge. Such sightings of a past not to be spoken of begin to proliferate as Sancho sees four hundred ghosts. They are the memories of a conflictive history, one where the converted hide their past and their practices. While Don Quixote's spectre rises out of his anxieties, Sancho's four hundred ghosts emerge from the anxieties of a land besieged by its own inability to accept the other. Suffice it to say that heterodox medicines impinge upon the matter of pious Christian tales and chivalric-epic pursuits, while spectres of a personal and political memory haunt the travellers. And yet, Don Quixote believes he is cured, not realizing that the means of the cure reveals the poison in the depth of his being. He believes himself a knight, and goes out of the haunted inn, out of his own mental anxieties, to fight new battles. Like Hamlet, he puts on a play for us, but unlike Hamlet he does not understand what the ghost has tried to communicate.

In order not to remember what has been erased, epic, the strongest and most powerful of genres, must come to the fore. Immediately after the haunting, an adventure must arouse Don Quixote's epic-chivalric expectations. As he travels with Sancho, he views in the distance a cloud of dust. This must be an approaching army, he concludes: 'Pues toda es cuajada de un copiosísimo ejército que de diversas e innumerables gentes por allí viene marchando' [it is raised by a prodigious army of divers and innumerable nations, who are on the march this way] (1978, 18.218; 1998, 127). Sancho actually reinforces his master's imagination by pointing out that there are actually two clouds of dust approaching. Don Quixote's use of the term *copiosísimo* and Sancho's response is a textual indicator that this episode will be one of *copia* or a copiousness or imitation through abundance. Indeed, it will arouse wonderment with the knight's ability to name numerous individuals in these two armies as well as their places of origin. In order to obtain a better view, Don Quixote asks Sancho to accompany him to the top of a hill. Using the device of teichoskopia, found in epics from Homer to Virgil, the knight tells Sancho about the Christian and pagan armies that are about to clash. As opposed to the Marcela episode, where epic women are to view silently, here we have a male *teichoskopia* where male speech from above is often demanded.[7] The knight even contaminates the epic speech with elements from rhetoric, a part of what Cicero and Quintilian label *evidentia*, giving the impression that one is actually looking at events: 'a quality which makes us seem not so much to be talking about something as exhibiting it' (Quintilian 2001, 6.2.32; 3.61). While in a speech it would be the speaker who envisions events, in a work of fiction, a character or narrative voice may pose as the one who sees and thus provides evidence of the event. Cervantes, in his clever use of rhetorical *evidentia*, provides the sounds and sights that may confirm the presence of two armies. Quintilian asserts: 'It is proper that the student should be moved by his subject and imagine it to be real' (2001, 6.2.36; 3.63). Don Quixote certainly does so, and as such he can be considered a good student of rhetoric – albeit one who believes in his own imaginings. But rhetoric does not necessarily search for truth. It can be at odds with the historical account as conceived by the ancients. Thus, Don Quixote can draw from his imagination as he enumerates the heroes on each side. For Michael McGaha there is a 'bizarre combination of musicality and humor in these names' (1991, 156). Indeed, teichoskopic moments are usually tied to a type of *enumeratio* typical of the classical epic, and later of the Italian romances and the romances of chivalry – the catalogue of heroes before a battle follows the epic tradition, and the division of armed groups by lands and rivers of their homeland is typically Virgilian.[8] The mention of the rivers Xanthus from Troy and Pactolus from Lydia are but some of the geographic markers found in the *Aeneid*.[9] Don Quixote's copious discourse then recalls epic and places him again under the mantle of epic and empire for Charles V was said to be a descendant of Aeneas. His triumphs were celebrated, according to Marie Tanner, with 'Vergilian rhetoric' (1993, 113). Unfortunately, there is no triumph to be celebrated here. Don Quixote seeks to intervene against the army of Alifanfarón, thus discarding his anxieties as he faces an Islamic king. But the armies turn out to be sheep, and the shepherds, seeing their flocks so ill treated, start to hurl pebbles at Don Quixote with their slings. The knight, feeling this onslaught, takes out the famous balsam to cure himself. But as he drinks of it, a large pebble hits him breaking three or four of his teeth. A Virgilian epic has turned into an epic of the defeated. Both 'valorous' knight and 'Christian' balsam fail in this parody of the epic and chivalric genres. Perhaps some consolation can be had by recalling that Ajax, when he is denied the armour of the dead Achilles, goes mad and also confuses sheep as armies.[10] And it is true that Don Quixote has been denied, so far, the helmet of Mambrino. But this is not the knight's excuse. Once again he turns to the evil enchanter in the *Belianís de Grecia.* It was he who turned armies into sheep. But none of this makes the pair feel any better as they seek shelter from the fateful tempests that assail them.[11]

No shelter is to be found as yet another storm gathers against the pair, while Sancho decides he knows the source of all this bad luck. He tells his master that he has sinned against the order of knighthood by not doing all the austerities he said he would do until he found the helmet of Mambrino (1978, 19.228; 1998, 134). Not long after Sancho mentions this Moorish talisman, the ghosts from the past reappear. It is as if the spectres of the knight's anxieties lie in wait to torment him. In the dark of night, Don Quixote and Sancho see stars or mysterious lights approaching. They turn out to be torches that lead a funeral procession. Don Quixote immediately reacts, trying to clear his melancholy mind of unwanted thoughts and apparitions. He attacks some of the mourners and succeeds only in breaking Alonso López's leg. The episode, as Arturo Marasso explains, recalls an episode in Mafeo Veggio's continuation or Thirteenth Book of Virgil's *Aeneid*, appended to Hernández de Velasco's translation. Here, we witness the procession that will take Turnus's body to his father Daunus. Many of the ingredients used by Cervantes come directly form the translation: the dark and silence of the night, the empty fields, the strange sight, the mourning of the participants, and the lighted torches. While Hernández de Velasco writes of 'de negras hachas todas encendidas' [black torches all lighted] (Marasso 1954, 239), Cervantes echoes these words. The black of mourning is transferred from the torches to the black coverings of the litter, the horses, and the mules. While in the past Don Quixote has been equated with Aeneas, here he seems to want to reverse allegiances. The hot-headed but valiant Turnus leads the battle against the Trojans in Italy. He even kills Aeneas's protégé, Pallas, the son of King Evander, taking his belt as booty and boasting of his deed. When in the twelfth and last book of the epic, it comes to a single combat between Aeneas and Turnus, the latter clearly shows his prowess in battle. But this is to no avail, as the Trojan hero vanquishes him. When the defeated son of the king of the Latins asks that he be spared, Aeneas considers this possibility, but on seeing that Turnus is wearing Pallas's belt, 'that memorial of cruel grief' (1978, 12.945), Aeneas turns away from mercy and 'buries the sword with fiery zeal' (1978, 12.950–1). Don Quixote, then, reenacts in his mind the procession that brought Turnus's corpse to his father.

In so doing, he also becomes a phantom of the emperor once again. Charles V challenged his rival Francis I to single combat at least twice, recalling how Aeneas was able to slay Mezentius in single combat and later repeated this feat with his main enemy, Turnus, thus ending the wars in Italy.[12] Don Quixote may have wanted to save Turnus, to turn Aeneas into a more compassionate hero, but, as stated above, he only succeeds in breaking Alonso's leg. His opponent is not a warrior, but an ecclesiastic who proceeds to excommunicate the knight. The epic grandeur of Charles V, who fights at Muhlberg for the Catholic cause, becomes a mere shadow in Don Quixote, whose mock battles are far from Catholic and whose trivial adventures mock an imperial past. Charles set free his rival, the French king Francis I, taking him at his word, when Francis reneged on his promises. Charles lost many of the advantages gained at the battle of Pavia. Don Quixote, instead, fails to abide by his own sworn statements.

The tempests are not yet at an end as the pair fails to find shelter that night. The phantoms still pursue them. In the dark of night, having survived the enchantments of Frestón and the ghostly procession, they rush to what they think is a stream only to hear the most dreadful sounds of clanging and chains: 'la soledad, el sitio, la escuridad, el ruido del agua con el susurro de las hojas, todo causaba horror y espanto, y más cuando vieron que ni los golpes cesaban, ni el viento dormía, ni la mañana llegaba' [the solitude, the situation, the darkness, and the noise of the water, with the whispering leaves, all occasioned horror and astonishment] (1978, 1.20.237–8; 1998, 142). Although this episode may derive from a ghost story, the terror felt by Don Quixote and Sancho when they hear the eerie sound may also stem from the episode of the Cyclops in the third book of the *Aeneid*.[13] Once again, different genres are commingled to produce unexpected results. To prepare himself for battle, Don Quixote evokes the myth of the Age of Gold which he is destined to bring back. He also calls upon Mars, the god of battle, for strength. All is for naught in a devastating blow to the knight's ego. After waiting all night to engage in battle the pair discovers that the noise is made by a fulling mill on a stream. At this point, laughter rings out from both Don Quixote and Sancho, and the reader may wonder why the knight did not transform these mills into a chivalric threat as he did with the windmills or into echoes of epic as with the procession. Perhaps the contrast of what he and Sancho expected and the resulting mill is too extreme to carry out the metamorphosis. Or perhaps the moistness of the environment has temporarily assuaged the madness of the knight, adding humidity to his dried body and brain. If this is so, it is disconcerting that it does not happen again with the helmet of Mambrino since there, a light rain is falling. There is a third possibility, which entails a knowledge of the history of technology, and this is something that we have already seen with the windmills. Fulling mills originated in Persia and came to Europe through Islamic Spain. As an Arabic invention, it could either arouse the wrath of the knight or trigger his anxieties. If this is the answer, then it melds well with the episodes of the balsam of Fierabrás and the upcoming helmet of Mambrino. No one wins here, except perhaps Sancho, who learns how to deceive his master. In the end, as Edwin Williamson asserts: 'The momentary anarchy of the fulling-mills episode is overcome, and the paternalistic distance between master and servant restored' (1984, 143). For Keith Budner, the clanging chains of the fulling mills also become the chains forged by Vulcan that trap Mars. The vision of a Golden Age is replaced by mocking laughter, a trapped and lustful god, and the inventions of an Age of Iron. An eclectic imitation, using ghost stories, chivalric tales, epic allusions, myths, and the concept of the ages of humankind (which appears in both Virgil's poetry and Pythagorean theories) come together to produce astounding effects and an unexpected conclusion.

In order to overcome the iron chains of polemical parody in which the Arabic historian wants to trap him, the knight decides that he must have the helmet of Mambrino. Manuel Durán states: 'He has seen, far away, a glimmer of gold that he relates to his rich literary background. He is no longer dealing with the forces of darkness and of technology, as in the previous adventure. He feels at home: a golden helmet brings to his mind the Italian Renaissance epic . . . the best of all possible worlds' (1995, 18). This object derived from the Italian romances of Boiardo and Ariosto, was made of pure gold and signalled invincibility to the wearer. It is strange, then, that paladins can be killed and dispossessed while possessing it: Rinaldo takes it from the Moor Mambrino. Sancho, in his folk style, hopes that it is true oregano, rather than fulling mills, by which he means that the object has true potency. Albertus Magnus, in his *Natural History*, for example, claims that oregano cures bites from poisonous snakes (1973, 98). Don Quixote, like Sancho, is searching for an object with talismanic power. The knight already possesses the balsam for a cure. Now he needs something for invincibility so as to stop his many defeats. While the squire thinks of oregano, the knight comes up with an even more appropriate tale.

When the barber abandons his basin on seeing the charging knight, Don Quixote compares this moment to the beaver that, on seeing the hunter, bites off his genitals and leaves them behind since he knows that this is what the hunter values. This *castoreum* was listed in many medical manuals. This time the knight does not need to turn to Moorish sources. This balm for potency is found, for example, in Marsilio Ficino's *Three Books on Life* (1989, 140). By taking the helmet, the knight acquires the potency to fight.[14] The helmet, then, represents both the magical power which, according to Edward Dudley, Don Quixote ascribes to it, and it becomes an emblem of the knight's illness, of his mental state, as Michael McGaha affirms.[15] Thus, the iron and gold of the previous episode reappear here, as they will again in the adventure of the galley slaves. Cervantes' knight is a Charles consumed by illness but steeling himself onwards, hoping for a miracle. The golden glow of the emperor, as portrayed by Titian's paintings of the ailing emperor, hid his sallow constitution, his debilitating illness.[16] And Don Quixote, yellowed by strife and melancholy, is but a reminder of past struggles as he reaches for the golden glow of a barber's basin. He believes that his anxieties, that the anguish he feels, will be assuaged by this Moorish magical talisman. This time, he turns to orthodox medical manuals instead of forbidden practices for his cure. And yet, what he wants to wear upon his head, although a spoil from battle, is still, in his mind, the helmet that was wrought for a Moorish king. It is Moorish magic that impels him forward. Paradoxically he sheds his anxiety and seeks to acquire the strength of a Christian knight through the magics of the Other. His secret, then, is implicated in this wavering back and forth between Charlemagne, Charles V, and their foes.

After six mostly disastrous adventures, where parody continues its polemical discourse, we are finally led to the culmination of this third narrative section of the novel. Don Quixote, buoyed up by the basin/helmet, decides to free twelve galley slaves. This is a far cry from a chivalric adventure, even if seen through the dazed vision of a crazed knight. The adventure, as Anthony Close has noted, is replete with folklore and lower genres. Close points to farce in the form of a 'burlesque tribunal' and to the use of double entendre in Don Quixote's interrogation of the galley slaves (2007, 15–17). Wordplay allows them to be viewed as victims while they are truly guilty. This is a far cry from the first part of the novel where hagiography, mythology, and Pythagorean numerology bolster the narrative. Nor is there anything here from Lucan's epic of the defeated except defeat itself. The iron chains of the *galeotes*, then, point to a fallen world where the Golden Age is far behind and where the Iron Age of lies and strife is very much in play. But Don Quixote fails to notice any of this. He even ignores the importance of the picaresque as Ginés de Pasamonte, whose story, we are told, can rival that of *Lazarillo de Tormes*, becomes the most prominent speaker among the galley slaves. The picaresque here produces a series of criminal traits: 'cynical contempt for the law, stoical defiance, truculence, and a characteristic style, including ruffian's slang and . . . euphemisms' (Close 2007, 18).

Not only does Don Quixote fail to notice all these traits, but he seeks to free galley slaves who have been condemned by the king himself. In doing so, he becomes, in Roberto González Echevarría's words, a 'fugitive from justice' (2005, 69). And yet, there are those that lay fault not just on the knight but on the flawed system of justice. For Kurt Reichenberger, 'the Crown was broke. At the deathbed of his father, Philip III learned that the State revenues for the following two years were already mortgaged by Genoese bankers. No money was at hand for the galleys. Thus the judges organized a bum rap: condemning men for minor crimes to the galleys. There was no need to pay them this way' (2005, 55). Whether hero or rogue, sacrificial victim or victim of a scam of words, Don Quixote must accept that he is a fugitive from justice. He cannot turn to Alfonso el Sabio's laws nor can he point to epic precedent. In spite of being deceived by rogues, this may still be his finest moment. He has perceived the Crown's injustice, and he returns as a vengeful ghost to mend the ways of the new Habsburgs. However we judge his justice, the narrative cannot proceed. We have reached a narrative impasse. The knight has gone beyond the chivalric books, which would forbid such an attack against those condemned by a ruler; and beyond the epic of the defeated since there is no appropriate enemy. As required by the ghostly emperor, two pillars make their appearance. On the one hand, we have the king's justice represented by the commissary's staff, which he lifts in order to keep order among the galley slaves, and Ginés de Pasamonte in particular. On the other hand we have Don Quixote, convinced of the innocence of the condemned. He raises his lance and attacks the commissary. While the first segment ended with the knight and the Biscayan holding up their swords, here there will be a battle. The pillars are not held high since the narrative has become highly unstable. Close sees the ending landscape in a different manner: 'The chapter ends with a brilliantly evocative image of two vertical figures and two horizontal ones in the now deserted *sierra*:

Don Quijote and Rocinante stretched out on the ground side by side; Sancho stripped of his cloak beside his ass, which stands pensive' (2007, 23). The standing pillars are Sancho and his beast. And this second set of columns is also apt. It will be Sancho who will lead Don Quixote away from this place, and it will be the theft of his ass that will add to the mystery of the next and fourth section of the novel.

This third segment of the novel, like the first, is divided into eight chapters. Eight, it should be recalled, is the Pythagorean number of justice (Agrippa 1987, 206). While in the first section the knight unjustly challenged the Biscayan, here he goes a step further, challenging the justice of the realm. The number of justice foregrounds Don Quixote's misdeeds and his audacious stand against the Crown. It may be difficult to separate him from the picaresque character in the episode, Ginés de Pasamonte – both are now fugitives from justice. However, there is one major difference: the knight does not disrupt the social fabric for his own gain. And yet, the questions can still be asked: How can a knight become an outlaw and still preserve his epic-chivalric stance? Are the seeds of his resentment to be found in the balsam and the helmet, objects of dangerous magic, the one becoming a *morisco* incantation and the second a golden treasure of Moorish power? Are these objects joined by the fulling mills of Islamic origin? From these uncertainties, other questions arise: is the gentleman from La Mancha a pursuing emperor rising from the past to right the wrongs of his successors, or is Don Quixote pursued by anxieties of blood, a cause of deep resentments? Neither solution can be envisioned as decorous or appropriate. The text must improvise. And this is as it should be since, as González Echevarría has noted: 'Cervantes' greatest innovation is to have let improvisation enter into his creative process and be apparent in the final product . . . There is an unfinished quality to the *Quijote*' (2005, 76). Of course, one may argue that this quality of improvisation is a form of *sprezzatura*, where what is apparently spontaneous has taken careful thought and consideration. The ghosts of the past call out their claims as the narrative must advance, striving to reach beyond so that the spectral cannot take hold of the many parodic objects that cement this chivalric, picaresque, and epic narrative.

6 Clues to a Narrative

I saw some animal tracks in the sand, and I could easily tell that they were those of a small dog . . . Other traces going in a different direction and apparently made by something brushing constantly over the surface of the sand beside the front paws, told me that she had very long ears. And as I noticed that the sand was always less indented by one paw than by the other three, I realized that the bitch belonging to our most august Queen had, if I may dare say so, a slight limp.

– Voltaire, *Zadig*

The 1605 *Don Quixote* is divided into four parts, reflecting the Pythagorean quaternities foregrounded in the creation of the narrative world. With the first three parts I have continued the division found in the Cervantine text. But when it comes to part 4, I will deviate and create an additional part, establishing the four of creation and a five of quintessence. In Cervantes' novel, the last part begins with chapter 28. This makes very little sense since chapter 27 ends the tale of Cardenio and chapter 28 takes up the tale of Dorotea, both part of the labyrinthine plot structure that surrounds Sierra Morena. So, I would move forward the fourth part to chapter 23 since this is the beginning of a radical change in the narrative. Here, the narrative moves from a linear tale to a labyrinth where many mysteries and narrative threads appear. Chapter 28 is a false division since it occurs in the middle of the labyrinth. The reasons for Cervantes' strange choice and what this alternative division reveals will be intimated in chapter 7. In addition, the fourth segment, comprising chapters 23 to 46 is so vast, that I have divided it into three chapters in this book. The present chapter will

6.1 Standard bearers, drummers, and trumpeters of a Saracen army on camels and horses. Thirteenth century. From Arab manuscript. Art Resource, NY.

take up the minidetective story that the pair encounters as they enter the mountains. Chapter 7 will look at the labyrinth of narratives, while the eighth will deal with the winding down of interlace as the chivalric pair goes to the inn and preparations are made for their return home.

In the previous chapter, the knight had met twelve galley slaves being led to become oarsmen for a specific period of time due to their infringements on the law of the land. On sensing their plight, Don Quixote stops to interrogate six of them and, on the basis of their elusive answers, he decides that an injustice has been committed and that he should free them. It makes no difference if he is correct in assuming that these men have been given too severe a punishment. What is important is that this is perhaps Don Quixote's major transgression in the novel. First, he does not understand the complex and bureaucratic legal system of the times, thinking that he is still in a world of chivalric prowess. Second, even if he were *illo tempore,* he is doing precisely what a knight should not do. Instead of defending his king, he flaunts his justice. And third, as Roberto González Echevarría has clearly explained, the knight goes against the law of the land and is seen to do so by the guards who carry the prisoners. He thus 'becomes a fugitive from justice' (2005, 69). Sancho, who clearly understands the problem, suggests they hide in Sierra Morena. The mountain can represent the primeval rock that Hercules had to destroy in order to move forward. While this time it is Sancho who leads the way, Don Quixote, intuiting his error, agrees to go along. Once they enter the forested mountains, the heart of the *despoblado,* the narrative begins to shift.[1]

As Don Quixote enters Sierra Morena, he finds it a place for adventure since it is remote and its geography intricate: 'Así como don Quijote entró por aquellas montañas, se le alegró el corazón, pareciéndole aquellos lugares acomodados para las aventuras que buscaba' [Don Quixote's heart leaped for joy at entering into the mountains, such kind of places seeming to him the most likely to furnish him with those adventures he was in quest of] (1978, 1.23.278–9; 1998, 175). This landscape also moves us to a new kind of genre, the sentimental novel. As Marina Brownlee has asserted, forbidding landscapes have been related to the inability to control through language (1990, 212), and this is exactly what has happened. Don Quixote had attempted to change a picaresque episode, the freeing of the galley slaves, into a chivalric one. The slaves' language overcame through wit the knight's own vision. And the knight's language could no longer control his downward shift to the picaresque, as he became a fugitive from justice. Now, in search of a new vision and a new language, knight and squire climb the mountains. As they go deeper into this realm, yet another genre (one that was not to be named until the nineteenth century) supplants the sentimental, albeit briefly. The pair becomes more like the detective pair of Sherlock Holmes and Watson who follow clues. In so doing, they lose some of their personalities as knight and squire who follow adventures. This chapter, then, is about the entrance into the Sierra Morena and the change in the characters. It will end with the appearance of Cardenio, a figure from the sentimental novel. Unfortunately, he cannot detain us for long. The next chapter will take up the full generic implications of this new topography. In order to fully understand what is transpiring in this introductory section, I will turn to a tale by Voltaire and use one of his *contes philosophiques* to look back at these mysterious episodes.

The mystery story or detective fiction has been said to derive from an ancient Persian tale that would eventually give rise to an episode in Voltaire's tale, *Zadig* (1748; rev. 1752). Although it is always tricky to search for origins, Carlo Ginsburg supports this genealogy of detection, and discusses what has come to be known as Zadig's method.[2] For him, it is a way of gaining knowledge that would inspire writers such as Edgar Alan Poe and Sir Arthur Conan Doyle. In this chapter, I would like to take as a point of departure Voltaire's famous story, in order to detect how Don Quixote moves from one way of looking at clues to a very different method. In so doing, I will argue, he unwittingly signals the transformation of how the novel itself develops the narrative. In addition, we will see how, for a moment, Don Quixote looks at empirical evidence rather than at his imagined memories. Furthermore, Voltaire's *conte philosophique* takes up the notion of optimism, pondering on Leibnitz's notion that the Creator only made the best of all possible worlds, the ones with the greatest good and the least possible evil. Although the happy conclusion of the tale supports this view, a number of Cervantine elements serve to question it. Even the tale itself, written by 'a sage of yore' – but not Cide Hamete – shows the virtuous and smart Zadig as a plaything of fortune. An appendix, a Seal of Approval, and the call for missing parts of the manuscript also destabilize the authority of the narrative to the point where an interpolation points to Zadig's 'sorry destiny' (Voltaire 2008, 177). While both Zadig and Don Quixote embrace some form of optimism, be it the desire for the Golden Age or the belief in the power of goodness to overwhelm the darkness, the narrative often destabilizes their views.

In Voltaire's novella, Zadig is a man of 'fine disposition' and great learning, with a penchant for 'natural philosophy' (2008, 110), who grows up in ancient Babylonia. As an optimistic youth, he believes that he can have a happy and prosperous life if he works hard and does good deeds, but he is disappointed to find that all his pleasures are fleeting and that his position in life is constantly menaced by circumstance. He is plotted against by the envious; he is imprisoned, jilted in love, made prime minister, and condemned to death, all the while dedicating himself to learning. In the end, he is able to solve a series of enigmas. This allows him to marry the queen of Babylon, Astarte. With her at his side,

Zadig lives happily 'ever after' and rules wisely: 'The Empire knew a time of peace, a time of glory, a time of plenty; it was the finest age the world had known' (2008, 171).[3] Very much like Don Quixote, he sought to establish a new Golden Age; and like Don Quixote, Zadig fails, leaving behind El Dorado. But, while the knight sickens and is taken home in an enchanted cart to recover from his adventure, at least the French protagonist seems to have succeeded in the end by clinging to virtue and using his evidential method.[4] He marries his beloved and rules a kingdom, like Don Quixote would have liked to have done. Voltaire himself sought to follow his hero and Cervantes' knight, attempting to right wrongs in eighteenth-century French society. But, as Jean Canavaggio explains, he ended up admitting that he might fail in his Quixotic endeavours, just as the Spanish knight had done (1990, 98).

Zadig's evidential method is most clearly presented in chapter 3 of the tale, where he discovers the king's horse and the queen's dog which had been missing. This is how the qualities of the dog are assembled by Zadig: 'I saw some animal tracks in the sand, and I could easily tell that they were those of a small dog . . . Other traces going in a different direction and apparently made by something brushing constantly over the surface of the sand beside the front paws, told me that she had very long ears. And as I noticed that the sand was always less indented by one paw than by the other three, I realized that the bitch belonging to our most august Queen had, if I may dare say so, a slight limp' (2008, 116–17).[5] He uses a similar method to recreate the horse, down to the fact that the animal had 'a tail three and a half feet long which brushed the dust off the trees when he swished it from side to side.' He also deduced the following: 'As for his bit, it must be made of twenty-three carat gold: for he had rubbed its bossed ends against a stone which I recognized as a touchstone and which I assayed myself. Finally I judged from the marks which his shoes had left on some small stones of a different kind that he was shod in finest silver.' As stated, Carlo Ginzburg locates in passages such as these, the 'embryo of the mystery novel' (1989, 116). The method used by Zadig and Sherlock Holmes consists in 'the ability to forecast retrospectively . . . When causes cannot be reproduced, there is nothing to do but to deduce them from their effects' (1989, 117). Sherlock Holmes tells Watson pretty much the same thing. He solves his crimes by 'reasoning from effects to causes' (Doyle 1953, 90).

From the very beginning of Cervantes' novel, Don Quixote is also engaged in seeking out clues. Obviously, Don Quixote is no Zadig and no Sherlock. But he does look at clues and he seeks to recreate the scene; and in a quirky way he thinks retrospectively. He departs from Zadig's method in that he does not seek to recreate a past scene that actually happened. His mental deduction is mediated by an imagination that is filled with objects and actions from the romances of chivalry. For him, fiction is history and he is a knight. If this is the case, all events must be in sync with his chivalric scriptures. Instead of considering all possible arts and sciences that would assist him in recreating the scene, he turns to chivalry, but expands his horizons by also considering epic, ballads, and the Italian romances. Thus he looks for ways to corroborate that an event similar to one from his many readings has taken place, or worse, is about to take place. Retrospection becomes projection as he decides that there is a lady in distress and thus he will save her. His evidence is metamorphosed into proofs of his monomania, as he constantly misinterprets his findings.[6] As Williamson asserts: 'He remains hermetically sealed within the circularity of his chivalric vision' (1984, 109). It takes no Sherlock Holmes to determine that the turning of the sails of a windmill is the result of the wind, although it did take millennia to conceive of these artefacts.[7] But for the knight, these mills are proof of the existence of giants. These hundred-armed giants move their extremities just as the sails of a mill. After such a blatant misuse of clues Sancho tells his master that his problem is that he has windmills in his mind (1978, 1.8.130; 1998, 60). This image is a circumlocution that allows Sancho to accuse his master of acting like a madman.[8] Zadig, instead, had learned 'that self-esteem is a balloon filled with wind, from which great tempests surge when it is pricked' (Voltaire 2008, 110). It may be that Don Quixote's windmills are not just a sign of madness but an indicator of an excessive self-importance that unleashes a 'tempest' of chivalric adventures.

In the next episode, there is no evidence to decipher when two monks of the Order of St Benedict come mounted on mules and followed by a carriage. Perhaps either Zadig or Sherlock Holmes would have found some flaw in the scene, some speck of dirt that would indicate that the carriage had been at a nearby castle and some physiognomic trait in the driver that would show his malice. Some important news of the day might have led him to deduce that the 'princess' in the carriage was in danger.[9] But for Don Quixote, the mules must be dromedaries, and the carriage that follows must be carrying an abducted princess (1978, 1.8.133; 1989, 62). He has no evidence, but constructs a scene from the romances.[10] At this point I will take one item in the knight's imaginings as a clue, as one of the minutiae that Holmes or Zadig savours.[11] The dromedaries are totally unnecessary for the scene; they are quirky supplements that will lead us back to Zadig's method. After all, Ginzburg has stated that the method depends on the gathering of 'small insights' so as to turn literary criticism from divination to a quasi-scientific endeavour (1989, 107, 115).[12] In a truly suggestive passage Ginzburg claims that one can juxtapose the pseudosciences of physiognomics and divination with 'sciences such as law and medicine . . . Something did indeed link these different methods . . . an attitude oriented towards the analysis of specific cases which could be reconstructed only through traces, symptoms and clues' (1989, 104).

It has been argued that Voltaire's *conte philosophique* has its origins in an ancient 'oriental fable of the three brothers who described an animal they had never seen by interpreting a series of clues' – they came up with a camel or dromedary (Ginzburg 1989, 116). Voltaire introduces the dromedary as a clue to his model when he tells us that Zadig and a servant had to flee Babylon on two of the fastest dromedaries at the court (2008, 132). I would argue that Cervantes might have done the same thing. The 'Persian' story became popular in the Renaissance through a couple of Italian versions, that of Christoforo the Armenian being particularly well-known. It was translated into French, German, English, Dutch, and Danish.[13] Cervantes probably knew this popular tale, and the transformation of the mule into a dromedary is the first clue as to the story's impact on the novel. Years later, when Horace Walpole invoked this tale to coin the term serendipity, he misremembered and stated that the three travelling princes had found clues as to the anatomy and whereabouts of a mule, not a camel/dromedary. For me, it is indeed serendipitous that the transformation of mule to dromedary or vice versa is linked to the method in both Cervantes and Walpole.[14] It is also interesting that the princes are accused of being 'stradaiuoli' (Armeno 2000, 19) highwaymen, and robbers (Remer 1965, 63), much like Don Quixote. In the Italian tale, the three princes gathered enough clues to deduce that the mule/dromedary was lame and had a missing tooth. The animal was loaded with butter and honey and carried a woman on its back. Taking as a clue that the camel would only eat grass to the left of its tracks, the princes also deduced that it was blinded in the right eye.[15] Emperor Beramo, most impressed by their sleuthing, kept them at court and spied on their conversations so as to marvel at their method.[16]

While the princes are very good at sleuthing, Don Quixote is a very poor detective. The knight does have the desire to solve a mystery, to detect a crime – but he does not eliminate all irrelevant factors to arrive at the cause of having a lady travel by carriage.[17] He does the opposite. He transforms the available clues so as to construct the chivalric adventure of an abducted princess. And he goes forth to battle the evil priests riding the dromedaries. As episode follows episode, Sancho comes to understand his master's flawed method and seeks to transform it. At the end of chapter 19, the pair is without wine or even water, and Sancho makes a discovery: green and fine grass (1978, 1.19.236; 1998, 141). This discovery leads him to affirm that 'estas yerbas dan testimonio de que por aquí cerca debe de estar alguna fuente o arroyo que estas yerbas humedece' [there must be some fountain or brook hereabouts to water these herbs] (1978, 1.20.237; 1998, 141). He has found clues or evidence for a brook. This may recall the importance of grass as a clue as to the dromedary's blind right eye in the Italian tale. It also recalls that Zadig 'did make special study of the properties of animals and plants, and soon developed an acuteness of perception which revealed to him a thousand differences where other men see only uniformity' (Voltaire 2008, 115). Although Sancho did not see a thousand differences, he saw what his master did not: the importance of the green grass. And through Zadig's method, he hypothesized the cause, a river or stream. And sure enough, Sancho proved to be correct. Knight and squire immediately hear the noise of water – further evidence to corroborate Sancho's evidential finding. Sancho then uses the stars to tell the time of night, recalling how Zadig 'steered his course by the stars' (2008, 132).[18] But Sancho's method fails as he is overcome by fear. Nevertheless the method serves to foreshadow its later use by the knight and his squire.[19]

Although we can see the importance of sleuthing throughout the novel, it is when the pair enters Sierra Morena that things truly change. Rather than using clues from reality to turn to the world of fiction, here the pair truly encounters a mystery. The clues are strewn all over this area: a saddle cushion, a portmanteau with shirts, linens, a handkerchief with gold coins, a pocket book, etc. They follow the evidence until they see a half-naked savage and finally a dead mule. This time, the knight does not transform it into a dromedary but views it as a real object of inquiry. This is one of the very few moments in the novel when Don Quixote's vision is not 'hermetically sealed.' Instead of following the authority of the book, he is tempted to use Zadig's method.

Still, Don Quixote is not much of a detective at first – he thinks that the evidence points to a traveller who has fallen into the hands of robbers, not even realizing that he himself could be called an outlaw. Sancho, again, is the better sleuth, reversing what we come to know as the perfect pair: a Holmes who is always searching for evidence and a Watson who serves as his foil. In Cervantes' novel the learned, lean, and melancholy character resembles the 'excessively lean' Holmes who would spend days in melancholy musings (Doyle 1953, 20). Christopher Weimer states: 'Physically they resemble one another: both tall and lean with strong features. Psychologically they are even more alike. Both are bachelors prone to melancholy, who have distanced themselves from the opposite sex by idealizing one woman' (1996, 197). Sherlock's chin, which 'had the prominence and squareness which mark the man of determination' (Doyle 1953, 30) also recalls that Don Quixote's original name was *quijada* or jaw, and that the deformed jaw of the Habsburgs, which Titian turned into a jaw of determination, has been linked to his features (De Armas 2006, 112–33). It is as if Conan Doyle, knowing the Spanish pair, delights in transforming their roles. The lean and pensive Don Quixote is no sleuth. It is his foil, Sancho, the later Watson, who first proves his mettle at this new science in spite of his reputed simplicity. Having sleuthed in chapter 20 in order to find water, he now turns to this new crime scene and realizes that his master's conclusion does not make sense. If it had been robbers, they would have taken the money – the gold coins wrapped in the handkerchief (1978, 1.23.282; 1998, 176).

The reading of a sonnet found in the pocket book intensifies the mysterious elements that call for a solution, while at the same time pointing to yet another genre in the novel. Sonnets, Lope de Vega reminded his public, were excellent vehicles for amorous discourse. And the sonnets that we find in Cervantes' novel are often of this type: two written by Cardenio, two declaimed by Lotario, and two written by the Captive. This first sonnet is addressed to Fili, which leads the knight to imagine who this lady might be. In his eighteenth-century English translation, Charles Jarvis renders the beloved's name as Chloe (1998, 177). This allows for Sancho's confusion of *Fili* and *hilo* to make sense in English. In the translation, Sancho now confuses Chloe for *Clue*. Sancho's confusion is actually a clever insight. As a number of critics have pointed out, this thread is used not to become lost in the labyrinth, that is, in Sierra Morena, a very rugged and disconcerting space.[20] In fact the thread is used over and over in the ensuing chapters, recalling how Hillis Miller imagined the writer in olden times, an author who 'sits at a desk and spins out on the page a long thread or filament of ink' (1992, 5).

This narrative line, he argues has been the source of numerous images: 'broken thread or dropped thread, line of argument, story line' (1992, 11). Cervantes' text plays with the meaning of *hilo* in the chapters that ensue: the narrative thread of Cardenio's story (1978, 1.24.292; 1998, 185); Sancho's stringing of proverbs (1978, 1.25.302; 1998, 194); the *hilas* that are used to bind wounds (1978, 1.25.310; 1998, 200); the thread of Perseus's/Theseus's labyrinth that Sancho must manufacture in order not to get lost in the woods (1978, 1.25.317; 1998, 206); Cardenio's laments that break the narrative thread (1978, 1.27.334; 1998, 221); the knot that seems to bind in marriage Fernando and Luscinda (1978, 1.27.339; 1998, 226);[21] and finally the combed and winding thread or yarn and the twisted tales that are told (1978, 1.28.344; 1998, 230).[22] This play of threads to form a tapestry out of many plots, as will be shown in the next chapter, derives in part from Ariosto's *Orlando furioso*, where the same image is utilized.

But these are not the clues or threads Don Quixote and Sancho are following on the way into Sierra Morena; the chivalric pair is simply trying to solve the case at hand. A letter and many more papers do not solve much, and the more Sancho scrutinizes the portmanteau, the less he finds. Although he gives up, he is satisfied by the gold coins he found earlier. Don Quixote is not to be outdone by Sancho. Competition teaches the knight the evidential method, if just for a moment. He now produces a correct hypothesis from all of the clues. The owner of the portmanteau with its shirts, coins, pocket book, and poems is or was 'algún principal enamorado, a quienes desdenes y alos tratamientos de su daba debían de haber conducido a algún desesperado término' [some lover of condition, whom the slights and ill treatments of his mistress had reduced to terms of despair] (1978, 1.23.284; 1998, 178). Don Quixote does not specify the terms of despair. He could have argued that, like Grisóstomo, this unknown person has died of love. But he does not, containing the cause so that it will fit the evidence. It is then that the knight sees a fleeing half-naked man. The text emphasizes that the knight 'todas estas menudencias miró y notó' [saw and observed all these particulars] (1978, 1.23.285; 1998, 179), including what little he was wearing. From these clues he surmises that the strange savage must be the owner of the portmanteau. Although the text goes on to use the verb *imaginó* (translated as 'fancied'), the reader is already aware that Don Quixote has noticed the details. Although in rags, the remnants of the strange man's breeches are made of velvet – denoting his ability to buy expensive garments. Thus once again, the knight takes over as the sleuth. And indeed, Don Quixote's imagination could be of assistance is sleuthing. After all, in order to put together all the clues and recreate the crime scene one needs, as Ginsburg states, some divination. I would say that some imagination is also helpful. But it must be reined in by the facts of the case. Now that they have a suspect, Don Quixote orders Sancho to help him search for the stranger and to make 'de los ojos linternas' [spying glasses of your eyes] (1978, 1.23.285; 1998, 179). As in any mystery story, once there is a suspect or 'a person of interest,' the chase is on.

The first important point that can be gleaned from these elements is that the shift from a metamorphic to an evidential mind-set alerts the reader to become an active participant and not be lost in Sierra Morena, which also becomes a space for the proliferation of tales and mysteries. The reader is to follow the thread, to search for clues as to the events that transpire and their meaning. Who is Fili/Chloe, the woman to whom a sonnet is addressed in the unknown pocketbook? Who is the naked madman swinging through the trees? Who is the youth whose long blond hair and beautiful foot are clues to a different gender identity?[23] And why is the labyrinth ascribed to Perseus rather than to Theseus (the slayer of the Minotaur)?[24] It is up to the reader, then, to reconstruct events as she slowly uncovers the many threads that are hidden in this mountainous and savage land. And as readers search for the clues, the very term Fili may lead them to wonder if this whole series of intertwined plots serves, in part, to make fun of Lope de Vega. After all, Fili was one of the poetic names he used for Elena Osorio, one of his beloveds, while Luscinda points to another of his paramours. The fact that Fili is the poetic name for Luscinda in Cervantes' text and that Cardenio is her lover (a poetic name used by Lope de Vega), may lead some readers to follow these clues to see how they relate to Lope's life story. They might also recall the many threads constructed in one of Lope's more convoluted plays.[25] Some of the very theatrical moments that will ensue in the interpolated tales that follow will recall Lope's dramas. But there are other immediate clues that take the reader in a much different direction.

As if to make the reader even more suspicious and attentive, Sancho's *rucio* disappears at some point, either in chapter 23 or chapter 25. Although some critics have pointed out that the second edition of 1605 corrects these 'blunders' by inserting both his theft in chapter 23 and his reappearance in chapter 30, Thomas Lathrop argues that the corrections were not made by Cervantes and that they were inserted in the wrong place.[26] Indeed, Cervantes in the 1615 novel explains the theft as if the readers did not know about it. For Lathrop this is proof that Cervantes rejected the insertions. After all, these chapters are all about clues and how to solve the mysteries. And this is what Cervantes has achieved yet again. In Lathrop's words: 'Es muy importante notar que ni Sancho ni don Quijote jamás tenían dudas; a ellos nunca les molestaba la misteriosa desaparición del rucio; sólo a los lectores les molestaba. Página tras página los lectores verdaderamente no sabían lo que estaba pasando, si Sancho tenía o no el rucio' [It is important to note that neither Sancho nor Don Quixote ever had doubts; they were not worried by the mysterious disappearance of the *rucio*; only readers were bothered. Page after page readers wondered what was happening, if Sancho had or did not have his *rucio*] (1984, 210). The readers only find out that he has recovered his beast in chapter 42. For Lathrop, the situation serves to question who is sane and who is mad, the knight or the readers? There are those who would object to this solution. Daniel Eisenberg, for example, asked Lathrop: '¿Tienes algún ejemplo de un romance caballeresco del caballo, o de un rucio, o de un camello, o de cualquier otra cosa que desaparezca y entonces reaparezca sin explicación?' [Do you have an example of a chivalric romance where a horse, a *rucio* or a camel or anything else disappears and then reappears without an explanation?] (Eisenberg and Lathrop 2009, 1199). I would answer the question by affirming that the theft of the *rucio* is a test. Once the readers are presented with the evidential method, they are asked to become active in the solution of the problem. Like Sancho and Don Quixote, they should use the clues to imagine the most likely event that could have occurred. One proof of this is that the text cleverly links the banishing beast to threads. When Don Quixote sends Sancho to search for Dulcinea, he wishes to keep with him some lint or *hilas* to heal himself while he does penance. Sancho must admit that he cannot provide it since these threads were lodged with Sancho's *rucio* (1978, 1.25.310; 1998, 200).The readers' curiosity as to the banishing beast would be satisfied in part 2. While it would have been nearly impossible to have deciphered the way in which the theft took place (unless the reader had a very good knowledge of the Italian romances), it would be a solid piece of sleuthing, and an excellent way to follow the threads of the narrative, to decide that Ginés de Pasamonte would have been the perpetrator. After all, he was as much a fugitive from justice as the chivalric pair; he was as close to Sierra Morena as Don Quixote and Sancho; he could well have followed them; and his picaresque bent would have led him to thieving. And what better item could he steal than an easy and comfortable ride?

We have then seen clues to two beastly mysteries: that of Sancho's *rucio* and of a dead mule. In foregrounding mysteries that deal with animals and are solved by humans the text may be pointing to what Charles Presberg calls 'symbolic quality and animality of that paradoxical creature,' the human being (2001, 233), to a mysterious mixture of passions, instincts, and desires. To these animal images must be added three more: the Minotaur, the dragon, and the dromedary. First of all, the Minotaur, half human, half beast, lurks in the labyrinth.[27] This monster, I would argue, hides within the narrative itself. These episodes do not just present linear mysteries to be solved. The entrance into Sierra Morena with all its twists and turns is an entrance into a new kind of labyrinthine narrative, a hybrid form that is in itself monstrous.[28] The cluster of clues in the labyrinth allows us to move from the repetitive and episodic chivalric adventures of the knight to something quite different. David Quint may not be interested in distinguishing a break in narrative form here, since he argues that interlacing, a technique in the romances of chivalry, occurs throughout the text and through the use of two different themes in the novel.[29] But literal rather than metaphorical interlacing does become a central feature of the narrative in Sierra Morena. In fact, it comes close to the many twists and turns of the Italian romance, to the 'serpentine structure' of the *Orlando furioso* with its many serpent images; to what Torquato Tasso labels as both monstrous and dragon-like (Looney 1996, 123–41). Although there are no dragons in Ariosto's romance or in Cervantes' novel, each hides this beast in its own way. In Ariosto's tale, cantos 10–12 are full of dragon-like monsters and figures. While at the end of canto 10 Ruggiero had saved Angelica from the orc, a sea-dragon or monster, now she must escape the knight since he envisions enjoying what he had wrested from the beast. After she escapes, it is Orlando's turn to save Olympia from the sea-dragon in canto 11. And if this were not enough, in canto 12 Orlando now believes he has heard the cry of Angelica, but he has no chariot with dragons like the one used by Ceres to find her daughter (1983, 116). Still, he follows the voice and is trapped in a magnificent palace by the sorceress Dragontina. Cervantes also hides his dragons in unlikely places. When Don Quixote and Sancho are discussing the squire's feigned visit to Dulcinea, the knight is convinced that Sancho was able to return so quickly because he was aided by a 'sabio encantador' [sage enchanter]. This is the way these enchanters protect knights who fight monsters like the dragon-like

endriago (1978, 1.31.385; 1998, 266). This allusion ties the Minotaur of Sierra Morena to the dragon-like creature of the *Amadís*. Both Ariosto and
Cervantes avoid actual dragons, but they both refer to a chariot led by
such beasts. In Ariosto, the chariot is a mere lack: Orlando does not have
Ceres's chariot. In Cervantes, the knight will travel from Sierra Morena
to Don Quixote's home in an 'enchanted' chariot. We will see how the
oxen that lead it can be also viewed as dragons. Just as we have dragon-
Minotaur and dragon-oxen, Cervantes' novel offers a third way to view
beasts from a double perspective. Even though in the Sierra Morena the
chivalric pair discovers a dead mule, previously Don Quixote had imagined mules to be dromedaries. And, in the source tale used by Cervantes
to present the ability to detect, the mule is a camel. Thus, the changing
shape of beasts is key to the novel. Camels or dromedaries, of course,
are the animals used by Muslims as they battle Christians. Don Quixote
always has a Christian reaction when he imagines they are present – be
they with the Benedictines or at the battle of the sheep. They are the
non-Christian Other that evoke such anxieties in the knight. At the same
time, both Ariosto and Cervantes incorporate otherness as part of their
narrative through images of dragons/Minotaurs, serpentine interweaving, and labyrinthine interlacing. While the narrative impels the reader
to accept change, the Christian knight is always fighting to keep such
dangers from his land.

The plot twists also recall the ancient Greek novel which Cervantes
will imitate in his *Persiles y Sigismunda*. As opposed to the chivalric, the
Hellenistic focuses on the passions, and this is precisely what happens
with the stories that cluster around Sierra Morena. Its convoluted plots
and interlaced actions call for a guiding thread to follow all the twists
and turns. In line with the Hellenistic, it is also in this tangled knot
that surrounds Sierra Morena that inexplicable desires arise.[30] Hillis
Miller reminds us that we as readers tend to read 'line by line from
the beginning to the end' (1992, 5). As the writer spins his lines, the
reader searches for clues that hint at their meaning. Thus, an active
reader is needed, one who can create scenarios based on the shifting
and tangled evidence. What is truly fascinating is that Don Quixote
and mainly Sancho have alerted us to Zadig's method, to a way of reconstructing the scene using the dead mule, the dromedary of ancient
times. The chivalric pair has also given us the thread with which to
link one event to the next without becoming mired in a labyrinthine,
dragon-like, or serpentine narrative. The reader must be like Theseus,
a rather ambivalent figure.

In addition, once Don Quixote and Sancho (as well as the readers) learn of the evidential method, other characters begin using it. We need only recall how Cardenio, the priest, and others watch as they hear the laments of a young peasant. Slowly, the evidence leads them to understand that this is a disguise. The beautiful feet he is washing in the river, the peasant's divine countenance, and his flowing golden hair lead them to conclude that they are viewing a woman, who turns out to be Dorotea (1978, 1.28.344–5; 1998, 231). These characters often misuse the evidential method to their detriment. Cardenio, spying on Fernando and Luscinda, concludes that he has lost his beloved to the knot of matrimony. Such an ending would recall the many tragic denouements of the sentimental novel. He departs on a mule before completing all observations. In his state of mind, Cardenio would not have been able to reconstruct the dromedary. Instead, he spied on his beloved with great jealousy and his worse fears were confirmed (or so he imagined). Nor did he have the agency of a true sleuth who would have intervened to stop the wedding and prevent any harm from coming to his beloved. And what is worse, at Sierra Morena and at the inn nearby there are those who would create not just one disguise but many, not just one lie but a lengthy fictional story. Thus out of the priest and the barber is born the Princess Micomicona. And Dorotea takes on this fiction. Again, it is a beastly clue that almost dismantles this deception, for when the barber falls from a mule, his pasted beard, made of the tale of an ox, falls off and comes close to revealing his identity. But all is fixed by the priest since Don Quixote is easily deceived and believes that the beard can be magically reattached (1978, 1.29.368–9; 1998, 252). While the reader is provided with the evidential method, this method is often put to the test by those who would disguise themselves and by a world that disguises its secrets in folds of science or magic.

Zadig's method did not stay with the Cervantine hero for long. Meeting Cardenio, another monomaniac, the knight's desire to break his fictional world dissolves. And yet, the image of the thread, so often foregrounded by narrator, knight, and squire, impels the reader to look at the clues within the novel, to become a diviner or a critic, to solve mysteries, riddles, paradoxes. But this may be one more quixotic trick, one more way to reassure the reader. The thread that leads us out of the quixotic worlds is yet to be found and the Theseus that wields it is a mendacious figure, as truthful and mendacious as Cide Hamete. And yet, readers continue to follow the clues, to look for Sancho's missing *rucio;* to wonder at Cardenio's madness. Cervantes' novel has presented us with a moment in which, through competition with his squire, the crazed knight has been able to break 'the hermetically sealed circularity' of his chivalric vision (one that includes a dangerous mystery to be divined but slowly, through future chapters). This is one of those moments that beckon readers to also break with their own monomania and follow the clues of what will be an increasingly serpentine and labyrinthine plot. It may be no coincidence that elements of an ancient mystery tale are found in Cervantes' novel and in Voltaire's Zadig. While Don Quixote assails chivalric monsters, the narratives of Cervantes and Voltaire suggest that there are other monsters that need to be perceived; that readers ought to become participants in the act of reading, and in the act of reconstructing their own world. The dromedary, the dragon, and other monsters may be clues to a larger mystery, to what drives Don Quixote onwards. While the fear of monstrous Otherness drives the knight to affirm his imperial and religious orthodoxy, the text invites readers to participate in the monstrous through its labyrinthine narrative and through deciphering the clues as to what motivates Don Quixote.

It may be no coincidence that in today's world, there is a major investigative agency based in Seattle called Cervantes and Holmes.[31] They welcome mysteries and assure the client that they will seek solutions. So, to the many different genres that have been pinpointed within Cervantes' novel, from the picaresque to the Hellenistic, from the sentimental novel to the Italian romances, from the epic to the chivalric, we can add retrospectively that of the mystery novel, and revel in the thought of the chivalric pair as predecessors of Zadig's method and Conan Doyle's characters.

7 Greek Interlace / Italian Interweaving

To catch every new lover in her net
The lady uses all the craft she can,
Not keeping always the same face for each;
She fits her looks and actions to the man.

Troy never beheld her shapeliness and poise;
Diana and Venus never were so dear.
Here the white veil enfolds a subtle glow,
But here, revealed, her locks of gold appear.

– Tasso, *Gerusalemme liberata*

The fourth section of the novel, then, begins with a mystery. As it progresses, the initial mystery turns into a mystery of clustered tales that become labyrinthine in their telling, while a second mystery, that of the knight's anxieties, emerges in the knight's penance. What slowly dawns on both knight and squire is that they have entered a kind of labyrinth, one so complex that the word thread is used over and over again as a way to sort out the labyrinthine confusions.[1] Indeed, Don Quixote advises his squire to use a method akin to Ariadne's thread, which allowed Theseus to emerge from the labyrinth after killing the Minotaur.[2] But this labyrinth is not just topographical in nature. The entrance into Sierra Morena presents a new kind of narrative that resembles the Greek or Hellenistic novel (sometimes misnamed as Byzantine) which Cervantes will imitate in his *Persiles y Sigismunda*.[3] At the same time, the narrative also recalls three other types of interlaced narratives: the

rather mechanical interlace of books of chivalry, the intrusion of interpolated tales in the pastoral, and the extremely intricate interweaving
of tales in the Italian romances, particularly the *Orlando furioso*. Thomas
Hart reminds us that 'Ariosto's favorite image for expressing the importance he attaches to variety is that of the weaver who needs many
different threads' (1989, 21). Like Cervantes, Ariosto foregrounds his
use of intertwined threads. In canto 2, for example, he states: 'But as
I have need of a number of warps and a variety of threads if I am to
complete the whole of my tapestry, I shall leave Rinaldo and his pitch-
ing prow and return to the tale of his sister Bradamant' (1983, 14). In
canto 13, Ariosto stops the tale of Bradamant at Atlas's enchanted castle
arguing that 'to complete the great tapestry on which I am working
I feel the need for a great variety of strands' (1983, 136). Cervantes, who
was clearly aware of the debates raging in Italy over Ariosto's use of
multiple plots, highlights his own interweaving in this fourth section
of the novel.

The cluster of episodes around Sierra Morena is replete with convoluted plots and interlaced actions that call for a guiding thread to
follow all the twists and turns. In line with the Greek, and Italian, it is
also in this tangled knot that surrounds Sierra Morena that inexplicable
desires arise, a trait that is also present in the pastoral and sentimental novels. Thus, an active reader is needed, one who can create scenarios based on the shifting and tangled evidence: who is Fili/Chloe,
the woman to whom a sonnet is addressed in the unknown pocketbook? Who is the naked madman swinging through the trees? Who is
the youth whose long blond hair and beautiful foot are clue to a different gender identity? And why is the labyrinth ascribed to Perseus
rather than to Theseus (the slayer of the Minotaur)? As the stories of
Fernando and Lucinda, Cardenio and Dorotea, and even the imagined
tale of Princess Micomicona slowly unfold, the narrative focuses on
their twists and turns.

What happens is that all of a sudden Don Quixote loses the role of
protagonist. He becomes a mere spectator as he tries to sort out the
different tales and bring together estranged parties. At the beginning
of this fourth narrative section he had become a detective, even surpassing Sancho in his search for clues. But once he discovers that the
'person of interest' is Cardenio, who, like Don Quixote, acts like a madman, the knight has a role model, a mirror in which he can see himself.
The Knight of the Sorrowful Figure embraces the Knight of the Woods.
They are as one. Seeing that Cardenio is crazed from what he thinks is

unrequited passion, Don Quixote decides that two can play the game. Both Cardenio and Don Quixote are now in the wild and forbidden landscape of the sentimental novel. Spurred by his new generic space, Don Quixote will find a place deep in the woods where he can do penance for his Dulcinea. And indeed, he finds what comes close to being a *locus amoenus* in these woods, a place that denies the impossibility of speech and the ruggedness of the genre. At the foot of a high mountain, there flowed a quiet stream, surrounded by a green meadow. It is here that Don Quixote decides to do penance for his beloved. His tears will feed the stream while his sighs will promote a sweet breeze. The rustle of the leaves will provide a testimony of his unending sorrow (1978, 1.25.307). While for Don Quixote this is the ideal place to do penance, for the narrative, this place signals how from Sierra Morena new narratives will spring and develop into streams of tales. It does not matter that Don Quixote is next to this small rivulet since it will not provide the knight with the humidity of consolation. Instead, Don Quixote will become drier and more melancholy as his tears feed the stream. And it, in turn, will humidify the narrative with the abundance of green vegetation, that is, with the abundance of new narratives that distance themselves from the knight.

The main decision Don Quixote has to make is whether to follow the example of Amadis, who became a melancholy knight and took himself to a remote and virtually inaccessible isle where he lived with a hermit in order to do penance for his Oriana, or whether to follow Orlando and go naked through the woods uprooting trees and killing cattle, crazed as he was when he learned that his Angelica was in love with the Moor Medoro. The narrative prepares us for this choice when Don Quixote surprisingly dismisses the *Belianís de Grecia* and claims that Amadis is the only excellent model of the chivalric (1978, 1.25.303). We may recall that in the first part of the novel, Belianís became the example of the choleric hero and the narrative itself, who was confronted with the melancholy aroused by Feliciano de Silva's intricate style. Now, we are once again faced with the opposition between the melancholy and the choleric humours. Both of these humours have dryness as a quality, reflecting the dryness of Don Quixote's body and brain. At the Sierra Morena, he chooses what he now calls the best of the Spanish chivalric books and contrasts it with an Italian romance rather than with the works of Feliciano de Silva. In the end, although he will use some of the elements from the *Orlando furioso*, stripping, tumbling, and hitting himself on rocks, he will mostly follow *Amadís de Gaula*. Thus he creates a simple rosary from a strip that hung from the bottom of his shirt, making eleven knots, and prays at least a million Hail Marys (or so the narrator states). For Hilaire Kallendorf, Don Quixote's penance is ambiguous. It points to Don Quixote as a sick person who must find faraway places to soothe his being. Even Don Quixote, in reply to Sancho's statement that they are in purgatory, replies that this is truly an infernal site (Kallendorf 2003, 169). On the other hand, the exchange also reminds her that this might also be a place for exorcisms: 'Penitence carries a great significance in both the Quijote and in exorcism manuals and the Sierra Morena exchanges remind us of demonologists' accounts of how the exorcist fasts with the demoniac and prays with him late into the night' (2003, 169). Don Quixote is certainly carrying out a metaphorical self-exorcism here, but not one that is at all Christian. It is blatantly heterodox as he tries to assuage the anxieties of Otherness.

The making of a rosary reflects the fact that Amadís had lived with a hermit during his penance; it also shows the religious anxieties that permeate the text. Even though Pope Pius V had placed the Holy League which won the battle of Lepanto under the protection of the Virgin of the Rosary, and Cervantes had participated in the famous battle, which is recounted in the Captive's Tale in *Don Quixote*, we know that Ave Marias had been used in a heterodox manner in the episode of the balsam of Fierabrás. Here, once again, the sacred is profaned. According to Roberto Véguez, all references to the rosary in the novel are satirical. As opposed to good Christian prayers that were meant to save the fleet and lead the Christians to triumph over the Ottomans, it is Maritornes in Cervantes' novel, with her rather dubious morals, who prays for the deliverance of Don Quixote from the Sierra Morena. And it is Don Quixote, in Sierra Morena, who creates a rather profane object that passes as a rosary. Indeed, Eric Graf, at the start of one of his essays, asserts: 'Attacks on religious practice abound in Don Quijote . . . Among the most blasphemous is the knight's decision to imitate the penitence of Amadis de Gaula by fashioning a rosary out of a particularly filthy piece of clothing' (2004, 949). The description of the knight's rosary was transformed in the second edition of the novel, where the rosary is made from the cork tree – someone must have worried about its lack of orthodoxy. Furthermore, the specific lines on how Don Quixote fashioned the rosary from the strips at the bottom of his shirt were censored by the Portuguese Inquisition in 1624. Véguez carefully explains how 'el rosario que se hizo don Quijote fue confeccionado con partes de su indumentaria que normalmente tendría funciones muy otras que las devotas' [the rosary that Don Quixote created was made from portions of his clothing that have functions very different than devotion] (2001, 93). They are linked to those parts of his body that not even Sancho wanted to see. The rosary thus becomes an erotic object. Véguez also reminds us that Amadís did not use the rosary during this penitence. Thus, the rosary is simply an added object that taints the parody with heterodox inflections. It shows how the novel takes a genre and a specific work, parodying it in a dangerous way.

While appearing to act as a Christian Amadís, the knight hints that his prayers have an erotic and thus heterodox component. When he turns to the Italian romance, he does the opposite. His reason for rejecting the *Orlando furioso* is that Dulcinea 'no ha visto en todos los días de su vida moro alguno' [never saw a Moor in his own dress, in all her life] (1978, 1.26.319; 1998, 208). And yet, in the poems that he carves on trees the knight emphasizes that his princess comes from Toboso: 'que debió de imaginar don Quijote que si en nombrando a Dulcinea no decía también del Toboso, no se podría entender la copla; y así fue verdad como él después confesó' [Don Quixote imagined, that if, in naming Dulcinea, he did not add Del Toboso, the couplet could not be understood; and it was really so, as he afterwards confessed] (1978, 1.26.321; 1998, 209). Why would Don Quixote need to confess? What is he hiding? Several clues are presented. El Toboso, first of all, was a town with a high *morisco* population. Eric Graf reminds us: 'Dulcinea's toponym Toboso was inhabited by a large number of Moriscos relocated from the kingdom of Granada after the Aplujarras War of 1568–70' (Graf 2007, 37; Castro 1966, 81). Second, the term *riscos*, used in the knight's amorous poems, while pertaining to the landscape of Sierra Morena, rhymes with *moriscos* and serves as a sign of his anxieties.[4] In Calderón's *El Tuzaní del Alpujarra*, for example, these terms are used in a rhyme: 'Caxas Españolas son / los que atruenan estos riscos, que no tambores Moriscos' [Spanish drums, these are / which resound in these rocks and crags, and not morisco drums] (1969, 366). In works from Lope de Vega's *Los cautivos de Argel* to Calderón's *El gran príncipe de Fez*, *riscos* is used in conjunction with the African Moors. Thus, while Don Quixote uses two genres, the Spanish chivalric and the Italian romance, he adds elements that evoke anxieties over religion. While Don Quixote ostensibly rejects the Moorish contaminations in *Orlando furioso*, he becomes complicit in them; and while *Amadís* is ostensibly used to foreground Don Quixote's Christianity, the knight's religious devotion is subtly questioned. In addition, the repeated allusions to Ariosto's romance are important since this work will serve to end this fourth segment of the novel. Indeed, the notion that Medoro, Orlando's rival, was a page of the African king Agramante, as well as the link between Dulcinea and Moorish culture, will play an important role in later chapters.

But for now it is Amadís that matters: Don Quixote is proud that his imitation goes beyond the models. While both Amadís and Orlando have done penance for a reason, Don Quixote decides to do it for no reason whatsoever: 'ésa es la fineza de mi negocio; que volverse loco un caballero andante con causa, ni grado ni gracias: el toque está desatinar sin ocasión' [and in this consists the finesse of my affair: a knight-errant who runs mad upon a just occasion deserves no thanks; but to do so without reason is the business] (1978, 1.25.305; 1998, 196). Here, the relation between narrative and character is foregrounded. While Don Quixote is imitating (and surpassing) other fictions, the narrative itself is also accomplishing this feat. The text presents us with a comic parody of the penance and madness of knights in chivalric books and Italianate romances, while at the same time having Don Quixote do something even greater. In this he also surpasses the Cardenio episode which can be associated with the sentimental novel. And, following the sentimental, the knight writes a letter to Dulcinea, thus mimicking the epistolary emphasis of this genre. Even though his voice will diminish in the woods, the letter (and his written bequest to Sancho) stand as proof that the knight can still voice genre.

The knight, although admitting to Sancho that Dulcinea is indeed the mannish peasant named Aldonza, also contends that in his imagination she is someone very different, a ladylike princess.[5] He compares her to Helen of Troy and to Lucretia (1.25.314; 1998, 203). The first is singled out for her beauty while the second stands out for her virtue. One is Greek, the other is Roman. In his mind, Don Quixote sets out to conquer the world through the conquest of a fictive woman. Henry Higuera finds the purpose of Dulcinea to be rather straightforward: 'Don Quixote wants to conquer the world out of love for Dulcinea del Toboso, his ladylove. His love for her, he thinks, inspires his whole imperial project' (1995, 185). Lisa Rabin also sees Dulcinea as a companion of empire: 'In these texts, the Petrarchan desire to possess the woman translates into a desire to possess new territory' (1994, 84). I would add that Don Quixote follows the principle of *translatio imperii*. As empires move west from Greece to Rome, and then to the Spain of Charles V and Philip II, so his beloved expands in his mind in order to encompass all three territories. What is striking, however, is that the Spanish empire is repressed, hidden. It is spoken of in terms of the ancients, perhaps out of an irrational fear that his Dulcinea might leap out of his imagination and lament her Moorish provenance.[6]

Alone in the woods, Don Quixote has sent Sancho to find Dulcinea in Toboso and give her a letter. Since Sancho is afraid of getting lost in the labyrinth, Don Quixote tells him to use branches as Perseus/Theseus had used a thread to come out of the ancient edifice in Crete. The departure of Sancho creates a rift in the narrative, as it now focuses on the squire. As he moves toward civilization and the inn, he will become a part of numerous new interlaced episodes. What we have, then, is a shift from linear fiction to labyrinthine interlacing. Although it started with the first part of Cardenio's tale, it will now accelerate.[7] One story starts, but does not end, taking us to the beginning of another, then returning to the previous one and so forth. What is new and particularly exciting in this accumulation of narratives is both the move from linearity to interlace and the fact that a series of Italianate *novelle*, when clustered, resembles the Greek novel and to a lesser extent, the Italian romances. In fact, I would argue that this section displays a series of genre contest between Greek interlace and Italian interweaving, and between chivalric books and the Italian *novelle*. Although Don Quixote remains in the midst of the labyrinth of Sierra Morena, other figures will appear in the woods in addition to Cardenio. The knight, isolated and alone, seems to be at the centre of adventures that have nothing to do with him and in which he, for the time being, does not play a role. He is delighted when Sancho brings him out of the woods and he meets the famous princess Micomicona (the disguised Dorotea). She tells the knight her tale of woe and how she has lost her kingdom. Only Don Quixote, she argues, can save her. In fact, she provides the signs by which she will know who can deliver her from the devilish giant Pandafilando: 'en camino de las Españas, donde hallaría el remedio de mis males hallando a un caballero andante, cuya fama en este tiempo se estendería por todo este reino, el cual se había de llamar, si mal no me acuerdo, don Azote, o don Gigote . . . que había de ser alto de cuerpo, seco de rostro' [for Spain where I should find a remedy for my distress, by meeting a knight errant, whose fame, about that time, should extend itself all over this kingdom and whose name, if I remember right, was to be Don Acote or Don Gigote] (1978, 1.30.374; 1998, 257). Don Quixote readies to go to her aid, but nothing can happen as yet since her kingdom is far away. The very inventiveness of Dorotea/Micomicona is mirrored by that of Sancho. The knight questions the squire about his meeting with Dulcinea and keeps correcting Sancho since his description of the 'lady' is not at all what the knight envisioned. The inventions by both Don Quixote and Sancho regarding this meeting are certainly an important part of the *inventio* in this narrative, featuring clashes between low and high style, chivalric elements, and quotidian minutiae.

A brief glance at the narrative world that surrounds Don Quixote shows that there are four 'interpolated' tales that create the narrative maze around the knight. Each deals with the tribulations encountered by a couple who is in love: Cardenio and Luscinda (told in two fragments by Cardenio with a final resolution at the inn), Fernando and Dorotea (told by Dorotea with a final resolution at the inn), *El curioso impertinente* (a tale read at the inn in two segments since it is interrupted by Don Quixote), and the Captive's Tale (told by the captive, continued in the present of the narrative at the inn, and left unresolved). A fifth and final tale, focusing on Luis and Clara, will be discussed in the next chapter since it leads to the resolution of this, the densest and most complex section of the novel. Cervantes foregrounds this proliferation of stories when he pens a brief introduction to what is labelled as the fourth part in chapter 28. The text reveals that the chivalric tale is accompanied 'de los cuentos y episodios della, que en parte, no son menos agradables y artificiosos y verdaderos que la misma historia; la cual prosiguiendo su rastrillado y aspado hilo . . .' [the stories and episodes of it, which are, in some sort, no less pleasing, artificial, and true, than the history itself: which resuming the broken thread of the narration . . .] (1978, 1. 28.345; 1998, 230). The narrative revels in its intricacy, pointing to the narrative threads that must be followed through the inclusion of separate tales. There has always been vigorous disagreement as to the function of these interpolations, as critics try to decide which ones are actual interpolations and which ones come closer to being episodes that are integral to the novel. For Edward Riley, except for *El curioso impertinente*, the stories serve to add variety without breaking the unity of the work. This variety is necessary since it reflects nature's diversity and gives pleasure to the reader through these adornments (1962, 191–213). I would add that the maze of stories also takes us back to the quaternities, particularly as they relate to the humours, thus foregrounding once again the medical manual of Huarte de San Juan. In this first part it was noted that the knight broke the harmony of quaternity since the two humours that predominated in him, melancholy and choleric, coincided in the quality of dryness. This term is repeated throughout the novel.[8] And it does not just belong to the knight – it also belongs to the narrative. In the Prologue we are warned that the author has composed, has given birth to, a dry text/child.

Epic and chivalric tales can be dry, and this one is particularly so, since it only deals with two main characters. In the 1615 *Quixote* we have the clearest explanation of the problems encountered by this kind of narrative, and how to solve the situation: 'por haber tomado entre manos una historia tan seca y tan limitada como esta de don Quijote, que parece que siempre había de hablar dél y de Sancho . . . y que por huir deste inconveniente había usado en la primera parte del artificio de algunas novelas' [for having undertaken a history so dry, and so confined, as that of Don Quixote, thinking he must be always talking of him and Sancho . . . and that, to avoid this inconvenience, he had, in the first part, made use of the artifice of introducing novels] (1978, 2.44.366; 1998, 745). Adornment and variety adds moisture or humidity to the text. Love stories are the best way to humidify a dry narrative. As Daniel L. Heiple reminds us, for Huarte de San Juan heat, dryness, and coldness are qualities that fortify the mind. Choler is related to a strong imagination, dryness is linked to judging, and coldness 'created a strong memory . . . The fourth quality humidity (phlegm) did not create a distinctive personality' (1991, 124). For Huarte, women, being cold and humid, were only good at memorizing. Huarte's theory, Heiple goes on to show, was challenged by both Lope de Vega and María de Zayas. The latter argues in her *Novelas amorosas y ejemplares* that coldness produces a sharper intellect while humidity allows trickery and deception to be carried out (Heiple 1991, 130).

Women's intellect is often reflected in a common topos of Eros or Cupid as a great teacher. He improved manners and he also showed the recipients of the arrows of love how to use disguise, deceive, and manipulate in order to achieve their goals. We need only look at Lope de Vega's *La dama boba* to see how love teaches the foolish and ignorant woman to use her intelligence. Many Spanish plays of the period show how women, although confined by their fathers, brothers, or other patriarchal figures, are able to create a free space in which to at least gain the husband they want through trickery, subterfuge, disguise, and other such methods. These techniques spill over into other aspects of life, as in women who disguise themselves as men to avenge themselves on a lying lover or those who create intricate stories to test others or to gain some favour. Many of these techniques are also used in the interpolated tales in Cervantes' novel: Camila learns how to disguise her secret desire for Lotario from her husband Anselmo; Zoraida learns how to deceive her father; Dorotea learns how to disguise herself; Dorotea as Micomicona knows exactly how to fabricate a chivalric fiction so as to deceive Don Quixote into helping her; etc. Thus it is through female agency that these stories provide the much needed humidity that serves to balance the excessively male and dry text. It may be that Cervantes begins his own part 4 of the novel with chapter 28 in order to emphasize these elements. Here the priest and those around him listen to the laments of a sweet voice. When they approach, they spy a young man dressed as a peasant. However, as they look closer, they notice that 'he' is bathing his feet in a stream. The beauty of the feet makes them doubt his gender and class. When they eventually see a beautiful face and long blond hair, they correctly deduce that they are looking at a woman disguised as a man. Thus, the narrative links the water of the stream with the physiology of a woman. As she tells her story, we seek to discover her moist manipulations to achieve her loving object, only to learn that a man, Fernando, has manipulated her disgrace and dishonour. Cervantes, then, accepts the humidifying aspect of love stories, but goes even further than María de Zayas would. He shows that both men and women use trickery to obtain their amorous desires.

While these tales are being told or enacted, the knight remains apart; his melancholy is such that it detaches him from the others. Only the imagined Dulcinea is worthy of his thoughts and speech. As his tears replenish the stream, he becomes drier, while the stream becomes the flow of many new narratives that humidify the text. As the maze becomes more complex and the humidity rises, the knight becomes more and more shrivelled by his penance. Finally, Sancho attempts to bring him out into the world: 'le había hallado desnudo en camisa, flaco, amarillo y muerto de hambre' [naked to his shirt, feeble, wan, and half dead from hunger] (1978, 1.29.361; 1998, 245). The colour yellow, as mentioned in the Spanish text, signifies melancholy and dryness, while thinness and lack of food also create dryness. In spite of this, the knight wishes to take on more adventures. To prevent this from happening, the inventive Dorotea weaves the tale of Micomicona and convinces the knight to stay with her. At first glance, it appears as if it is just one more tale of chivalry that is going to use its threads to lead Don Quixote out of his introspection and toward home. However, a closer inspection shows that the Micomicona tale derives from Torquato Tasso's *Gerusalmme liberata* (1573). While the poem attempts to follow Aristotelian rules, as its recent editor and translator, Anthony

M. Esolen, asserts: 'The tales of Erminia and Tancred, and Rinaldo and Armida threaten to run away with the poem' (2000, 12). Accused of precisely what he wished to avoid, Tasso spent years revising the poem to the point that he went mad. Cervantes takes the fictitious story of the enchantress Armida and has Dorotea/Micomicona deliver it. Armida comes to the Christian camp desiring to conquer through her beauty and her false tale of woe the armies led by Godfrey:

> Lovely Armida, proud of her peerless form,
> Of the charms of her youth and womanhood,
> Takes up the challenge, leaves that very night,
> Traveling ever along the hidden road
> And in her woman's habit nursing hope
> To rout armed legions never yet subdued.   (2000, 77)

She does so by telling how she is the daughter of Arbilan, ruler of Damascus, who, upon the death of her parents, had to rely on her uncle's care. Not wanting to abide under his 'secret malice' (2000, 81) and being 'haunted' by dreams, phantoms, and her mother's shade, who warned her of murderous intent, she flees her kingdom and faces many misadventures. She thus comes to Godfrey as a damsel in distress: 'You are my refuge, sir, / I a poor maiden orphaned, innocent' (2000, 84). Armida's Islamic veil veils the eyes of her opponents who fail to even intuit her purpose. Her beauty and her woeful tale catch many a Christian fighter and slowly reduce the store of heroes in Godfrey's camp.

Dorotea's tale is not so different from Armida's and her purpose is similar: to distract Don Quixote from his quest, just like the enchantress sought to distract Godfrey from the siege of Jerusalem. Like Armida, Dorotea acts like a damsel in distress, weaving a tale of woe. But Dorotea cannot be fully equated with Armida. She is not standing against Christian expansion, just against Don Quixote's misguided quest. Indeed, as if to further the link between Don Quixote and the Habsburgs, Dorotea has shifted the narrative from Asia to Africa. It is from the African shores that Islamic corsairs threaten Spain. Iberia repeatedly attempted to conquer these coasts, and one of the great successes in this struggle was Charles V's conquest of Tunis. Is the knight viewing himself as a new emperor, liberating the shores of Africa? Whatever the answer, the narrative delights in clashes. As in the third segment of *Don Quixote*, where two forms of epic vie with each other, here the contest is between two types of Italian romance. Since Tasso had written against

Ariosto's excessive tales and excessive marvellousness, Cervantes uses Tasso against himself, developing Armida's tale to include even more marvellous events. And to further confuse genres, he portrays the African princess Micomicona as white, thus introducing echoes of the Greek romances where, in the *Aethiopica*, Chariclea, although she is the daughter of the king of Ethiopia, is white.[9] But it is all so seamless that the episode of Micomicona seems like a playful game as its clashing generic and even racial underpinnings are disguised.

In spite of these genre wars and the proliferation of narrative threads, Don Quixote does not see himself as a void, as nothingness out of which the creative impulse of the labyrinth of tales emanates. He is still focused on his vigils and future adventures. But part of him wants to regain narrative control, although he is too exhausted from his penance. He sleeps while the tale of *El curioso impertinente* is told at the inn.[10] One of the main impulses of the story comes again from Ariosto's *Orlando furioso*, which was one of the models for the knight's penance. In the Cervantine tale, Anselmo wants to test the faithfulness of his wife Camila. In order to do this, he asks his best friend Lotario to serve as bait. In order to emphasize the literariness (and foolishness) of the test, Lotario reminds his friend Anselmo how Rinaldo, in the *Orlando furioso*, rejected such a test. Lotario thus admonishes his friend to be prudent since nothing would be accomplished by such impertinent behaviour (1978, 1.33.407). The advice will not be accepted and the tale will end in tragedy. This is the only full-fledged tragedy within the novel, and it can exist since it is totally detached from the action. It is narrated as a fiction, and one that takes place outside of Iberia, in Florence. The tale also exhibits a number of genres. Divided into three different chapters it recalls the three acts of a Golden Age Spanish play. And within it, there is the play created by Camila to deceive her husband – metadrama being a common aspect of Spanish plays of the period. Although it would fall under the category of tragedy, the play also incorporates its opposite. When Lotario tries to dissuade his friend Anselmo from testing his wife, he recalls the tale of Danae, who even when imprisoned by her father was able to find her man (in this case Jupiter the god, found her) (1978, 1.33.409). By using the example of Danae as told in a play, Lotario is pointing to the famous use of the myth of Danae in Terence's *Eunuch*. The narrative threads within this tale, then, include the Italian novella, and the Italian romances, tragedy, and comedy. And if this were not enough, it points to an interpolated tale in Apuleius's *Golden Ass* as well as to the story of Giges in Herodotus's *Histories*.[11] Cervantes succeeds in creating a unified and compelling narrative while imitating so many different forms. *El curioso impertinente* may stand alone, as a centrepiece, since it is truly a tour-de-force which takes us and bends genres to serve a very specific narrative focus.

But something extraordinary will happen in the middle of the story. The knight will face an extreme moment of estranged spectatorship. As he sleepwalks and battles with wine skins, he imagines, or dreams, that he is battling giants – even the Pandafilando of Princess Micomicona. For Juergen Hahn, this serves to point to an intertextual link between Anselmo in the tale and Don Quixote in the novel. While the first is ruled by his curiosity and must test his wife's faithfulness, the knight seems to be totally faithful to a lady he has only imagined. On the other hand, the wineskin episode is modelled after Apuleius's *Golden Ass* in which Lucius, like Don Quixote, battles three wineskins which he describes as giants (Scobie 1976, 75). Diana De Armas Wilson asserts that the link between Apuleius and Cervantes is thus reinforced by what she calls 'the rhetoric of double interpolation' (1994, 89) where both the *Curioso* and the wineskins interruptions utilize Apuleius as a model. The episode of the wineskins only reasserts the general view at the inn that Don Quixote is mad and must be returned home.

Once the tragic tale is over, it is time for resolution. Four men in black and a woman in white, all wearing masks, arrive at the inn. A new mystery arises to puzzle those who had listened to *El curioso impertinente*. Cardenio, from afar, recognizes the woman's voice. She, on seeing him, faints and her mask falls off. Dorotea sees the man who holds the fainting woman and she also faints, and so on. The scene is the perfect ending of a Greek romance or a Roman comedy with a series of *anagnorisis* and a final happy conclusion. It also feels staged, carefully crafted to create a moment of perfect theatre. As in Camila's metadrama, theatre erupts into the narrative. For Manuel Martín Morán, it is as if Cervantes were recasting some of his early plays into a narrative, while Jill Syverson-Stork prefers to study the theatricality that pervades the whole novel, thus infusing into narrative the techniques of theatre. Many critics believe that Cervantes experienced great frustration when Lope de Vega 'conquered' the stage, and his plays were forgotten. He says as much in the Prologue to his *Ocho comedias y ocho entremeses* published toward the end of his life. First he praises Lope: 'Tuve otras cosas en que ocuparme; dejé la pluma y las comedias, y entró luego el monstruo de la naturaleza, Lope de Vega, y alzóse con la monarquía cómica' [I had other things to occupy me; I left pen and plays, and soon afterwards Lope de Vega, the monster of nature entered the scene, and became king of the comic stage] (1982, 93). Cervantes then reveals that in later years no producer was interested in his plays: 'no hallé autor que me las pidiese' [I could not find a producer that would ask me for them] (1982, 93). In the end, Cervantes uses a double strategy to rival Lope. He publishes his plays and he uses the *Quixote* as a vehicle through which the author can exhibit his theatrical techniques.

Even though genres, including theatre, proliferate without Don Quixote, there seems to be some gain for the crazed knight as he navigates this maze with the help of his squire. It is as if the Greek and Italian interlace become the knight's true penance for Dulcinea. By listening to some of these tales he is faced with the meaning of the world around him without being able to alter the situation: 'Weakness, ambition and, above all, lust, twist human destinies, separate lovers, impose the will and desires of the powerful upon the helpless. This is the condition of suffering humanity in the Age of Iron, so different from the peaceful and trusting one of the Age of Gold' (Herrero 1981, 55). The knight who had once given a speech on how to bring back the Golden Age is now silent, watching, listening. Through the stories that unfold around him, he witnesses what it is to love, what it is to betray a friend for a whimsical desire,[12] what it is to lose one's love and to regain it.[13] Whether he understands the world or is still consumed by his monomania is of little concern. The labyrinth still revolves around him. Continuing the analogy between novel and empire, the maze can be linked, in part, to the many lands under the sovereignty of Castile and Aragon. It can also reflect the complexities of governance in Spain itself. As a 'composite kingdom,' the laws and systems of governance in Castile were different from those in Aragon, and the latter was itself tripartite, with Catalonia, Valencia, and Aragon proper retaining their own councils, estates, and ways of governing. Thus, governance was a maze that few could comprehend.[14] As J.H. Elliott reminds us: 'In the Crown of Aragon, laws and constitutions forbade the appointment of non-native officials' (2009, 10). Indeed, Elliott points to 'a brittleness about composite monarchies which is bound to raise questions about their long-term viability' (2009, 11). Add to this the fact that Charles V was an emperor who was raised outside of Spain and had to learn its many intricate customs and laws, and we can understand how the Spanish kingdoms could be viewed as a dangerous labyrinth. After ruling for decades, Charles came to believe that his whole empire was too large and thus divided it at his abdication. But Philip II still had to deal with the composite kingdoms of Spain, Naples, and Sicily as well as areas of less conformity in customs and beliefs such as the Netherlands, America, and parts of Asia. The increased bureaucratization during his reign is due to an attempt to control through writing his labyrinthine empire: 'Philip was drowning in a sea of paper' (Parker 1998, 29). An anecdote told by the historian Geoffrey Parker in which Philip complains that he has to remain awake most of the night trying to come to terms with his writings and his archives (Parker 1998, 42) has led Jesús Botello to posit that there is a connection between Philip II's excesses and Don Quixote's. After all, the knight spends his nights reading books of chivalry (Botello 2009, 206). I would expand Botello's insights and assert that the excess of words and tales in this segment of Cervantes' novel also reflects the proliferation of governmental documents produced at this time, with all the many different petitions, each with its own story. This 'sea of paper' to which Parker refers may be calling for the reinstitution of the *non plus ultra*.

The fourth segment of the narrative began with clues to a mystery in Sierra Morena. Don Quixote, a fugitive from justice, is now turned detective and he, together with Sancho, attempts to solve the mysteries of the abandoned portmanteau and the dead mule. Once Cardenio becomes a person of interest and once he tells his tale of love, Don Quixote decides that he is much like the crazed lover and must do penance in Sierra Morena. He stands alone, shedding tears that dry him up further while impelling the stream of narratives. While he is alone, he is surrounded by a narrative labyrinth as interlacing tales become more and more frequent, with different characters telling their parts of the story. The mixture of genres is accentuated: a conglomerate of Italianate *novelle* can be read as Greek interlace or even as the interweaving of the Italian romances. High drama and the exchanging of roles insert theatre into the mix. In the midst of all this confusion, punctuated by peripeteia and anagnorisis, the knight remains apart, consumed by his own riddle or mystery. Anxieties over the Moorish Medoro, over Sancho's trip to the *morisco* town of Toboso, and over the knight's heterodox construction and use of a rosary further infuse a sense of mystery and ambiguity to the parodic tale of a Christian knight who seems to echo the imperial journeys of Charles V.

8 Palinurus and the Pleiades

And if longing seizes you for sailing the stormy seas,
when the Pleiades flee mighty Orion
and plunge into the misty deep
and all the gusty winds are raging,
then do not keep your ship on the wine-dark sea
but, as I bid you, remember to work the land

– Hesiod, Works and Days

A Mariner I am of love
And in his seas profound,
Toss'd betwixt doubts and fears, I rove,
And see no port around.
At distance I behold a star,
Whose beams my senses draw,
Brighter and more resplendent far
Than Palinurus e'er saw.

– Don Quixote 1.43

Emerging from the mountains, Don Quixote, yellowed with melancholy, dry, and lacking protagonism, hopes to regain some health and authority at the inn. This chapter will show how he begins to do so in ways that are somewhat heterodox. As he slowly regains voice, other stories are told which impinge on his plight. His troubled spirit had tried to stop proliferation as he stopped the telling of the tale of the *curioso impertinente*, fighting giants in his sleep. But this only irks the innkeeper and confounds the guests. In the meantime, Dorotea/Micomicona continues to attract the knight with tales of chivalry although he is not at all recovered, albeit dressed for war: 'Salió en esto, don Quijote, armado de todos sus pertrechos, con el yelmo aunque abollado de Mambrino sobre la cabeza . . . su rostro de media legua de andadura, seco y amarillo' [By this time Don Quixote sallied forth, completely armed with his whole furniture; Mambrino's helmet, though bruised and battered, on his head . . . his tawny and withered lantern-jaws] (1978, 37.458; 1998, 332). As noted previously, Dorotea/Micomicona takes on the role of Armida in Torquato Tasso's *Jerusalem Delivered*. While Don Quixote had toyed with Ariosto in the mountains, Dorotea counters with a more correct and Counter-Reformation text, one where paganism is replaced by the Christian marvellous and where the conquest of strange lands is substituted by the Crusades. And yet, Dorotea will play the role of the evil enchantress Armida. She comes to the Christian camp to distract the warriors from their cause. The made-up story that the enchantress tells of her childhood and lost kingdom is clearly imitated by Dorotea in her tale.[1] Don Quixote, then, like many of the Christians in Tasso's poem, falls for a beautiful woman and an alluring lie. Thus, we can say that the initial revivification of the knight derives from a pagan enchantress who would distract the Christian knights from their quest. Indeed, all wait to hear what he has to say about Dorotea's fictions: 'y estuvieron calando hasta ver lo que decía' [and they stood silent to hear what he would say] (1978, 1.27.328; 1998, 332). The second impetus to regain agency comes from an unexpected quarter.[2]

Although Dorotea's fictive plight has animated his spirit, Don Quixote regains his power of speech with the arrival of new guests at the inn: a man whose attire reveals that he has recently returned from Moorish lands, and a veiled woman (1978, 1.37.461; 1998, 335). Although the guests at the inn are most curious to know their story, they offer instead their hospitality. At dinner, it is Don Quixote who now chooses to speak 'movido de otro semejante espíritu que le movió hablar tanto como habló cuando cenó con los cabreros' [moved by such another spirit, as that which had moved him to talk so much when he supped with the goatherds] (1978, 1.37.464; 1998, 337). This second speech, then, parallels the discourse he pronounced on the Golden Age. While before he had contrasted the mythical age with the present, now he contrasts two careers or life choices: arms and letters. Here, he praises the soldier over the scholar. While both may suffer wants and travails, soldiers are greater and their danger greater still since they can lose their lives. Linking this discourse to that of the Golden Age, he decries modern inventions such as gunpowder, which make prowess with the sword less likely (1978, 1.38.471; 1998, 342). It is curious, then, that Don Quixote will speak just when travellers from Moorish lands arrive. While he speaks to Micomicona, not realizing that her tale is enchantingly pagan, he also speaks when travellers from Moorish lands arrive. This second tale seems to have a mirroring effect: 'Together, Zoraida and the Captive arrive at the inn as realistic figurings of a modern Christian knight and his chastely silent Lady' (Garrett 2000, 141). While the captive, Ruy Pérez de Viedma, will tell of his plight as a soldier in foreign lands, Don Quixote must also foreground the role of the Christian knight when faced with potential enemies. In some ways, then, the veiled lady recalls the knight's Dulcinea. This mirroring can spur speech through anxiety since Dulcinea can be seen as an Other. Equally curious is the fact that when the new arrival starts to tell his story, it echoes Don Quixote's discourse on the paths in life. The former captive tells how his father, having three sons, told each to follow a different path: arms, letters, and the mercantile arts. The oldest and the teller of the story, chooses the army, the second decides to go to the Indies, while the third would finish his studies in Salamanca and join the church. Don Quixote, of course, would leave out merchandising. In the first chapters of the novel, the merchants from Toledo had aroused in him a 'Catholic' reaction, since merchants were often suspected of being of 'impure' blood. They also engaged in trade, and this separated them from both the court and the church. Don Quixote's conservative stance, then, is modified by the captive's father who accepts the mercantile.

The Captive's Tale, although it can still be assigned to the genre of the Italianate novella, also wavers in genre, as a textual Proteus who changes shapes from this to that. It recalls the idealized Moorish romances and ballads that arose as a reaction to the unseemly historical reality in Spain when the *moriscos* were marginalized and were threatened with expulsion – seen in such works such as *Abindarraez y la hermosa Jarifa*. But in its grounding in present realities, it can also call up the chronicles of captives from North Africa, such as the famous work by Antonio de Sossa, *Topografía de Argel*, where the Portuguese doctor describes his five years of captivity in this city and shows not only the horrors of captivity but also how Algiers stood at the crossroads of civilization, with a population more diverse than any European city of the period. Cervantes, also a captive, calls on his own life experiences to further impart upon this tale a sense of immediacy.[3] Another genre is also evoked within this tale. The important role played by Zoraida's white hand in the text, the change in skin colouring from brown (as would be expected of a Moorish woman) to pure white, recalls Greek romances. In the *Aethiopica*, Chariclea is white although her parents are black rulers from Ethiopia. This allusion serves to familiarize the reader with Zoraida and render her less threatening and more like a heroine of romance. The interlacing, as will be shown, is very tight and revealing in the three storiesabout Micomicona, the captive and Zoraida, and Luis and Clara. While Micomicona quoted from the Italian Christian 'epic' by Tasso, the Captive's Tale quotes from the *Aethiopica*, which was considered at the time a prose substitute for epic. To conclude the weave, the story of Luis and Clara clearly evokes Virgil's *Aeneid*, thus continuing with the epic thread. In addition, all three stories have to do with voyages or pilgrimages. In the Micomicona story, she has come from faraway lands to search for her deliverer, Don Quixote. Of course, this is merely a ploy to divert him from chivalric adventures. In the Captive's Tale, Zoraida will journey with her beloved to Christian lands through many dangers and rough seas; in the Luis and Clara story, although the route only takes the lovers within Spain, the allusions to Virgil expand the geography, as Luis must make his way through the rough seas of love to encounter his beloved. The tight weave keeps Don Quixote in check. But more and more he regains his agency and voice. Micomicona compels him to intone chivalric promises, but these are meant to trap him. His discomfort with Zoraida leads the knight to deliver his discourse on arms and letters so as to assuage his anxieties. While the Virgilian aspects of Luis's tale (together with Maritornes's trick) seem to marginalize him again, the violence that erupts at the inn gives him the perfect opportunity to take charge and to deal with the demons of his past, to come to terms with the anxieties of Otherness. All these tales, then, include a clash of civilizations, beginning with the allusion to Tasso's epic on the Crusades, continuing with the present clashes between corsairs, renegades, Moors, and Christians in the Mediterranean of Cervantes' time, and ending with a Virgilian epic that is suddenly metamorphosed into an Italianate romance dealing with Saracens.

The Captive's Tale centres on both love and war. It is also a story that in many ways mirrors Cervantes' own captivity in Algiers. Thus, to the many genres already encountered, we may add a kind of fictional autobiography. Like Cervantes, Ruy Pérez de Viedma joins the Spanish armies in Italy; like the author, he participates in the famous battle of Lepanto; and like Cervantes, he becomes a captive in Algiers. The tale of the heroic soldier, however, is not all about prowess in war, or about

Cervantes' own glory as a veteran of the most famous war of his time. The tale combines praise with critical views. As Roberto A. Véguez explains, the fact that Viedma, in a departure from Cervantes' biography, serves the duke of Alba in Flanders introduces a critical perspective. The duke's quelling the rebellion and his execution of Egmont and Horne earned him the name of 'butcher of the Low Countries' (2005, 104). The captive, however, simply praises the duke: 'Tuve nuevas que el gran duque de Alba pasaba a Flandes. Mudé propósito, fuime con él, servile en las jornadas que hizo, halléme en la muerte de los condes ded Eguemón y de Hornos' [I was informed that the great Duke of Alva was passing into Flanders with his army. Hereupon I changed my mind, went with him and served under him in all his engagements. I was present at the death of the Counts Egmont and Horn] (1978, 1.39.476; 1998, 346). The reference to the double execution which shook Europe does not have any qualifying adjectives or any kind of description whatsoever. This elision of comment appears as a kind of censorship that highlights the events and the duke's harsh justice. The cruelty of Spaniards must be taken into consideration in any account of clashes, particularly with those who were considered Others such as Muslims. If Spaniards can be cruel with those who partake of their own religion and culture, how would they act against the Other? If the captive is not outspoken on matters of Christian cruelty at this point, he does criticize Spanish policy. At one point he disapproves of the fleet for not pressing on at Navarino: 'Ví y noté la ocasión que allí se perdió' [I saw and observed the opportunity that was then lost] (1978, 1.39.478; 1998, 347). Later, he is actually pleased that the Turks regain the fort of La Goleta: 'eso a muchos les pareció, y así me pareció a mi, que fue particular gracia y merced que el cielo hizo a España en permitir que se asolase aquella oficina y capa de maldades, y aquella gomia o esponja y polilla de la infinidad de dineros que allí sin provecho se gastaban, sin sevir de otra cosa que de conservar la memoria de haberla Ganado la felicísima del invictísimo Carlos Quinto' [But many were of the opinion and I was of that number, that heaven did a particular grace and favour to Spain, in offering the destruction of that forge and refuge of all iniquity, that devourer, that sponge, and that mouth of infinite sums of money, idly spent there, to no other purpose than to preserve the memory of its having been a conquest of the invincible emperor Charles the Fifth] (1978, 1.39.479; 1998, 349). Both of these references show that Ruy Pérez de Viedma, as soldier, does not merely follow orders but is deeply concerned with the politics of the Mediterranean struggles. Marina

Brownlee goes further in her assessment: 'Indeed, the trajectory posited by the Captive (from Lepanto to Navarino to La Goleta) points to Spain's decline as a military power' (2005, 570).[4]

Although the captive condemns (without saying so) Spanish cruelties, he clearly points to the cruelty of Turks, Moors, and renegades. For example, the cruelty of the renegade Hassan Pasha, ruler of Algiers, is described in great detail. Véguez reminds us that 'the captive mentions impalings, hangings, and beatings' (2000, 105). This notion of cruelty and savagery goes hand in hand with the perceived horrors of the land. Eloy Martín Corral explains the Spanish view of North Africa and its inhabitants: 'De ahí que, recogiéndose la tradición medieval de los bestiarios, los países islámicos fueron habitualmente presentados como morada de fieras terribles y sanguinarias que devoraban miles y cientos de miles de musulmanes en cada uno de sus continuos ataques . . . castigo a la equivocada religión que profesaban sus moradores' [In this way, taking up the medieval tradition of the bestiaries, the Islamic countries were habitually presented as the home of terrible and sanguinary beasts who devoured thousands and hundreds of thousands of Muslims in each of their attacks . . . a punishment for the wrong religion professed by its inhabitants] (2002, 38). Hassan Pasha and his cohorts can be viewed as part of this savage landscape, as beings as cruel as the beasts spawned by the region. Furthermore, the heroes of the tale are not necessarily without fault. Although Zoraida claims that she wants to convert to Christianity and wants to worship the Virgin, taking her name, Maria, and although the captive is spurred by yearnings of freedom and a desire to return to his own more 'civilized' culture, both Zoraida and the captive perform an act of great cruelty. They abandon Zoraida's father (as well as some Moors that they have taken captive) in a deserted area as they make their way to Spain with the family jewels. Cruelty toward a father is often construed in Spanish texts as a sign of damnation, since the paternal figure mirrors God, *pater noster*. Caring for the father carries the opposite result. In Tirso de Molina's *El condenado por desconfiado*, for example, the ruffian Enrico is saved only because he cares for his father, while the pious hermit Paulo is condemned.

Indeed, the place where Zoraida's father is abandoned is not without significance: 'llegamos a una cala que se hace al lado de un pequeño promontorio o cabo que de los moros es llamado el de la Cava Rumía que en nuestra lengua quiere decir la mala mujer cristiana' [we came to a creek by the side of a small promontory or head, which, by the Moors, is called the cape of Cava Rumia, that is to say, in our language, 'The wicked Christian woman'] (1978, 1.41.506; 1998, 373). Thus, the father is abandoned in a place that has for its name that of a bad Christian woman. Are the act of abandonment and the location where it takes place a signal that Zoraida is not the idealized figure she appears to be? This is a site that was feared by Christians since here La Cava is buried, the woman who in legend was said to have been the cause of the Moorish invasion of Spain. So, is Zoraida marked with this evil, or is she the opposite, is she reversing the invasion and signalling the conversion of Muslims? Michael Gerli asserts that Cervantes reverses the myth of La Cava through Zoraida's tale; he rewrites it from an apocalyptic narrative of violation, ruin, and exile into a new Revelation centring on faith, hope, and return – of homecoming and of closure. Supplanting the old, he endows the story of destruction of Spain with a new teleology founded on the ethos of love, charity, and personal sacrifice that repudiates La Cava's fundamental message of violence, vengeance, and devastation – of pollution and banishment for trespass symbolized in sexual defilement – dispensed through usurpation by an oriental race (1995, 57). In this reversal of La Cava's myth images, Zoraida emerges in a positive light: 'Zoraida's abandonment of her father in sight of La Cava's tomb, more than a cruel act of personal tragedy, constitutes ... an act in the name of faith symbolizing the rejection of a patrimony of carnality, infidelity, vengeance, and enslavement in favor of a matrimony in Christian peace' (1995, 55). Of course, the question still remains as to why the positive conversion is from Islam to Christianity. Cervantes clearly shows that in Algiers, conversion to Islam was common since it allowed for social mobility. What, then, is the difference? Since Zoraida's future baptism is to take place at a time when Spain is considering the expulsion of the *moriscos*, it may mean that Zoraida does not have a place in Spain, and that the peace and freedom she seeks is not to be found in Iberia. Does her idealization of Christianity have no place in the clashes between civilizations? Nothing is ever simple in Cervantes' fiction. A play of mirrors asks not only who is the most beautiful, the most Christian, but also who is the cruellest of them all.

The Captive's Tale seems to be three tales at once: a story of war and piracy in the Mediterranean; a story of captivity which images Cervantes' biography; and a story of love triumphing over religious differences. Of course, love triumphs in order for the couple to be Christians and not Muslims. But, as always, there are subtleties in Cervantes. To emphasize the cross-cultural love affair, Zoraida has to write to the captive in Arabic. The letters are actually translated by a renegade from Murcia – and the captive insists more than once that he and the renegade are friends. For the Spanish of the times this must have been quite shocking. A renegade was derided not just because he abandoned his religion, but also because he lived in a society where there was an intolerable freedom to ascend the social scale. Indeed, twenty-one of the thirty-five corsair captains in Cervantes' time were renegades, from such places as Genoa, Murcia, Naples, and Venice (Garcés 2009, 556). And the very governor of Algiers was a Venetian renegade. The complex situation of the renegade is highlighted, as Maria Antonia Garcés explains, when he asks the captive for a letter saying that he is a good renegade, one who is kind to Christians and wants to return home (2009, 562–3). Thus, the renegade serves as a 'go-between' in this cross-cultural love affair. Just as letters are used between Zoraida and the captive, letters will be used between the renegade and the Spanish authorities. The double epistolary exchange, points to the conflictive doublings of Spain and the Mediterranean. At the same time, the Other as monster will be pitted against the Other as perfect beauty, as Madonna and even as saviour. Zoraida becomes a kind of Madonna and saviour, helping to bring the captive back to Spain and changing her Moorish name to María.[5] In spite to the tale's 'epic' sweep of battles in the Mediterranean, it has a flavour of immediacy, of something that is happening right then. And so it should. Clashes with the African Moors and anxieties of *moriscos* living in Spain were problems of the moment. The story of Zoraida begins *in medias res* with her arrival at the inn. It is here that the text immediately shows her Otherness – her monstrous self. Indeed, the tale has been compared to an interpolated story in Mary Shelley's *Frankenstein*. Both fictional tales include a Muslim woman who has a Christian lover who must somehow interpret the beloved's Arabic language. The Safie episode in Shelley is an imitation of Zoraida's tale. And both women seem to have a place outside of society, like Frankenstein's creature who is called monster. But his is not the place she desires to have. Garrett explains: 'In both *Don Quixote* and *Frankenstein*, a female figure who is half Moor (the body) and half Christian (the soul) enters into self imposed exile from her home culture in order to actualize a hidden and purportedly European self' (2000, 141).

    Don Quixote is a novel about metamorphoses. The knight is always transforming what he sees into something else. And so it is with this story. A Muslim woman is not what she appears to be, much like Micomicona who is the disguised Dorotea.[6] Following in the footsteps of other characters, Dorotea becomes a sleuth who tries to figure out who this woman who arrives at the inn really is. This is precisely what others had done with her. Although dressed as a man, her beautiful foot and her long blond hair revealed to those spying on her that Dorotea was a woman. In this case, Luscinda and Dorotea marvel at the strange dress worn by the woman who arrives at the inn. Dorotea immediately asks: '¿esta señora es cristiana o mora? Porque el traje y el silencio nos hace pensar que es lo que no querríamos que fuese' [Is this lady a Christian or a Moor? For her habit and her silence make us think she is what we wish she were not] (1978, 1.37.462; 1998, 336). The signs or clues are her language (in this case her silence) and her clothing (face veiled, turban on her head). These are signs of an Other, and it is thus that Dorotea claims that she is something that is not welcome in Christian Spain.

This perspective is immediately countered by Ruy Pérez de Viedma who asserts: 'Mora es en el traje y en el cuerpo; pero en el alma muy grande Cristiana, porque tiene grandísimos deseos de serlo' [She is a Moor . . . in her attire and in her body; but in her soul she is already very much a Christian, having a very strong desire to become one] (1978, 1.37.463; 1998, 336). Very much like Don Quixote's vision, where appearances hide the 'real' chivalric world, Zoraida's body, language, and clothes hide her Christian soul, according to the captive. Her desire to be Christian, her desire to be baptized after she learns the dogmas of Christianity, and her assertion that she does not want to be Zoraida but Maria are the steps that dispel the image of a dangerous or wanton and exotic Oriental princess (Garrett 2000, 143). Taking off her veil, she 'reveals' her soul through a beautiful countenance. The characters that show a strong distrust of the embodiment of another civilization begin to change their minds. Zoraida as María is not dangerous but one of the many figures that in hagiography and chivalric tales have converted to Christianity. As the captive tells their tale, her white hand recalls the beautiful white foot that pointed to Dorotea's beauty. A Moorish white hand like Dorotea's white foot takes us to other genres, to Tasso's epic with its pagan enchantress and to Heliodorus's prose epic where Chariclea is a white beauty born of black parents. These metamorphoses signal genre disruptions as well as clashes of culture, creating instability in both text and characters. The hybrid has become the sign of questionings and protagonisms. Echoing hybridity, Zoraida's white hand and other clues such as the cross and the gold coins are at first woefully misinterpreted by the captives who think that she is a renegade married to a Muslim (1978, 1.40.487).[7] Clues once again serve to engage an active reader, who, like the characters in the fiction, attempt to decipher these signs. As Brownlee asserts: 'The gesturing hand, along with the symbols of religion and wealth that it bears, present the reader with a strikingly hybrid mystery' (2005, 572). When her truth emerges, we learn that Zoraida is a Muslim who wishes to become a Christian because of the lessons and inspiration given to her by her Christian slave-governess. The tale, then, is all about discovery, both in Algiers and at the inn. It is indeed about the hybrid as Brownlee states, but it is also about familiarity. In both sites, as she is 'unveiled' she becomes more and more familiar, more and more to be appreciated and loved. And this may be one of the key elements here. The tale familiarizes the characters with the figure of the Other, taking away fear and the sense of danger. The Other is ready to be part of Christian Western civiliza- tion. Indeed, for Martha García, Otherness is averted in the tale since Zoraida becomes a true subject, whose agency delivers Ruy Pérez from Algiers (2005, 85). I would add that she is a subject because she wants to become a Christian. If conversion had not been an issue, the tale would have been even more non-narratable than Don Quixote's extravagances with Maritornes at the inn.

Zoraida as an alluring and complex figure has been the subject of many other interpretations. Is she a monster of lust and cruelty reflect- ing the monsters spawned by the African lands? Is she a hybrid fig- ure as when the captive calls her Lela Zoraida? Brownlee explains: 'lela being a term used exclusively to signify the Virgin Mary or a sultan's wife' (2005, 575; Asín 1948, 322–3). Is her desire for conversion a politi- cal move? Is it simply a desire to be free from her father and her culture? Does she simply want her independence as Alison Weber asserts? Can her desire to be a Christian stem from her genealogy? Is her ancestry truly Muslim or does her white hand point to something else? After all, the tale is based on a historical account where a woman named Zohara was 'nieta de cristianos tanto por su padre como su madre' [a grand- daughter of Christians both on her father and her mother's side] (Asín 1948, 254). Or is she a Madonna and a saviour? Some critics would see her as a figure akin to the Virgin of Loretto;[8] and some associate her with a miracle attributed to Notre Dame de Liesse (Cirot 1938; Vaganay 1937). Indeed, Brownlee shows that 'the Christian romance vignette with which we are confronted at the inn, [is] a calque on Joseph with Mary on the donkey, who are told that there is no room at the inn' (2005, 580). This critic, however, problematizes this scene, concluding that Zoraida is 'a floating signifier' (2005, 581). Others, however, take the Christian calques even further and consider Zoraida as the force that will redeem humanity. For George Camamis she represents Christ, since she starts her journey of deliverance at a garden on a Friday (1977, 81–2).

Given that the novel is constantly pointing to naming, perhaps it is here that we may find a clue as to an aspect of her identity. While she is always intoning the name she wishes to take at the time of her baptism, that of María, she is still called Zoraida. I would ask: what is the significance of this name that she would leave behind? Zoraida corresponds to the Arabic name Turayya or al-Thurayya 'the many little ones, associated with abundance and plenty produced in the pastures and crops by rains'; in other words, the Pleiades (Camamis 1977, 81).[9] Although Alberto Montaner Frutos problematizes this association (2006, 256–9),[10] he partially accepts both Luis A. Murillo's idea that she is the captive's 'guiding star' (1983, 240) and María Antonia Garcés's notion that her name evokes 'striking brilliance, one that speaks of the non-representable nature of this desired other. This luminous vision recalls the symbolism of Zoraida's name: pleiad, cluster of stars' (2002, 215). I would like to elaborate on Zoraida as the constellation of the Pleiades, which is one of the earliest constellations on record, mentioned in China (2357 BCE) and India (1730 BCE). It appears in Homer, Euripides, Sapho, Aratus, and Hesiod to name a few authors from the classical world. It is 'one of the most noted objects in the history, poetry and mythology of the heavens' (Allen 1963, 392). There are several stories told regarding the transformation of the seven sisters. They may have committed suicide, saddened by the plight of their father (or of their sisters, the Hyades). More often, it is said that Orion pursued one or all of the Pleiades, seven sisters, and daughters of Atlas, after the Titan started to carry the weight of the world on his shoulders. As with many persecuted women in mythology, they are transformed before they are seized. But they had to wait seven years until the god heard their laments. Zeus changed them first into doves, and then into stars. As an astromorphosis or catasterism (the transformation of divinities, objects, or human beings into stars), this event is recounted by Aratus. Curiously, Ovid, who relates a number of such transformations in his *Metamorphoses,* does not describe what happens to the Pleiades, although he alludes to them. He mentions them, for example, when he describes Achilles' shield with 'The constellations in the height of heaven, / The Pleiads and the Hyads and the Bear' (1998, 303). But even in the heavens, these seven sisters do not find needed rest from flight. They revolve along with the other constellations, and to make matters worse, with Orion's demise, he was placed behind them in the

heavens to immortalize the chase. But what has this to do with Zoraida? The myth itself appears to tell us very little about her since it is
the story of seven sisters who are chased by a mighty hunter. She is not
pursued by Ruy Pérez de Viedma, but instead pursues him. Why then
utilize this name?

Achilles' shield, as described in the *Iliad* and recalled in Ovid's *Metamorphoses*, is associated with four constellations:the Pleiades, Hyades,
the Bear, and Orion (18.483–9). J.H. Phillips asserts that these constellations, through 'their sequential heliacal risings and subsequent cos-
mical settings' point to a specific period, approximately from May to
November (1980, 179–80). This is a time for plowing and for the harvest,
and these activities are found in other parts of Achilles' shield (18.541–
72).[11] The Pleiades also mark the harvest in the *Georgics* (1978, 1.4.233).
But the seasonal import is also of a different kind. More important for
our purposes is Virgil's statement that the constellation is visible in the
Mediterranean only during sailing season (1978, 1.1.138). These stars
rise with the sun in the eastern sky around 15 June and set with the
rising sun in early to mid November. As early as Hesiod's *Works and
Days*, a poem that, according to its editor and translator Apostolos N.
Athanassakis, delves into 'the right time of the year for the undertak-
ing of various types of work' (2004, 63), the reader is warned that once
the Pleiades plunge into the sea fleeing Orion, the sailor should return
home and not brave the tempestuous waters:

> And if longing seizes you for sailing the stormy seas,
> when the Pleiades flee mighty Orion
> and plunge into the misty deep
> and all the gusty winds are raging,
> then do not keep your ship on the wine-dark sea
> but, as I bid you, remember to work the land   (2004, 80, vv. 618–23)

Richard Hinckley Allen summarizes the many meanings of the Pleiades
asserting that they are a sign of rain, harvest, sailing season, and also
catastrophic destruction (1963, 391–403). Zoraida, then, is associated
with sailing, with the battles in the Mediterranean, and with captivity and piracy that take place at the time they shine in the sky. But she
is an ambivalent sign – she represents possible bounties coming from
peace or a great catastrophe augured by the cruelty to her father and
the name of the place where he was abandoned. Her story is open-
ended since this chapter in history is yet to be concluded. She could

soon become a *morisca*, a Christian Moor, at a time when there is talk of their expulsion. The reader could also envision a scenario where her father's rage, like that of Don Julián, father of La Cava, precipitated an invasion of Spain. Cervantes has thus presented us with a sympathetic figure that conceals opposing signs. And he leaves her to wander in Christian lands.

There is little time for Don Quixote to intervene in the goings-on at the inn, since a new arrival sets the stage for another novella that will also use the inn as a place for further development while its initial complications will be told, once again using the *in medias res* technique. A judge arrives at the inn with his daughter, whose beauty shines just like that of Zoraida. Don Quixote is allowed to sing her praises, stating that her beauty is such that it would cause 'no sólo abrirse y manifestarse los castillos, sino aparterse los riscos, y devidirse y abajarse las montanas; para dalle acogida' [to whom not only castles ought to throw open and offer themselves, but rocks to separate and divide, and mountains to bow their lofty heads, to give her entrance and reception] (1978, 1.42.515; 1998, 381). Although Don Quixote, as usual, is referring to events in books of chivalry, the splitting of rocks and mountains recalls the formation of the Pillars of Hercules. Indeed, the arriving gentleman announces that he will be going on to be a judge in the courts of Mexico. Thus he will be going *plus ultra*. It is as if the pillars are starting to emerge again in preparation for a new segment of the novel. But there is yet a story to be told, that of Clara (the judge's daughter) and the yet unknown Luis. Before the lover makes his appearance, the inn will become the place of another *anagnorisis*. Ronald Paulson defines the inn as one of two 'basic metaphors of eighteenth-century fiction' (1984, 200). Cervantes, even before Fielding and Hogarth, sees the inn as the gathering place where unfathomable contingencies and coincidences brought about by fortune take place.[12] Fortuna and her wheel keep bringing people together here: from Fernando's re-encounter with Dorotea to Cardenio recognizing the veiled Luscinda. And now we discover that the judge is none other than Ruy Pérez de Viedma's brother. As the captive reveals himself to his brother Juan in a very theatrical moment, the scene is set to present the story of the father and the two brothers, the one who studied letters and the one who became a merchant and became rich in Perú. *Anagnorisis*, of course, is a common device used from Greek novels and comedies to the books of chivalry. The inn, then, is a place to unveil people, relationships, and motivations.

This is the time, then, to unveil one last relationship, one that will connect the mythology of the Pleiades, found in Homer's and Ovid's epic and Virgil's *Georgics*, with another image of the sea derived from the Virgilian epic. The arrival of a love-struck youth both quickens interlace and, in the end, brings back Don Quixote's voice and vision. According to Raymond Immerwhar, there are seven interpolated tales in the 1605 novel. The first constitutes most of the second segment of the novel, the tale of Marcela and Grisóstomo. Five of the tales occur in this fourth part, and a brief and final one can be encountered in the fifth and final segment of the novel. In fact, we could say that there is a sixth tale in this fourth part, that of Dorotea, who claims to be the princess Micomicona. If we accept this, then the novel has yet one more Pythagorean element in its structure. There are eight *novellas*, replicating the eight chapters of the first part and the eight chapters of the third part. Eight, as has been explained, doubles the quaternity which represents cosmos and is also the Pythagorean number for justice. It is the seventh tale, the last or sixth tale of the fourth section, which will lead to the return home of the knight. As we have seen, it is prefaced by a *plus ultra* remark on the part of Clara and, as will be discussed in the next chapter, it will end with a clash so severe that there seems to be no way out, *non plus ultra*.

Let us turn then, to the tale of Luis and Clara. Dorotea is wakened by a song. Outside of the inn a youthful voice is heard. The poem begins with the line: 'Marinero soy de amor' [A mariner I am of love] (1978, 43.521; 1998, 386). In the verses that follow, the young lover, Luis, represents himself as a new Palinurus, the helmsman of Aeneas's ship. The epic hero had abandoned Dido in order to pursue his quest. He must reach Italy, even though a storm is coming. Palinurus, his helmsman, exclaims: 'Alas! Why have such clouds girt the heaven? What wilt thou, Father Neptune?' (1978, 5.13–14). These words by Palinurus foreshadow his dark future. Putting aside passion is not Aeneas's only sacrifice. Palinurus will also have to die since Neptune will only permit the hero to reach his destiny if the god is given a sacrificial victim. In the middle of the night, once the waves have quieted and all is calm, Somnus whispers to Palinurus, impelling him to nod off and go to sleep: 'Lay down thy head and steal thy weary eyes from toil' (1978, 5.845). But the determined helmsman is wary of even a calm sea. Not putting his fate in this 'monster' below, he continues to steer the ship and follow the stars (1978, 5.849). A sleeping draught eventually overcomes Palinurus, who falls into the sea dragging the helm with him. The ship is without direction. David Quint explains: 'It is Neptune who brings the fleet to Italy. The hero's individual agency is illusory, at best greatly diminished, even when he appears to promote his destiny . . . he goes with the flow of historical necessity that will not allow him independent action' (1993, 91–2).

Thus, in spite of the disappearance of the helmsman, Aeneas can arrive in Italy, led there by the winds of fortune, the winds of destiny, the will of the gods. Quint also argues that 'Palinurus is, in fact, a surrogate for Aeneas in the hero's capacity as a leader, as head of the ship of state' (1993, 86). Although it is true that Palinurus steers the ship and is thus an image of Aeneas's governance, I would add that there is at least one key difference between the two. Palinurus is well acquainted with the art of navigation. As someone who is proud of his art, Palinurus seems to have more agency during this voyage than Aeneas. He knows the seas and the heavens, and he can follow the right course. In a sense, he is a tragic hero. Even though he follows his stars, even though he is determined to fulfil his duties, the gods will impede this. Through no flaw of his own, he falls asleep. His art has led him to his death since the epic poem is in the hands of the gods. It is Neptune, not Palinurus, who will guide the ship to where it needs to go. In the Cervantine adaptation, Palinurus (Luis) is a mariner impelled by love. As Antonio Barnés Vázquez asserts: 'Él es un marinero y el amor es su mar. Su amada es su estrella, y las nubes los obstáculos que ella interpone' [He is a mariner and love is his sea. His beloved is his star and the clouds are the obstacles that she creates] (2009, 230). Palinurus must follow specific constellations so as to steer the ship correctly: 'He marks all the stars gliding in the silent sky, Arcturus, the rainy Hyades, and the twin Bears, and he scans Orion, girt with golden armour' (1978, 3.514–16). The Hyades, the Bear, and Orion are the constellations associated with the Pleiades in Hesiod, Homer, and Ovid, among others.[13] Virgil's poem, however, substitutes the Pleiades for the star Arcturus, the 'Bear Watcher.' According to mythology this brightest of stars is positioned to guard Callisto (*Ursa maior*) and her son Arcas (*Ursa minor*). Like the previous constellations, this star was used in ancient calendars and as a provider of directions for the mariners. And, like the Pleiades, it could have adverse effects. In fact, while the Pleiades are both fortunate for agriculture and warn of storms at sea, Arcturus seems much more ominous. Studying the omens surrounding the battle of Actium, Christopher M. McDonough points to Aristophanes' *Rudens*, where Arcturus as Prologus creates a storm: 'I raised a howling winter storm, and stirred the ocean's waves – for I am Arcturus, the most bitter constellation of all, stormy when I rise and stormier when I set' (McDonough 2003, 254).

While Zoraida as the Pleiades is an ambiguous sign for navigation, Palinurus, in following Arcturus, may be viewing his own disaster. Perhaps it is for this reason that Luis rejects Palinurus's stars. Luis has only to follow one star, Clara. Love has thus become an epic quest. Luis's poem rewrites the Virgilian epic where love (Dido) must be abandoned in order to pursue the epic path. As a lover, he is totally committed to his pursuits. Luis claims that his sailing is unsteady and he has little hope of arriving at a safe harbour: 'navego sin esperanza / de llegar a puerto alguno' [Toss'd betwixt doubts and fears, I rove, / And see no port around] (1978, 43.521; 1998, 387). The port, of course, is Clara's welcoming presence and love. Luis's poetic song ends with the fear that she will abandon him: 'Al punto que te me encubras / será de mi muerte el punto' [If thou withdraw'st thy cheering day, / In night of death I lie] (1978, 43.522; 1998, 387). His death would not be caused by Neptune or Somnus, but by Clara's indifference. While Aeneas has to abandon Dido and Palinurus to achieve his destiny, Luis only needs to follow his starry beloved and have her shine her love on him. She must not veil herself in the clouds, but must shine forth with her love. Once again, unveiling is key to success. Only if she rejects him will he find death like Palinurus. If there is a Neptune in this story, it is the father who may withhold permission to marry. Thus the possible demise of the helmsman has little to do with epic adventures or questions of governance (the helmsman of the ship of state). It has to do with dying for love if either Clara turns away from him or Luis's own father rejects their marriage.

It seems as if Luis has been as artful a helmsman as Palinurus. Disguised as a muleteer, he has guided his steps (albeit not his ship) to find his beloved in a faraway place, at a small inn close to Sierra Morena. In spite of many obstacles he has reached safe harbour. The difficulties in Cervantes have little to do with the gods. Instead of falling asleep, the Spanish Palinurus actually wakes up his beloved: 'Clara despertó toda soñolienta' [Clara awoke, quite sleepy] (1978, 43.522; 1998, 387). And Clara is not about to turn away from the amorous youth. She is, however, worried that their love will come to naught, given his high position in society: '¿qué fin se puede esperar, si su padre es tan principal y tan rico, que le parecerá que aun yo no puedo ser criada de su hijo, cuanto más esposa?' [what conclusion can be hoped for, since his father is of such quality, and so wealthy, that he will not think me worthy to be so much as his son's servant, and how much less his wife?] (1978, 43.525; 1998, 390). Even though it seems that Palinurus has arrived at a safe harbour at the inn, this is really not the case. He has arrived at a strange and confusing place. Let us remember that Virgil's Palinurus does not die at sea. Instead, he reaches a savage land in the south of Italy where he is murdered by the native tribe of the Lucani. Indeed, this new land where Clara abides is also full of danger. Four servants of Luis's father have followed him to the inn with the command to take him back home. In a confrontation, Luis asserts that he will not return home alive. He will die like a new Palinurus: 'si no es llevándome muerto, aunque de cualquiera manera que me llevéis será llevarme sin vida' [except you kill me; and, whichever way you carry me, it will be without life] (1978, 44.534; 1998, 398).

But Luis is saved; he is heard by the *Oidor*, the judge. This character, as Carroll B. Johnson has perceptively shown, links the previous interpolated story, that of the captive, with this one. As noted above, he is Ruy Pérez's younger brother Juan, who studied at Salamanca and has become a prosperous judge. As Johnson explains: 'Even after the Captain has ascertained that the *Oidor* who has just arrived with his daughter and retinue is in fact his brother, he refuses to come forward and effect the reunion. He is afraid his brother will reject him because of his poverty' (1982, 143). Not only is the brother afraid, but also the innkeeper. The reason has to do with the power and influence exerted by such officials: 'He is a successful member of the *letrado* class which controlled the new imperial bureaucracy, on his way to Mexico to take possession of an important post in the *Audiencia* there' (1982, 144). In addition, Juan is already a rich man, having inherited a substantial sum after his wife's demise. And he is not afraid to use his power and influence to get the best room at the inn. While Juan Pérez has been successful in letters, his brother, in spite of his bravery, was a captive and is poor. It is up to the priest to narrate (again) the captive's tale so that his brother can be moved to compassion, and this is precisely what happens with the consequent *anagnorisis*. The *Oidor*, having heard his brother's tale, will eventually be led to listen to Luis's story. For, Juan Pérez (in yet another coincidental encounter at the inn) is actually Clara's father. Our poetic Palinurus is faced with a clever and rich judge who judges him most suitable for his daughter. The problem is that Luis's father is of even greater social position. Cervantes, then, presents us with the miseries of the captive soldier – the misery of many in the dangerous career of arms – so as to contrast him not so much with his lettered brother, but even more with a youth who believes that his amorous adventures are worthy of being sung as a Virgilian epic of love.

The many confusing tales at the inn are told in rapid narratives that are suddenly cut off to turn to the next one, only to return to the earlier tales later. The changes in tone are equally conflictive. We move from the poetic to the comic; from the idealized epic to contemporary social and monetary concerns; from the chivalric to the picaresque (as two travellers want to leave the inn without paying). Don Quixote even becomes the object of a particularly clever and cruel trick played on him by Maritornes. As the knight, his hand tied with a rope, hangs from the window all night attempting to keep Rocinante under him, we can view the event as one of the threads or ropes that entangle the narrative. This comic, even burlesque, scene had as its cause in the knight's belief that a princess wanted to hold his hand. Don Quixote's false chivalric imaginings and eventual humiliation contrasts with the higher style of Luis's amorous and even epic love. The inn certainly resembles the savage land to which Palinurus drifts from the sea. The quarrels and confusions rapidly escalate, and as they do, interlacing becomes more frequent. There are at least five instances of it in chapter 44, culminating in a total breakdown of order in the following chapter: 'El cura daba voces, la ventera gritaba, su hija se afligía, Maritornes lloraba, Dorotea estaba confusa, Luscinda suspensa y dona Clara desmayada. El barbero aporreaba a Sancho, Sancho molía al barbero' [The priest cried out, the hostess shrieked, her daughter roared, Maritornes wept, Dorothea was confounded, Lucinda stood amazed, and Dona Clara fainted away] (1978, 45.544; 1998, 406–7). In this breakdown of order, Cervantes may have taken into account the fact that Palinurus, like many literary helmsmen, represents governance in the ship of state. But who can bring order at the inn? Who is the Aeneas who can follow the winds of fortune or the Palinurus who can steer this chaotic site? The reality is that the new Palinurus is now on savage land and is in great peril.

In spite of the move from mountain to inn, genre confusion continues to prevail as Don Quixote seeks a voice amid so many. He hears Micomicona, only to be drowned by her trickery; he tells of arms and letters only to be supplanted by a 'real' story that pits brothers in these professions. The Captive's Tale, with its Moorish background, takes the reader away from the knight while at the same time exploring Don Quixote's anxieties regarding the Other. The story is never finished signalling that Spain's engagements with Africa and with its own *moriscos* is still an ongoing problem. While this story is left hanging, another one takes its place as mayhem continues to reign at the inn. Many genres come into play as wide-ranging *novelas* are told in the claustrophobic inn, adding to the confusion. We move from Tasso's epic and chivalric inventions in Micomicona's story to Homer as clue to Zoraida's name and to Heliodorus as a quote for Zoraida's white hand. We then turn to Virgil in order to reveal Luis's 'epic' amorous ·plight – and this tale in turn is punctuated by picaresque adventures. Theatrical moments and farcical scenes impinge upon these genres. Verbal and thematic variations keep threading the plot, while heavenly stars ask to be deciphered: Zoraida as the Pleiades and Luis as a new Palinurus following Arcturus. Veiling and unveiling, confusion and *anagnorisis*, the perils of the sea, and the many struggles that emerge from the lands that surround the Mediterranean seem to burst forth at an insignificant site, hidden away from civilization. Indeed, the clashes of genres and civilizations have reached such a crescendo that it is time for the narrative to cross the Pillars of Hercules. And here, it is Don Quixote, who had lost his voice and agency in the tangle of adventures, who comes to the fore. His strange resolution of the situation will be the subject of the next chapter. Indeed, this resolution will also unveil a deep secret that the knight has been hiding deep in chivalric battles, in clashes of genre, and in the folds of the narrative.

9 Don Quixote among the Saracens

When these Christian authors wish to understand Islam, they will turn rarely to Muslims themselves, normally preferring those time-honored authorities, the Bible and the church fathers. Medieval Christians, with very few exceptions, did not use the words 'Moslem' or 'Islam'; instead they used ethnic terms such as 'Arab,' 'Saracen,' 'Ishmaelite.' Information about these people could be found in the venerable books of old.

– John V. Tolan, *Saracens*

For the influence of persecution on literature is precisely that it compels all writers who hold heterodox views to develop a peculiar technique of writing, the technique which we have in mind when speaking of writing between the lines . . . But how can a man perform the miracle of speaking in a publication to a minority, while being silent to the majority of his readers?

– Leo Strauss, *Persecution and the Art of Writing*

More than a quarter of a century has passed since Carroll B. Johnson published his controversial book, *Madness and Lust: A Psychoanalytical Approach to Don Quixote*. One of its basic tenets was clearly summarized by Daniel Eisenberg: 'A bachelor, with only women sharing his house, he is disturbed by the maturation of his niece, and takes refuge first in literature, then in a radical change of life and the deflection of this unacceptable desire to a new object, Dulcinea' (1983, 155). Eisenberg follows this summary with two basic objections to the book, mainly that Johnson is psychoanalysing a character from fiction and that there is no textual proof of the gentleman's sexual obsession with his niece. Having said this, Eisenberg pronounces it a very good book since it is thought provoking. Other critics follow suit.[1] And even to this day, the book triggers much discussion. In a memorial to Carroll Johnson in the journal *Cervantes*, Anne Cruz begins her discussion of Johnson's 1983 book calling it 'infamous' and 'scandalous' (2007, 7, 8). She does, however, turn this around, praising 'Carroll's impressive analysis' and his refusal to concede his point, driving 'with California plates that defiantly read "SOBRINA"' (2007, 8).[2] In this chapter, I will return to the knight's anxieties. As noted previously, this term was often used in the seventeenth century and need not relate to Freud's theories. The knight's anxieties can be gleaned from a careful textual analysis, one that focuses on his actions and imaginings, and also on imitation and parody. Reworkings of different genres thus hold a key to a secret held by the knight and the novel. Instead of searching for the *sobrina*, I will pay particular attention to an episode that includes a *sobrino*. Chapter 45 of the 1605 *Don Quixote* could well include an important clue regarding a mystery as dire for the knight as the one that Carroll Johnson once posited. It may be that throughout the novel, the narrators have been guarding the same sort of 'essential secret' (Todorov 1977, 145) that Todorov finds in Henry James and Eric D. Mayer gleans in Cervantes' *Novelas ejemplares*. Such a mystery, according to Todorov, is presented through a narrative by a double movement: one of veiling and the second of disclosure. The first always trumps the second as the reader is left with clues but no stated solution to the mystery. In *Don Quixote*, a whiff of mystery surfaces at the very beginning of the novel, when the ancestry of the crazed gentleman is withheld. Is the purpose simply to parody the deterministic but opposite genealogies of *pícaros* and knights? But let us begin *in medias res*, and then move backwards and forwards mimicking the double movement of the mystery itself.

In the previous chapter, we encountered a Don Quixote without a voice. He was drowned out by the maze of stories around him and finally, he became a comic figure, humiliated by Maritornes. At this point, the contentiousness at the inn is aggravated, in part, by the claim from a barber that Don Quixote has stolen his basin and he must return it. Those present at the inn must decide if it is truly a prized helmet or merely a barber's basin. Those who know Don Quixote's mad imaginings, favour his cause, while the others find it untenable. When the answer favours the chivalric, Don Quixote can once again be at the centre. The knight insightfully views the verbal battles at the 'enchanted' inn as a struggle that replicates the ones that took place at the camp of King Agramante, whose chief counsellor was King Sobrino. Since Don Quixote imagines his adventures as stemming from fiction, it is fitting that he turn to Agramante for his example. After all, as Michael Murrin states, this very young, ambitious, and fierce African king, who invades France and lays siege to Paris, is a fictional being, with no history whatsoever: 'In one respect Matteo Maria Boiardo differs from other writers of romance in the late fifteenth century, for he invented a purely fictional world . . . Boiardo told a story without precedent in the old chronicles. It is doubtful that anyone in his audience would have believed that Agramante had ever existed or led a huge African army into France' (1994, 57). The Agramante imagined by the knight from La Mancha is far from historical, an invented African king, the main antagonist in the *Orlando inamorato* (1495). The Agramante in Boiardo, who, at a council of war 'gives.two speeches, which open and close the debate' (Murrin 1994, 59) is further developed by Ludovico Ariosto in his *Orlando furioso* (1532). The twenty-seventh canto, tells of the discord at Agramante's camp, a topic that reappears throughout Western literature and culture, as in *Waverly*, the romantic saga by Sir Walter Scott; the caustic *Memoirs* of Laure Junot, duchess d'Abrantes (1831–4), detailing the Napoleonic period in France; and Theophile Gautier's famous travel book *Italia* (1852) where a play at a theatre in Venice shows a handsome French officer in a seraglio as confusion ensues.[3] Ariosto narrates the scene after a great battle, where the Saracens push back the Christian armies into Paris:

> The shrieks and wails of widows and little orphans and bereaved old folk ascended from this murky air to where Michael sat in serene eternity; they showed him how the faithful were prey to wolves and crows – how the dead of France, England, and Germany lay covering the whole field. / The holy angel blushed, for it seemed to him that he had ill obeyed the creator; he reckoned himself deceived and betrayed by faithless Discord, to whom he had entrusted the duty of sparking quarrels among the pagans. (1983, 327)

The archangel Michael immediately plucks the winged figure of Discord out of a monastery where she is delighting in causing monks to throw breviaries at each other in anger, and forces her to sow disputes at Agramante's camp. It is her baleful influence that ignites a series of quarrels, and there are so many instances of conflict and each is so fierce that Agramante can only arrange the order of the contests to follow. Discord first kindles the sparks of conflict as the warriors contend who should be first in the field of battle: Rodomont (the fierce African king of Sarthia and Algiers), Mandricard (the clever king of the Tartars), or Ruggiero (a descendant of Troy's Hector). Ruggiero would fight Rodomont over a horse, while Mandricard would battle Ruggiero over a shield.[4] Agramante can only persist in rearranging the disputes. The first to fight would be Rodomont and Mandricard over their love for Doralice. As they prepare to engage in combat, matters become even more muddled, as each of the two opposing camps is set into further confusion. Gradasso, who is helping Mandricard dress for battle, sees that he has Orlando's sword, Durindana, which he has pledged to find, while Sacripant tells Rodomont that the horse he is riding is not Frontino, but his own Frontalact.[5] And it is indeed so, having once been stolen by Brunello. Discord has won the day. She sends a message to St Michael on high telling him of her triumph. The Saracens are too busy fighting each other to think of taking Paris. Eventually Rodomont leaves the camp despondent as Doralice chooses Mandricard; but this is to no avail since then Ruggiero slays Mandricard (canto 30). By canto 31 the Saracen army is in flight along with King Agramante; and by canto 38 Agramante must call a Council of War on the news that Charlemagne's paladin, Astolfo, has invaded Africa.

Don Quixote's choice of Agramante to envision what is happening before him at the inn is both fitting and awkward. It is fitting because the confusion at the inn resembles in its many different contests and struggles the confusion in Agramante's camp, albeit in a debased and parodic fashion. It is awkward because Agramante was the leader of the Saracens who were fighting against Charlemagne and the Christian army.[6] And it is not Cide Hamete, the unreliable narrator who tells this. The comparison seems to come from Don Quixote's recollection of his readings. Perhaps this is a case of sacramental imitation on the part of the knight. What he reads must be true, and thus he must imitate it without question. As Barbara Fuchs reminds us: 'The frequent Italian diatribes against the Spaniards, who had an increasing military presence in Italy in the sixteenth century, routinely describe them as *marranos*, infidel Moors . . . Ariosto implicitly echoes these characterizations in his *Furioso*, where all Spaniards are simply Saracens . . . In the eyes of other Europeans, Spain's distinctive national identity was Moorish' (2009, 119). Don Quixote's imitation is 'sacramental' in the sense that he never questions how Christians can act as Saracens. Nor does he seem to remember that it was St Michael who brought about this confusion to take down the infidels.

My question then, is, given all the many medieval chronicles that narrate the battles between Saracens and Christians, and given all the Christian treatises that rail against infidels and Saracens, why does Don Quixote, all of a sudden, imagine himself as a leader of the Saracens instead of the Christians, and why does he suddenly regain his voice in doing so?[7] Perhaps Don Quixote feels that he is entitled to be surrounded by Saracens since Bernardo del Carpio, who is often invoked in the novel, served at the side of the Moorish King Marsil of Zaragoza in order to defeat the advances of Charlemagne in France. In a number of Spanish versions, Bernardo kills Roland/Orlando at Roncesvalles. As early as the first chapter of Cervantes' novel the knight imagines the great chivalric heroes among whom is the Spanish victor over Orlando: 'Mejor estaba con Bernardo del Carpio, porque en Roncesvalles había muerto a Roldán el encantado, valiéndose de la industria de Hércules, cuando ahogó a Anteo, el hijo de la tierra entre sus brazos' [He was better pleased with Bernardo del Carpio for putting Orlando the Enchanted to death in Roncesvalles, by means of the same stratagem which Hercules used, when he suffocated Anteus, son of the Earth, by squeezing him between his arms] (1978, 1.1.74; 1998, 23). Possibly utilizing the *Segunda parte de Orlando con el verdadero suceso de la famosa batalla de Roncesvalles*, written by Nicolás Espinosa, Don Quixote envisions how Bernardo, not being able to kill Orlando with a sword, had to raise him from the ground and strangle him.[8] Thus, the Orlando who battles against the Saracens is also the Orlando that must be defeated if the designs of Charlemagne to conquer Spain are to be averted. As Ryan Giles has shown, twelfth-and-thirteenth-century Spanish texts tended to 'downplay the role of Charlemagne in driving the infidels from Christian territory. The legend of Benardo del Carpio and works like the *Poema de Almería* (c. 1150), for example, construct a native alternative to the storied heroes of "the matter of France"' (2009, 132). In the *Primera crónica general*, Bernardo and his followers 'más queríen morir que entrar en servidumbre de françeses' [preferred to die rather than be subservient to the French] (cited in Giles, 2009, 132). It is this confusion as to who is Spain's greatest enemy, the Saracens or the French, that allows Don Quixote to envision himself among the Saracens.

Don Quixote can also have a second excuse. During the fifteenth and sixteenth centuries the French, as they attempted to acquire dominion in Italy, did so through the image of Charlemagne. For example, Pope Leo X had members of Raphael's workshop create a magnificent fresco at the Vatican, *The Coronation of Charlemagne* (1516). This paint-

9.1 Raphael's stanze: *The Coronation of Charlemagne* (1516). Art Resource, NY.

ing, as Robert Morrissey shows, has a definite political thrust. With it, 'the pope gave striking proof of his support for Francois I's imperial project by having Charlemagne represented with Francois's features, while lending his own face to Pope Leo III' (2003, 108). This fresco, of course, was meant to diminish Charles V's claim to the imperial crown and control of Europe. Since Charles is one of Don Quixote's models, he could well oppose the uses of Charlemagne as an image of a future French emperor. However, nowhere in the episode does the Spanish knight verbalize either one of these concerns. Don Quixote fully envisions the inn as a space where those surrounding him are Saracens under king Agramante.[9]

This is one of the most neglected chapters in the novel, and yet, I believe it contains more than a hint of an answer to what Todorov has called an 'essential mystery' in narrative – in this case, the secret that has to do with Don Quixote's quest. The search for a solution takes us back to Carroll Johnson's question as to why the gentleman from La Mancha became a knight and left home. We have seen how in chapter 22 of the novel, the knight becomes a sleuth chasing clues over the labyrinthine topography of Sierra Morena. The labyrinth will eventually become a narrative one, with its proliferation of stories. But the knight is not involved. Having ascertained that one can go mad from love after hearing Cardenio's tale, he chooses to do penance for his lady Dulcinea. In this wild and deserted space, as Don Quixote is set to do penance, the reader is asked to become a sleuth in order to follow the many narratives that erupt around him. But perhaps the reader should do more. Perhaps the sleuthing that the text demands should include a bit of detection regarding the knight and his motives. His penance, as we have seen in the previous chapter, borrows more elements from the *Amadís de Gaula* than from the *Orlando furioso*. He claims to choose Amadís since Orlando was in love with Angelica, who in turn loved a Moor, Medoro, something that Don Quixote cannot tolerate. And yet, there is contamination from the *Orlando furioso*. In Ariosto's poem, there is also sleuthing, as Orlando uncovers evidence that his beloved has taken up with a Moor. As he came upon a meadow, 'he saw inscriptions on many of the trees by the shady ban; he had only to look closely at the letters to be sure that they were formed by the hands of his goddess' (1983, 278). Looking elsewhere, he saw the names of Angelica and Medoro carved on trees. He still rejected the possibility of betrayal. Then, he came upon a hidden cave, and inside, there was their name again 'inscribed within and without, sometimes in charcoal, sometimes in chalk, or scratched with the point of a knife' (1983, 279). Only when he detected an inscription in verse written in Arabic by Medoro himself, extolling the pleasures of love with Angelica, did he finally believe his eyes. For Orlando could read not only Latin, but also Arabic, the language of the triumphal love poem.

Orlando's rage is immense; his epic violence spreads through the countryside as he uproots trees, kills peasants, cattle, and whoever or whatever comes his way. Don Quixote does follow Orlando to a point. He takes off his outer clothing and acts with crazed violence. Harold Bloom asserts: 'Don Quixote is mad because his prototype, the Orlando (Roland) of Ariosto's *Orlando furioso*, fell into an erotic madness . . . His madness is a poetic strategy worked out by others before him, and he is nothing if not a traditionalist' (1994, 126). Although Bloom points to Don Quixote's main models, he ascribes the cause to a poetic strategy. As we investigate the figure of the knight we will see that it is much more than that. As with Orlando, the image of Dulcinea with a Moor arouses deep feelings in Don Quixote: 'Porque mi Dulcinea del Toboso osaré yo jurar que no ha visto nunca en todos los días de su vida moro alguno, ansí como él es, en su mismo traje' [for I dare swear that my Dulcinea del Toboso never saw a Moor, in his own dress, in all her life] (1978, 26.319; 1998, 208). This may well be the response of a Christian knight who is always poised to battle the infidel. Certainly the ideal Christian knight is on a perpetual crusade. But Don Quixote is only imagining his status. In this sense, the 'essential mystery' here, like the one signalled by Todorov, has a double movement toward and away from revelation. Yes, Don Quixote thinks of himself as a knight. This reveals nothing. But the mystery begins to insinuate solutions once the reader learns more about Don Quixote's status and his actions. He has been knighted by a picaresque innkeeper in his hurry to leave his home. Thus his status is more than suspect. As he sets to do penance in Sierra Morena, he confesses to Sancho that he had been enamoured of a peasant woman, Aldonza Lorenzo. She is the basis for the knight's construction of Dulcinea. Of her Christian background, Don Quixote assures Sancho: 'en lo del linaje importa poco, que no han de ir a hacer información dél para darle un hábito' [as to her lineage, it matters not; for there needs no inquiry about it, as if she were to relieve some order of knighthood] (1978, 1.25.314; 1998, 203). When the knight asserts that Aldonza/Dulcinea does not have to prove her lineage, he is actually bringing up one of the greatest anxieties of Counter-Reformation Spain, that of *limpieza de sangre* or purity of blood. Many feared that their families may have married Moors or Jews; the nobility consistently married moneyed families with *converso* hidden backgrounds; while others knew quite well that their parents or grandparents observed forbidden practices, and had only converted in name and under duress – they knew that they came from converts who decided to stay in Spain after the decree against the Jews in 1492 and the one against Muslims in 1502. These *cristianos nuevos* or 'new Christians' were second class citizens. *Moriscos* or converted Muslims were even more suspect since they clung to ancient customs and practices. Many were being watched by the Inquisition for any sign of relapse and were unable to obtain privileges such as membership in the Christian Knightly Orders such as Santiago or Calatrava. So, what Don Quixote is telling Sancho is that Aldonza/Dulcinea's background does not matter since she is not going to be requesting a habit from these orders. Consequently, she could well be a *morisca,* or even one who still practised the Jewish or the Muslim religion. Even though some studies have attempted to downplay the extent of the damage done by the *limpieza de sangre* statutes of 1547, claiming that they were often evaded or ignored (Kamen 1986, 322–56), there is no question that the fear of being labelled as the Other was pervasive. We need only remember Cervantes' own theatrical interlude, *El retablo de las maravillas*, in which the Sage Tontonelo has created a theatrical entertainment that will be invisible to the person 'que tenga alguna raza de confeso, o que no sea procreado de sus padres de legítimo matrimonio' [who is tainted with convert blood or has not been born to a legitimately married couple] (1982, 220). As Teresa Kirschner affirms, the interlude dramatizes the fear of not being able to see the spectacle, as it focuses on the audiences' reactions to an invisible action. Michel Moner, on the other hand, stresses that some of the figures that are supposed to be seen are a way to satirize such fear.[10]

Furthermore, Don Quixote takes great pains to tell Sancho who the parents of Aldonza are: Lorenzo Corchuelo and Aldonza Nogales. The two trees evoked by the last names of the parents evince Aldonza's rusticity according to Augustin Redondo (1998, 232–3). After an exhaustive investigation, this critic portrays her as 'una rústica hombruna, recia y lúbrica' [a manly rustic with strong sexual impulses] (1998, 237).[11] Don Quixote flees La Mancha and transforms her into Dulcinea because of the 'imposibilidad' [impossibility] he explains to Maritornes when she sits on his bed at the inn. For Redondo, this impossibility means impotence. However, I would add that the trees that make up her parents' last names provide us with a second possibility. In general, it was thought that the peasant class was of old Christian stock. Many plays of the period, and in particular the famous peasant plays of Lope de Vega such as *Fuenteovejuna* and *Peribañez*, contrast the *limpieza de sangre* of the peasants with the tainted and non-Christian blood of the nobility. Such a background, then, would show her to be an old Christian (with a family not 'tainted' by Jewish or Moorish ancestry). At the same time, Cervantes, in his interlude, *El retablo de las maravillas*, shows that even villagers and peasants were obsessed with such purity of blood, afraid that they too could be tainted. During the Age of Cervantes, many people changed aspects of their family trees in order to obscure any connection with Moorish or Jewish ancestry. By using different kinds of trees as last names of Aldonza's parents, Cervantes may be playing with all the fake family trees that had to be reviewed to obtain high positions in the government, and also the ones reviewed by the Inquisition as they searched for heterodoxy. The remarks on lineage made by the knight provide one plausible solution as to why he leaves home. He desires a woman whom he knows to be of a non-Christian family. As he tries to avoid contact at a time when the state readies to expel all *moriscos* from Spain, he still cannot fully forget her. She becomes Dulcinea del Toboso. She is a sweet and honeyed woman whose ancestry comes from the wrong side of the Mediterranean. In order to give some hint of his knowledge, the knight situates her in the geography of Spain. The town of El Toboso was known for its *morisco* inhabitants. Thus Don Quixote's madness is no mere poetic strategy, as Bloom contends. The knight may claim that he is doing penance for no reason in the Sierra Morena. But this is not the case. The Christian knight does penance and even fashions a rosary out of strips from the bottom of his shirt because his beloved may be of Moorish descent. And this penance, although it follows that of Amadís, who went with a devout hermit to Peña Pobre to atone for his indiscretions, is also contaminated with elements from the *Orlando furioso*. The Spanish knight strips like Orlando, who 'tore off his clothes and exposed his hairy belly and all his chest and back' (1983, 283). While Orlando amazes, Don Quixote's act arouses mirth. But there is danger in this laughter. His undergarment is contaminated by the strip from the bottom of his shirt, one that is fashioned like a rosary. The rosary becomes an erotic instrument of meditation and prayer, thus subverting the knight's Christianity.

Don Quixote also carves wondrous poems on trees where his name and that of Dulcinea can be found. But he does not just carve the name 'Dulcinea.' The text tells us that he confessed later that he had added her place of origin. The verbal confession points to the confessions under torture made by many. They confessed their tainted origin and their relapse to the forbidden religious practices. The term can also refer to *confesos*, which also means those who converted. And, the carving on trees imitates but radically transforms the episode in the *Orlando furioso* where the hero destroys all the trees that carry the name of Angelica and Medoro (1983, 281). This inversion makes Don Quixote into a new Medoro, pining for his Angelica. In the Italian romance, Angelica is a pagan princess from Cathay (China or India), who is sought after by the Christian hero, Orlando. But she prefers the African prince, Medoro, eventually returning with him to Cathay. While Don Quixote dismisses the African as 'un morillo de cabellos enrizados' [a little Moor with curled locks] (1978, 26.319; 1998, 207), his anxieties over Angelica and Medoro may well reflect his own anxieties over Dulcinea/Aldonza's lineage. And what are we to say about our gentleman from La Mancha? Perhaps he protests too much. We know nothing of his background, of his family tree. Perhaps there is a stain, a *mancha* that he wishes to atone for. The text points to different last names for him and totally erases all elements of a family tree. This is worse than what we have seen with Aldonza. While some critics see this as a way to reject chivalric determinism, it could point to a form of determinism that the knight is escaping, his own tainted lineage. The erotic rosary and his pursuit of the forbidden are signs or clues of his divergence from orthodoxy.

And there is more. As we have seen, Don Quixote tells all that he possesses the balsam of Fierabrás, the two barrels stolen by a gigantic Saracen containing the substance in which Christ was embalmed. In the novel, however, Don Quixote does not need to fight a Saracen giant in order to obtain it. When wounded, he brews it with oil, wine, salt, and rosemary. Instead of imitating this pious legend, Don Quixote prepares the elixir as an *ensalmo,* a rite with words and herbs that was considered heterodox. It was said to cure through the powers of the devil. And *moriscos* as well as Muslim physicians used this form of healing. Don Quixote then inverts the Christian balsam and performs a heterodox ritual. His cure may not be an indication that his knightly powers are back. They may point to the comfort he receives from a *morisco* practice. Equally curious is why the chivalric pair believes that the inn is haunted by Moors. While Don Quixote searches for the 'moro encantado' [enchanted Moor] who beat him in this enchanted castle, Sancho, mimicking and attempting to surpass his master, asserts that he was beaten not by one, but by four hundred Moors (1978, 17.208; 1998, 118). This enchantment may have to do with the anxieties that haunt the knight. Not long after he leaves the inn, there is a curious episode in which Don Quixote cannot envision a chivalric enemy. It is that of the fulling mills. Since these contraptions were introduced to Europe through Islamic Spain, this may yet be another indication of the knight's ambivalence and anxiety toward the other. It is then conceivable that he left home not only because of his anxieties over his beloved's origins, but also to show to the world that he is a Christian knight and not a heterodox figure. And yet, hauntings, magics, and fracas pursue him through La Mancha, pointing to a possible stain in his or his beloved's lineage. After all, Christians over the centuries envisioned Saracens as possessing violence and magic. John V. Tolan asserts that Christians 'would find a series of images of Saracens or Arabs, who are descendants of a common ancestor, Ishmael. Ishmael is variously portrayed in these sources as a bastard son of Abraham, a first idolater, a magician, and especially a "wild man," whose "hands will be against every man and every man's hand against him" ' (2002, 20).

According to a number of critics, Cervantes' novel, in a veiled manner, espouses tolerance toward Islam.[12] Eric C. Graf, for example, takes two scenes from the novel and conjoins them to arrive at this kind of conclusion. He contrasts the black dress of the Virgin in chapter 52 with the white skin of the Moorish Zoraida in the captive's tale: 'In this context, Zoraida-Mary . . . And the statue of the Virgin . . . combine to symbolically interrogate Don Quijote's affirmations of Dulcinea's purity' (2007, 83).[13] I would add that the interrogation is one of Dulcinea's purity of blood and perhaps includes the knight's own suspicions as to his own ancestry. In addition, Judith Whitenack has wondered why Cervantes' novel, which follows so closely the major motifs of the books of chivalry, fails to include the ever-present forced conversion. She decides that this is due to the parodic nature of Cervantes' book: 'Making the conversion battles comic might even have verged on the dangerous' (1993, 69). And then she adds: 'One might also account for the absence of episodes in which the knight is the agent of conversion by applying Marie Cort Daniels's conclusions on Feliciano de Silva, i.e., that the distinct lack of enthusiasm for conversion in his *Amadís de Grecia* and others of his chivalric romances might be explained by his *converso* heritage' (1993, 69). It is not my intention here to discuss the possible *converso* origins of Cervantes.[14] I think that a much more intriguing element to be considered is the play of narrators, one that includes a Saracen and a *morisco*. If the full manuscript was written (fictionally speaking) by Cide Hamete Benengeli, then this Arabic historian purposefully leaves out forced conversions as a radically dangerous tool of the oppressor. If Cide Hamete is also the author of the first few chapters, it is he who leaves out the knight's ancestry, thus making possible Quixote's heterodox family tree. It is also Cide Hamete, this time through the words of the knight, who actually provides hints as to Aldonza/Dulcinea's background. Thus, the Arabic narrator delights in punishing a hero who goes to great lengths to avoid any contact with the Other. We can even imagine Cide Hamete laughing as Don Quixote does violence to friars from the order of St Benedict. These friars are particularly appropriate victims since they were known as hounds of God – they were often sniffing out heterodoxy. And the narrator would laugh again when a *bachiller*, who is angry about a sprained ankle, excommunicates Don Quixote while citing a Counter-Reformation law. These events may be signs of the confusion that reign in Don Quixote's mind. A Christian knight who imitates the actions of a Holy Roman Emperor is in reality contending with his own amorous-religious fears and desires.

It is only toward the very end of the 1605 novel that an important truth is revealed to an attentive reader. The Christian knight is at home with the Saracens. Indeed, he recovers his own voice by taking up a passage in the *Orlando furioso* where Agramante tries to settle a terrible discord in the African camp. Lest we forget, when the knight turned away from imitating Medoro, he stated that this African prince was a mere page of Agramante (1978, 26.319; 1998, 207). It is as if he finally decides to accept the anxieties that plague him, and while ignoring Medoro, he takes up the cause of his powerful leader, Agramante. The discord at the Saracen camp was initiated by St Michael, who brought Discord herself in order to prevent the Africans from taking Paris. The knight's internal discord comes to an end when he finally comes to tolerate his Otherness, be it his desire of a non-Christian Aldonza or an acceptance of his own self as perhaps tainted by what the Counter-Reformation saw as dangerous. And the joke is on the author himself. And I am not speaking of Cide Hamete's laughter at so subtly incorporating Don Quixote's transformation. I am speaking of Miguel de Cervantes' narrative trick to include himself in the discovery of his knight's secrets. Lest we miss the point, right before Don Quixote decides to call the confusion at the inn the discord at Agramante's camp, Clara, Luis's beloved, tells us that she is not yet sixteen, but will have her birthday on St Michael the Archangel's day (1978, 1.43.525; 1998, 390). Miguel de Cervantes is thus named after the St Michael who brought about the discord of the Saracens. And yet, he presents his protagonist as one who will fight against St Michael and bring peace to the inn around the time of the feast of St Michael. To further the confusion, which now falls upon the reader, it is notable that Michael is an archangel in the Hebrew, Islamic, and Christian traditions. He was also considered the patron of Christian knights (thus aiding Charlemagne and his companions). After so many battles, after so many laughs, and after so many feats of generic metamorphoses, both Cervantes and Cide Hamete show us something of extreme importance, but only in passing. The very crux of the knight's character is glimpsed in a single moment. Then it dissipates as if it had been a nightmare, a vision, an insubstantial moment, a spectre. And this is as it should be. Leo Strauss explained long ago that some authors learn to write between the lines. In order to present a heterodox view, such writers expound extensively on this and that. Only at a very specific point would the author write 'three or four sentences in that terse and lively style that is apt to arrest the attention' (1988, 24). These few sentences would serve as the basis for examining the rest of the text: 'Reading the book for the second and third time, he would detect in the very arrangement . . . significant additions to those few terse statements' (Strauss 1988, 25). And this is precisely what happens in Cervantes' novel. Don Quixote's terse statement on the confusion among the Saracens can easily lead to a reading of genealogical gaps, of magics, of the Other, of the other side of the Mediterranean. The reader who has been caught in a humorous and 'exoteric' text all of a sudden is confounded by the dangers of a possible esoteric reading.

At Agramante's camp they fought mainly over a horse, a shield with an eagle, and a sword. But no such objects are truly present at the inn. Don Quixote, as he looks around him, seems to perceive all three objects, but adds a fourth one, a helmet: 'Mirad como allí se pelea por la espada, aquí por el caballo, acullá por el águila, acá por el yelmo, y todos peleamos y todos no nos entendemos' [behold how there they fight for the sword, here for the horse, yonder for the eagle, here again for the helmet; and we all fight, and no one understands one another] (1978, 1.45.544; 1998, 407). This added object, the helmet of Mambrino, provides a further link with Ariosto's story. Although there is no helmet which causes discord in Agramante's camp, it is easy to understand how an avid reader like Don Quixote would place it there. Let us recall that when Don Quixote saw the barber running away from him, leaving behind the basin/helmet, he compared him to the beaver that cuts off his genitals so as not to be caught. After all, hunters wanted to acquire the coveted *castoreum* since classical authors from Pliny (*Natural History* 8.47) to Juvenal (*Satire* 12) claimed that they had curative powers.[15] By the sixteenth century Peter Martyr was calling the tale into question, while in the middle of the seventeenth century, writers such as Sir Thomas Browne in his *Pseudoxia epidemica* were correcting this myth (1658, 93). In reality, beavers did no such thing and what the hunters prized was the secretions from the animals' sacs or glands that even today are used in perfumes. No matter. The helmet is Don Quixote's *castoreum*, his healing balm. He must believe in its efficacy. And curiously, this same comparison is used in Agramante's camp. Mandricard has obtained the sword Durindana because Orlando (and all who possessed it including Zerbin) chose to abandon it because they knew they would never stop fighting for it: 'The count had imitated the beaver, he explained, who rips off his genitals if he sees the huntsman closing in, well knowing that these are all he is after' (Ariosto 1983, 329). Gradasso will now fight Mandricard for it, much like Don Quixote will once again fight the barber for his basin. One more knot must be added. When Zerbin tried to take the sword from Mandricard, he could not do so even when he struck a deadly blow: 'had his helmet not been enchanted, his skull would have been cracked in two' (1983, 290). In Don Quixote's mind, the alchemy that produces Mambrino's helmet derives from Ariosto's many tales: Mandricard's enchanted helmet, the sword Durindana, which had power like the genitals of a beaver; as well as all the knights and objects circulating in Agramante's discordant camp.

Perhaps drawing power from the imagined helmet of Mambrino, the mad knight's command is able to silence all: 'Tense todos; todos envainen todos se sosieguen; óiganme todos, si todos quieren quedar con vida' [Hold all of you! All put up your swords; be pacified all, and hearken to me, if you would all continue alive] (1978, 1.45.544; 1998, 407). Once the room is silent Don Quixote explains that this is a situation akin to that in Agramante's camp. As he reviews the four items of contention, none object. It is as if this new quaternity which embraces the magic helmet has recreated the quixotic worlds. With a few more words, Don Quixote makes the priest into a new King Agramante and the judge, Clara's father, into a new King Sobrino, Agramante's most trusted advisor. Although he does not persuade all, his voice triumphs (with the help of many clever negotiators). His verbal victory, I would argue, reflects his newly acquired tolerance toward the Other. He can now visualize an adventure in which Christians act like Saracens. He may not have incestuous desires for his niece, his *sobrina*, but he can stand side by side with the king Sobrino. As the knight abides among the Saracens, his voice grows strong like that of Agramante, and his counsel is wise like that of Sobrino. Having seen the many star-crossed lovers in the labyrinths of narrative, he may not feel quite as anxious as to the true identity of his beloved. It is not that Don Quixote is going to change his ways and become a Saracen; it is simply that he can abide with them while continuing his fictitious chivalric quest, now stripped of some of its anxieties. Don Quixote's parody of Ariosto's romance is certainly polemical.

The helmet of Mambrino is the tangible object that, in part, brings about the transformation. Discussing this contentious object, Italo Calvino explains: 'In realistic narrative, Mambrino's helmet becomes a barber's bowl, but it does not lose importance or meaning . . . We might even say that in a narrative any object is always magic' (1988, 33). While

Edward Dudley believes that the helmet gives Don Quixote a kind of magic to help sort out the 'Byzantine' love adventures (1972, 363), I would argue that it does not fully come into play until after the tales; it resurfaces in these chapters so as to acquire new value in its ability to take us back to a chivalric world, the world of Ariosto. The fusion barber's basin plus magic helmet represents the coming together of opposites. Mambrino was a Moorish king. Perhaps it can be seen as a war trophy, but perhaps it can also be viewed as an object that makes Don Quixote whole, an object that temporarily cures him of his anxieties. Possessing the helmet may imply that he is at peace, having conquered the Otherness of himself and of his beloved. Indeed, among those who sat with King Agramante to view the contests between his great heroes, one is singled out, the king of Spain. In addition: 'To accompany the Queen of Castille there were queens, princesses, and noblewomen from Aragon, Granada, Seville and the lands towards the Pillars of Hercules' (Ariosto 1983, 329). If the battles in the *Orlando* mirror the contest for control of Italy between the French and the Spanish, led by Emperor Charles V, then the Saracens could stand for Spain and Don Quixote's choice of the camp of Agramante would allow the knight to be at home with the Saracens and an embodiment of the emperor and the kings of Spain. Indeed, the episode serves to recognize that Spain's culture cannot be embraced without accepting the *moriscos* and the Saracens. The magical power of the Iberian lands calls for their objects of culture: the ingredients for a new heterodox Balsam, the Moorish helmet of invincibility, the eagle of the Habsburgs. Only when together can power return to the land. For a moment, at least, Don Quixote's anxieties have been laid to rest. He is at peace among the Saracens.

The reference to the Pillars of Hercules in the Agramante episode would also serve to point to an ending of yet another section of Cervantes' novel. The Greek interlace must now give way to the ways of the knight. The interminable and excessive narrative of empire must be contained, must find its *non plus ultra*. After all, the Other is within the self. The narrative must become linear once again in order to reach its destination, in order to return home. To do so, it must pass by the columns as represented by helmet and basin and thus return us to the beginnings.

10 *Thymos* and the Chariot

In Plato's story of Leontius and Havel's fable of the greengrocer – at the
beginning and the end of the Western tradition of political philosophy – so
to speak – we see a humble form of *thymos* emerge as a central factor in
political life. *Thymos* appears to be related to a good political order in some
way, because it is the source of courage, public-spiritedness and a certain
unwillingness to make moral compromises.
    – Francis Fukuyama, *The End of History and the Last Man*

Having passed through the last pillars, the narrative takes us back to its
beginnings, but not quite so, even though we enter into the linearity of
the denouement in this fifth and last segment of the novel. Don Quixote,
having regained a central place in the narrative, does so by seemingly
losing agency. Although he has regained authority through the helmet
of Mambrino, this seems to be a mere ruse on the part of his companions. He soon discovers that he has once again lost his power to move
the action. Those at the inn, including his friends, the priest and the barber, and many of the characters in the labyrinthine tales, plot to take him
home by a very clever method. Don Quixote suddenly finds himself in a
cart led by some oxen. Those around him encourage him to believe that
he is trapped in an enchanted and moving contraption. As Edwin Williamson asserts: 'When he is carried back home in a cage he finds himself happily arguing with Sancho that he is truly enchanted' (1984, 109).
Williamson adds that his arguments are consistent: since he is a knight
and cannot move, this can only happen if he is enchanted. I would add
that he is happy because enchantment is actually a proof that he is a chivalric figure of sufficient worth to be plagued by evil enchanters.

I would add that Don Quixote's 'happiness' also has to do with his coming to terms with the anxieties that have haunted him since the beginning of the novel. Indeed, this happiness reflects that of the Spanish *moriscos*, who, according to Louis Cardaillac felt that the time of their deliverance from Spanish rule was soon to arrive (2001, 172). Of course, Don Quixote does not want to be delivered from Spanish rule, but from the anxieties within. Let us briefly recall this journey. Cervantes set out from home in order to become a knight – a profession long neglected, except for ceremonial purposes. Imagining that he would bring back a new Golden Age and even become emperor, he becomes a shadow, and parodic ghost of Charles V and Philip II. As a man named Quijada, he displays onomastically the Habsburgs extremely prominent jaw. But in the initial trinomial of possible names attributed to him, the name Quejana points to possible *converso* origins. Thus he is not only haunted by imperial desires, but also by anxieties concerning his ancestry. Perhaps it is for this reason that the 'historian' that tells his tale says nothing of his background. Is his family tree 'tainted' with either *morisco* or *converso* ancestry? Is the Arabic author trying to protect this secret while exhibiting his anxieties through his desire to become a knight at all costs? Or is Cide Hamete showing the consequences of a Christian empire – the repression of the Other even within the confines of the self. As adventures follow one another we come to see the conflicts in the knight's psyche as they are acted out through the clashes in genres and in the parody of forms. He turns the balsam of Fierabrás, a holy object from the Carolingian cycle, into a heterodox *ensalmo*, a curative magic often used by *moriscos* and *conversos*. From the Italianate romances he picks out the helmet of Mambrino and wishes to use it as a talisman, even though its owner was a Moor and he would be engaging in heterodox magic. He even attacks windmills, thinking that they are giants as their sails configure the arms of the giant Briareus consigned to Dante's *Inferno*. At the same time, the sails of these 'infernal' mills represent the sign of the cross which the knight attacks. The cross, it appears, is useful for heterodox cures as the knight makes crosses in the air over his suspect balsam. Don Quixote even dares to confront friars, priests, and other clergy, being excommunicated for one of his attacks. The world is upside down as the knight seeks to recreate Charles V's Christian empire while he is hounded by melancholy phantoms of Otherness and heterodoxy which lead him to act in erratic, esoteric, and revealing ways. Like Charles after he abdicated, the knight is the ghost of all power – his power is that of illusions. As a ghost of empire he is hounded by the phantoms of the excluded. His crosses fail to exorcise anxieties since they become signs of his Otherness.

Even in Sierra Morena, when he attempts to fabricate a rosary to do penance, he reveals his own sacrilege as he leads the reader to question why he must do penance. Is it because his beloved is from Toboso, a place known for *moriscos*? Is it because he both embraces and rejects the image of his beloved as a new pagan Angelica in love with Moor Medoro/Don Quixote? While he is undergoing penance, Don Quixote loses his voice and protagonism. The geographical labyrinth that surrounds him is much like the labyrinth of tales told around him. The intricacies of the literary and spatial surroundings also reflect the labyrinth of his mind. Emerging from Sierra Morena, he is still yellowed with melancholy and suffering. He can easily fall for Dorotea/Micomicona's trickery. Taking her cue from Tasso, she is a new enchantress who would derail the quest of worthy knights. But Don Quixote is no true knight. He was once knighted by a picaresque character, and such folk were known for their 'impure' genealogies. The arrival of a captive and a Moorish woman at the inn spur him to speak, to recount the glories of arms and letters in a Christian empire. He cannot allow the Other to take his place. But the captive's tale is much more alluring than the knight's speech. And the beauties of other civilizations threaten to destabilize the world as represented by the inn. Here, confusion arises and many scuffles ensue. Finally, Don Quixote shakes the ghosts that haunt him. Turning to Ariosto's *Orlando furioso* once again, he imagines the scuffles at the inn as the conflicts that took place in Agramante's camp. No matter that he was a Moorish king. His imagination now views all the Christians around him as Saracens from Ariosto's poem. This final feat of the imagination brings him out of the closet, so to speak. He is now both a Christian and a Saracen. It may be that in this moment he creates a new Golden Age, one where the clashes of civilizations come to an end and all are seen as equal through the power of his vision. Indeed, it is at this point that he regains full voice and protagonism. He is free from the ghosts of Charles and the phantoms of anxiety. It matters not that he is imprisoned in a cage and thus taken home. His mind is at liberty to roam the fields of culture regardless of race or religion. He is free to attack Christians or Moors; he is free to be a captive or a knight. Incarceration is nothing to him since his new self has found a space of imaginative expansion. Thus, he is happy as they take him home, for he has, to some extent, exorcised the demons that brought him forth.[1]

To put it in a different way, the anger he felt at himself and at others throughout the novel has faded since he has recognized that part of his inner self that was subjected. In a way, he has acquired *thymos* or self-worth. Explaining the meaning of *thymos* in Plato's *Republic*, Francis Fukuyama asserts: '*Thymos* is something like an innate human sense of justice: people believe that they have a certain worth, and when other people act as if they are worthless . . . then they become angry' (2006, 165). Throughout the novel, Don Quixote has been angry. Perhaps part of his choleric disposition comes from the fact that his humours are out of balance. More important, he is an impoverished hidalgo, and he feels he should be shown more respect. And it has not helped that when he sets out on a quest those around him have thrashed him and laughed at him. Fukuyama explains just this result: 'He is driven into a bloody rage when that sense of self-worth is denigrated' (2006, 165). But Don Quixote's self-worth is also tied to his inner anxieties. Only when these are somewhat appeased can he feel a kind of happiness. This is the opposite of what happens to Leontius in Plato's *Republic*. Leontius 'saw the executioner with some corpses lying near him. Leontious felt a strong desire to look at them, but at the same time he was disgusted and turned away' (1974, 439e). When he succumbs to his unsavoury desire, he feels angry at himself and addresses his own eyes: 'Look for yourselves . . . you evil things, get your fill of this beautiful sight!' (1974, 440a). Leontius excoriates his eyes and himself because he has not acted according to his self-worth. This passage has captivated scholars from David Hume to Fukuyama, exposing the divided self. Don Quixote's problem is also related to sight and conflict. He does not want to see that mutilated part of himself which causes anxiety. He does not wish to contemplate the other, that which must be discarded and rendered mute and defunct in a Christian society. Only when he envisions himself among the Saracens can he feel happy, can he acquire a new voice. As opposed to Leontius, seeing or envisioning is liberating for Don Quixote because it provides him with a 'thymotic pride' in himself (Fukuyama 2006, 165), an emotion that goes beyond recognition by others. He now recognizes himself as worthy in the very act of subtly subverting the very tenets of a Christian knight. Fukuyama relates Leontius's tale to that of the greengrocer as told by Havel as an emblem of communist Czechoslovakia: 'Communism humiliated ordinary people by forcing them to make a myriad of petty, and sometimes not so petty, moral compromises with their better nature' (2006, 168). This affront to *thymos* has been with us since the beginnings of Western civilization; it has been the plight of many in constrictive political systems. It was part of daily life in seventeenth-century Spain where one had to forever disclaim any appreciation for values that were not the ones proclaimed by the most Catholic Crown and church. The limits of dissent and scepticism were quite narrow. Don Quixote's many compromises encounter a parenthesis in this one vision of the Saracens. It becomes the space for *thymos*.[2]

As he travels home, Don Quixote meets the canon of Toledo with whom he has a lengthy conversation regarding books of chivalry. Here both men show that they have enough wit and intelligence to carry out a most lively debate. Don Quixote, upheld by his new-found happiness, can challenge the strong and intelligent arguments of the canon with alluring visions of chivalric quests. The books he cherishes, however, are called monstrous, without form, without rhyme or reason. The canon would see new books written in a more classical manner. Perhaps Don Quixote favours the chivalric not just because they tell the never-ending adventures of Christian knights; he may favour them for their monstrosity. After all, *moriscos* were often accused of being monsters (Cardaillac 2001, 176). Although the knight cannot perform any of these adventures for the canon, Williamson asserts that he is still happy: 'The mad knight is in good spirits, for he is still confident that the day is not far off when he will realize his chivalric destiny' (1984, 110). There is, and this must be stressed once again, a second motive for happiness. The knight has been able to shed ghostly anxieties while espousing knighthood. In a mental tightrope that may be one of the causes of his madness, he is happy because he has regained his self-worth by playing the Saracen. The Moorish magical devices have provided him with the ability to have both helmet and basin; to be Christian knight and Moor in disguise; to feel happy at Christian contests and paradoxically at Moorish deliverance. He is now free to explore his future in a less anxious manner. The Arabic historian, this sage who once denigrated him, is now providing him with the ability to be himself.

The company that takes him home only knows of their own trick on the knight. They know nothing of the subtle variations of Don Quixote's mad but perspicacious intellect. Nor are they aware that the Arabic historian is also playing a joke on them. The invention of the chariot seems to derive from the characters that plot to take him home. And yet, this very device hides its true purpose and the joke is on the perpetrators of this ruse. The novel had started by poking fun at enchantment and magic, the stuff of the romances of chivalry. At the same time it had subtly inserted Pythagorean mathematical correspondences and even the esoteric magic of the Other. Now, the novel returns to the beginnings by subtly injecting magic into the text. While the characters and the novel itself seem to be parodying the romances of chivalry as Don Quixote is placed in an 'enchanted' chariot (a cart pulled by oxen), the sage Cide Hamete knows better. He is carefully infusing the ending with astral magic, a type of magic encountered from the Arabic *Picatrix* to the Renaissance treatises by Marsilio Ficino. Perhaps it is the fusing of helmet and basin, the grudging acceptance of this impossible object that evokes the magic of the end. Perhaps the Pythagorean quaternity has led us to the quintessence. We are faced now with a human being who, in glimpsing his own *thymos*, is embraced by the heavens, for the cart becomes a planetary chariot.[3] Discoursing on *The Dignity of Man*, Giovanni Picco della Mirandola recollects how Abdala the Saracen had asserted that the most wonderful thing in the world was man. Picco explains that this happened because God, at the end of his creation, had placed man in the middle. Unlike other creatures and objects, he was not confined, but allowed to move upwards or downwards – to act as a brute beast or to commune with divinity. Don Quixote recalls this portrayal of the Renaissance man who represents all possibilities. By accepting the *thymos* of his higher soul, the knight can become attuned to the heavens.

The novel has carefully prepared the reader for such an event. It has shown how Zoraida is under the sway of the Pleiades and Luis is attuned to the stars like Palinurus. Don Quixote need not look up, for the heavens descend to embrace his new vision. The astral adventure begins right before this final section of the novel, at the end of the very chapter when Don Quixote performed his own magic by evoking the dispute in Agramante's camp. It is at this point that the tricksters construct a cage with wooden bars and shut him up. It is then yoked to some oxen. Don Quixote recalls countless examples in books of chivalry where knights are transported through enchantment. He imagines them enclosed in dark clouds, carried in chariots of fire or flown by winged hippogryphs (1978, 1.47.557; 1998, 418). But he cannot think of an example of a knight who is incarcerated and carried in a cart led by oxen. In the end, he is content to acknowledge that in modern times, such a new type of conveyance is part of the chivalric world. Perhaps he knows more about magic than he is letting on.

But we have seen that what Leo Strauss calls 'exoteric' readings conceal the esoteric, by which I mean not only the magical but what Strauss would conceive as the dangerous and heterodox.[4] In classical antiquity as well as in early Islamic thought, planetary gods were depicted as riding in chariots, led by the animals assigned to them. Venus, for example, is often seen in a chariot drawn by either doves or swans.[5] Renaissance Latin versions of treatises by Albumasar (Abu Ma'Sar) depict her with doves. She is also presented thus on the cover of the seventeenth-century Spanish translation of Boiardo's *Orlando inamorato*, as well as in numerous Renaissance paintings, including one by Pietro Perugino at the Collegio del Cambio in Perugia.[6] In order to allude obliquely to what is transpiring, there is a prophecy intoned by the barber, disguised as enchanter, where he speaks of Dulcinea as 'la blanca paloma tobosina' [the white Tobosan dove] (1978, 1.46.432; 1998, 416). While Dulcinea may be viewed as conducting Venus's chariot, the cart in which Don Quixote is riding represents quite a different planet. The narrative explains that it is being pulled by oxen who are 'perezosos y tardíos animales' [lazy, heavy animals] (1978, 1.47.556; 1998, 418). This quality is again underlined when the text refers to the 'el paso tardo' [slowness] of the animals (1978, 1.47.560; 1998, 421). These attributes belong to Saturn, who was considered as the furthest and slowest of planets in Ptolemaic astrology. He was said to be the most malefic of planets, responsible for delays and incarcerations.[7] In his *Genealogía de los dioses paganos* Boccaccio states: 'Es además el que indica . . . las largas y fatigosas peregrinaciones, de las cárceles, de las tristezas y de las penas' [He is also the one that indicates long and exhausting journeys, incarcerations, sadness, and woes] (1983, 485). Thus we find Don Quixote in his cage, 'delaying' his chivalric quest. Indeed, Saturn was often portrayed in a cart drawn by the slow and slothful oxen. As Salvador Fajardo has noted, the ox-drawn Saturn can be found in works as different as Boccaccio's *Genealogía de los dioses paganos* and Baccio Baldini's account of a Medici wedding in Florence in 1565 (1986, 249). But just like Venus, who could be led by doves or swans, Saturn could be conducted by slothful oxen or by terrifying dragons, creatures that would certainly impress Don Quixote much more than the oxen. Pietro Perugino painted Saturn's cart as drawn by two dragons. Two rather terrifying beasts are seen in Noel Coypel's *The Triumph of Saturn* (1670–2) at Versailles. But on this canvas, Venus is keeping Saturn's malice in check as her cupids harness the momentarily pacified dragons. In Cervantes' text, the Venus-like Dulcinea never intervenes since she is a construct of the knight's imagination.

Saturn was said to be the planet of delays, frustration, and even death. Andrés de Lí's calendar describes its characteristics thus: 'Muestra destruycion, muerte, tristura, lloro & sospiro' [It denotes destruction, death, sadness, tears, and sighs] (1999, 62).The skeletal and sickly knight returns home, an image of the last days of the emperor. It was said that Charles V's seclusion at Yuste was the result of his melancholy, and the knight's yellowish countenance betrays signs of this humoral imbalance. The emperor, as noted, has been described as a ghostly figure once at Yuste: 'Restless and sleepless, ghost like, he would roam the corridors of the convent' (Stirling 1851, 533; Franklin 1961, 467). Don Quixote may view the ghost of old age lurking around the corner; thus he seeks the power of emperors so as not to become, like Charles at Yuste, 'the symbolic ghost of all power' (Franklin 1961, 463). But, like Charles V, he runs into Saturn, the planet of melancholy. His journey on this planetary chariot will take up the last segment of the novel. There are six chapters in this last section, thus recalling the second part of Cervantes' novel where we witnessed Marcela's apotheosis and Grisóstomo's demise. Six is 'called the number of man, because the sixth day man was created' (Agrippa 1987, 191). It is also the 'Scale of the World' and is extolled as the last day of creation. What this may portend, is hard to fathom, other than the fact that the knight comes home from an imperial quest that has led to excess, to the impossible labyrinthine proliferation of narrative. Rather than continue this textual and territorial journey, the knight now seems to break the barriers between earth and sky. He has become, just for a minute and in parodic fashion, the ideal Renaissance man who can reach the heavens and envision a more perfect world.

Cide Hamete is not just adding magic for its own sake, or because it is found in the Arabic *Picatrix*, and certainly not for an emperor such as Charles who fought against Islam. He wishes to show that Don Quixote's melancholy is guided by Saturn, the planet that gives its children, through suffering and intense work, the gift of wisdom. Don Quixote, in the end, has acquired a wisdom that projects beyond his own culture and civilization in order to embrace the Other. He has come to know the Other's magic. Astrologers considered Saturn as the mark of a great criminal or a great artist, and as a marker of great changes in empires and religions.[8] This second belief goes back to Abu Ma'Sar (Albumasar), a ninth-century astrologer who studied in Baghdad. His theories were well known in medieval and Renaissance Europe, where he was often referred to as Albumasar, creating furious debates in scholarly settings such as the University of Paris. In the Spanish Golden Age, this Arabic astrologer was at times used against himself by sermon writers who prophesied the end of Islam.[9] Indeed, his treatise *On the Great Conjunctions* shows that the conjunctions of Jupiter with Saturn were markers of great events to come. In 1603, two years before the publication of *Don Quixote*, a major conjunction of Saturn and Jupiter could be seen in the skies. Coupled with the appearance of a nova or new star the following year, this created a furor of astrological predictions, culminating in the notion of 'nova stella, novus rex' [new star, new king].[10] As Don Quixote rides home he is pleased with the knowledge that changes are coming; he is happy that he is riding the chariot of transformation. What these changes may be he does not know. Campanella had predicted that since the conjunction was to take place in Sagittarius it would make Spain exalted since the country was under the tutelage of this particular constellation (1982, 26). His assertion would have been opposed by Abu Ma'Sar: 'We say that if the conjunction occurs in the fiery triplicity, it indicates power for the eastern people, and that the strongest of their signs is Sagittarius' (2000, 1.91). Abu Ma'Sar was wrong. The changes that do come do not favour the east and much less the notion of *convivencia* within Spain. They do not follow the knight's secret opening of vision to encompass *conversos* and *moriscos*. The great changes that he expects turn out to be the expulsion of the *moriscos* from Spain six years after the conjunction. The 'nova' signifies destruction, and the conjunction points to the demise of Moorish culture in Spain.

No matter. Don Quixote can continue his happy journey home, for he also knows that Saturn is the planet of esoteric knowledge, of strange and compelling visions. Boccaccio asserts that the planet presides over magicians and gives its children 'de la mayor reflexión y de profundo pensamiento . . . tuvo influencia con su pensamiento y astucia' [comprehensive reflection and deepest thought . . . he influences with thoughts and cleverness] (1983, 485, 486). The knight knows that the planet belongs to the Other, that it guides *conversos* and *moriscos*, and that his chariot will bring him not just the woes of this malefic planet, but also the blessings of the highest of wandering stars. After all, Girolamo Cardano had stated that 'the Jewish religion is controlled by Saturn or its star, or rather both' (Grafton 1999, 62). And, according to Ibn Abī l-Riŷāl, the birth of Islam religion was marked by the Saturn-Jupiter conjunction in the year 571 (Samsó 2009, 7–39).[11] It may be that, as some medieval and Renaissance astrologers have argued, Saturn rules the Hebrew religion, Mars and Venus rule Islam, and Jupiter and Sol reign over Christianity.[12] But the knight, in his chariot, must remember that he has all the required influences. He is travelling under Saturn, planet of the Hebrews, the heterodox, the magical and the Other; he abides with this planet at a moment of conjunction, one that portends great changes for Moorish Spain. Also, Don Quixote has clearly stated that he was born under Mars, which brings to him the influences of Islam, while his love for the Moorish Dulcinea places him under Venus.

As noted above, as he is being placed in his enchanted chariot the knight heard a prophecy that affirmed that he would someday encounter his dove from Toboso: 'No te de afincamiento la prisión en que vas, porque así conviene para acabar más presto la aventura en que tu gran esfuerzo te puso. La cual açabará cuando el furibundo león manchego con la Blanca paloma tobosina yoguieren a uno' [Let not the confinement you are under afflict you; for it is expedient it should be so, for the more speedy accomplishment of the adventure in which your great valour has engaged you; which shall be finished when the furious Manchegan lion shall be coupled with the white Tobosan dove] (1978, 46.555; 1998, 416). The dove, then is a figure of Venus and thus of Islam. The mystery that the novel seems to reveal in veiled terms is the knight's anxiety over his ancestry (Saturn/Jewish; Saturn conjunct/Moorish) and over the religion of his beloved (Venus/Islam) that had forced him to leave home and to invoke Sol/Apollo to make him a Christian knight. In reality, the greater secret might be that he embraces all three key religions that once thrived in the Iberian peninsula. At a time when forced conversion and expulsions have occurred and continued to occur, he rides in an 'enchanted' chariot to a mysterious place where three faiths and two civilizations can abide in his heart and in his vision.

Furthermore, the prophecy of Dulcinea as the dove may yet bring to mind a *morisco* myth. Mary Elizabeth Perry tells us of the beautiful maiden Carcayona, who, as she is worshipping an idol in India, is visited by a golden dove who tells her of a true religion, instructing her on the basic tenets of Islam and assuring her that upon her death she will go to the seven heavenly castles. When she tells her father that she believes in Allah instead of the paternal polytheistic pantheon, Carcayona becomes the subject of mutilation. After she repeatedly refuses to worship an idol, her father cuts off both of her hands and abandons her in a mountainous wilderness. There Allah leads her to a cave, where she is eventually found by the king of Antioch, who is hunting in these regions. He marries her and converts to her religion, but once she gives birth, calamity befalls her again. While the king is away, a mysterious letter supposedly from the monarch, orders that she be banished. Once again, a dove appears and tells her to pray to Allah to restore her hands.

This she does and she is able to live and care for her child in this cave until her husband finds her. She returns to him only when he promises to build a new city where the religion of Allah will prevail (2005, 21–37). In this classic tale remembered by the *moriscos* of Spain, the dove, then, is a clear symbol of deliverance, of Allah's gifts to Moorish women. In Cervantes' novel, Don Quixote may be tied to his chariot, but he waits for the moment in which he can rescue Dulcinea/Carcayona from his imagination, making this Moorish princess his bride. In a recent article, Mary B. Quinn has shown how *moriscos*, at a time of peril, rewrote the legend of the handless maiden into the tale of Carcayona: 'Circulated in Aljamía-Spanish written in Arabic letters that reads from right to left – the Carcayona legend was part of a corpus of secret Morisco literature that was hidden under floors of private homes' (2008, 214). Indeed, for Quinn, this tale serves as model for Cervantes' Captive's Tale. But while Zoraida will convert to Christianity, Carcayona will turn to Islam. Both do so in defiance of their fathers.

I would not only agree with this assertion but also locate the tale at another point in Cervantes' narrative. For those who knew the tales of Moorish Spain kept alive through the oral tradition, the prophecy that foresees the joyful union of the dove from Toboso could well recall this ancient story. Indeed, the maiden praises the dove's words: 'su dulzor han entrado a mi corazón' [their sweetness has entered my heart] (Cuadra 2000, 251; Quinn 2008, 214). Thus the name Dulcinea may derive from this 'dulzor' and may have as one of its origins the Moorish tale. Both the dove of Allah and the site of Toboso can be pointers to a Moorish legacy. Don Quixote must go to Toboso, a town renowned for its Moorish inhabitants, and rescue his beloved dove, a bird who teaches of Allah and of celestial castles. And indeed, Don Quixote is forever constructing castles in the air.

But of course, the prophecies dealing with his beloved dove are not fulfilled during Don Quixote's travels in the chariot of Saturn. Instead, before he reaches home, he is treated to one more interpolated tale and he will be allowed to have one last adventure. Both can be taken as signs that, under Saturn, he is shown portents of the Other. The interpolated tale, like that of the captive and Zoraida and that of Luis and Clara, is left without an ending. Here a goatherd reveals himself as Eugenio, who loved the beautiful Leandra, but had a rival named Anselmo. However, it is the returning son of a poor peasant that forever shatters this rivalry. The lad, transformed into a soldier named Vicente de la Rosa, captures Leandra's heart. His tales of heroism amaze the whole village, although his deeds seem patently false: 'No había tierra en todo el orbe que no hubiese visto, ni batalla donde no se hubiese hallado; había muerto más moros que tiene Marruecos y Túnez, y entrado en más singulares desafíos, según él decía que Gante y Luna, Diego García de Paredes y otros mil que nombraba' [There was no country on the whole globe he had not seen, nor battle he had not been in. He had slain more Moors than are in Morocco and Tunis, and fought more duels, as he said, than Gante, Luna, Diego Garcia de Paredes and a thousand others] (1978, 1.51.592; 1998, 448). In addition, he had become a musician and a poet, a gallant who dressed exceedingly well, calling attention to himself with his colourful wardrobe. The result is that Leandra elopes with him. The people of her village find her three days later without her clothes or the money and many jewels she had taken. Once her father sends her to a convent, Anselmo, Eugenio, and all who desired her turn to the hills where they establish a new Arcadia. There they celebrate her beauty, lament her loss, and condemn her fickleness. It is as if Cervantes' novel, coming to a close, is eager to recall the early pastoral episode of Grisóstomo and Marcela. But this time, there are no epic overtones, only a parody of heroism in the figure of the *miles gloriosus*, the braggart soldier.

Other than a parodic recapitulation of an early pastoral, this tale has a series of important features that place it under Saturn. First, it is a tragic tale (or so Eugenio states unequivocally). Tragedy and separation are often the result of Saturn's baneful influence. Second, it places the men who admired Leandra in a pastoral Arcadia where all express their sadness: 'No hay hueco de pena, ni margen de arroyo, ni sombra de árbol que no esté ocupada de algún pastor que sus desventuras a los aires cuente' [There is no hollow of a rock, nor brink of a rivulet, nor shade of a tree that is not occupied by some shepherd, who is recounting his misfortunes to the air] (1978, 1.51.595; 1998, 450). Sadness is clearly a trait of the seventh Ptolemaic planet. Don Quixote thinks that he can free others from Saturn's influence and fetch Leandra from the nunnery. He wants to be the *deus ex machina* of this tragedy, although he knows better. In addition, the tale has a heterodox tone much like Grisóstomo's. At the very start, when Eugenio first makes the acquaintance of those who are leading Don Quixote home, he does so by accident, trying to catch a she-goat speckled with black, white, and gray and thus named *Manchada*, who has escaped him (1978, 1.50.588; 1998, 444). Could this be a sign that refers back to Don Quixote's pursuit of Dulcinea, of the taint of Moorish blood in his beloved? Finally, this brief tale links with the adventure that follows. In both there is a distressed lady and they wear black – Leandra may have assumed the habit of her convent.

Even though Don Quixote is 'enchanted,' this magic is so peculiar as to allow him to partake of one last adventure. 'El son de una trompeta tan triste' [The sound of a trumpet so dismal] (1978, 1.52.598; 1998, 452) alerts him to his task. He sees disciplinants in their strange garments who are carrying an image of the Virgin in a procession as they plead for rain in a scorched landscape. Don Quixote, as usual, transforms reality into a chivalric adventure: 'se imaginó que era cosa de Aventura . . . y confirmóle más esta imaginación pensar que una imagen que traían cubierta de luto fese aluna principal senora que llevaban por fuerza aquellos follones y descomedidos malandrines' [he imagined it was some adventure . . . and he was the more confirmed in his fancy by thinking, that an image they had with them covered in black, was some lady of note whom those miscreants and discourteous ruffians were forcing away] (1978,1.52.599; 1998, 453). As Dinda L. Gorlée explains: 'Every time the Knight of the Rueful Countenance encounters puzzling events, persons, and objects, he advances a "logical" explanation as he produces an array of malevolent sorcerers, invisible magicians, devils, ghosts, giants, enchanted Moors, and other supernatural agencies' (1988, 57). Indeed, Gorlée cites the episode of the Virgin and claims that Don Quixote is a trickster. I would say that Don Quixote's action still reflects a man under the influence of Saturn, although the 'signs' of this adventure are puzzling, reinforcing the mystery hidden in the text. Don Quixote, in many ways, acts as usual. This would not be the first time that he attacks men of the cloth. This would seem to reveal that his anxieties are returning; that the parenthesis of visionary amplitude may be closing; that the ghosts of Otherness still pursue him, transposing Christians and foes. However, all is not as it appears. Like the chariot, the woman hides a secret.

Cervantes' prose is constantly hiding mysteries between the lines, hiding an esoteric truth. The economy of the prose does not allow the reader to ensure that her interpretation is correct. In a previous episode, he encountered the veiled Zoraida and came to know her as an Islamic woman. Now, on seeing a woman incarcerated and veiled, he feels he must free the Other. This impulse is triggered by yet another series of images. The procession is calling for rain on a sunny and dry day. Thus, the Virgin's beauty shines under a brilliant sun. Throughout the literature of the period, the shining beauty of a woman dressed in black has been related to the planet Saturn. For example, at the inception of Claramonte's *La Estrella de Sevilla*, the king enters the city and perceives seven women on their balconies, denoting the seven Ptolemaic planets. Each is described in terms of her planetary qualities. The last one is Estrella herself, dressed in black. James F. Burke writes: 'She is described in terms of a black light which can eclipse the bright light of the sun. The one remaining planet is Saturn, which in astrology and alchemy was considered a black star and a *sol niger*' (1974, 144). When Don Quixote views the Virgin dressed in black, he may well think that she, like himself, shines with the dark light of Saturn. Thus, she is both an image of Saturn and a veiled image of the Islamic Other. He must free her from the incarceration, although such a plight comes from the planet's influence. This act would have a double purpose: he would be able to abandon the chariot of Saturn and he would allow her to also relinquish her enchanted placement. Of course, this is not to be. And his jailers will not allow him to have a final chivalric triumph. He is quickly defeated and returns to his cart. He knows quite well what all this has been about. Don Quixote tells Sancho: 'y será gran prudencia dejar pasar el mal influjo de las estrellas que agora corre' [and it will be great prudence in us to wait until the evil influence of the stars which now reigns, is over-passed] (1978, 1.52.601; 1998, 456). Don Quixote, then, knows that he is under Saturn. He knows of the astral magic that has led him to this point and has allowed him to catch a glimpse of his true ghosts, of his anxieties. Briefly freed from them, he now relapses into melancholy. A moment of illumination is covered by the dark light of Saturn.

As the incarcerated knight arrives in his village he is described as 'flaco y amarillo' [skeletal and yellowed] (1978, 1.52.602),[13] conditions typical of the melancholic. And indeed, Boccaccio asserts that melancholy falls under the sign of Saturn (1983, 486). The fact that he arrives home on a Sunday, the day of the Sun, points to the most famous of celestial chariots and imbues the scene with a new celestial meaning. At the start of the novel, Don Quixote imagined himself as a solar being, riding out under the auspices of Sol/Apollo. Under his guidance he would become the brightest and best of Christian knights, fighting the infidel. What he does not understand at the start is that his Ptolemaic planet is the Sun's opposite. It was said that Saturn was the old Sun, turned cold. And, as stated above, it was called a *Sol niger*.[14] Don Quixote is a phantom of imperial conquest rendered powerless and an icon of Saturn, the planet of the other. When he finally comes to envision himself among the Saracens, the visions of Saturn are revealed to him.

He is rewarded with a moment of *thymos*. But now, as he arrives home, the sun shines bright. He is back in the cultural and political milieu that allows no infringements. He must again conform to the rays of a Catholic Crown and make the compromises necessary to continue a quotidian existence unencumbered by any taints. So let us leave the knight as he reposes at home dreaming of chivalry and magic while incarcerated by the ways of his times. With this sleep, the 1605 novel comes to an end, pointing to the knight's death – and death is one of the traits of Saturn, often represented with his scythe. But such a death will be long delayed. The knight has yet other foes to quell, other adventures to pursue. These will be caused by different anxieties, different ghosts.

The 1605 novel does not narrate all the episodes of the knight. The author tells us that there was a third sally, but this one has not yet been found. The book ends with some poems that were unearthed by a physician: 'un antiguo médico que tenía en su poder una caja de plomo, que según dijo, se había hallado en los cimientos derribados de una antigua ermita que se renovaba; en la cual caja se habían halado unos pergaminos escritos con letras góticas, pero en versos castellanos, que contenían muchas de sus hazañas' [an aged physician, who had in his custody a leaden box, found, as he said, under the ruins of an ancient hermitage then rebuilding: in which box was found a manuscript of parchment written in Gothic characters, but in Castilian verse, containing many of his exploits] (1978, 1.52.694; 1998, 458). Of these only a very few could be read and are reproduced at the end of the text. This discussion is much more than a play between history and fiction, or between the existence of different narrators with their own versions of the story of Don Quixote. What is important here is that the findings come from a hermitage where they were discovered in a leaden box. Such a find immediately recalls the *libros plumbeos* or lead books discovered at Sacromonte in Granada. In 1588, as *moriscos* were tearing down a minaret of a mosque to make room for their nave of the Cathedral of Granada, a lead box was discovered containing an image of the Virgin Mary dressed in the Egyptian or gypsy manner and also a parchment written in Arabic, Latin, and Castilian dealing with St Cecil. Philip II approved the translation of this unusual find. And then, starting in 1595, the caves around Valparaíso, Granada, yielded what seemed to be important finds just when Cervantes was completing his novel. These finds went on for years, as the now sacred site took on the name of Sacromonte. It is very likely that the reference to the unearthing of a leaden box in the *Quixote* would bring to mind the famous discoveries in Granada. Here, tablets as well as more than twenty books were eventually unearthed – the latter in circular lead sheets, each book with its leaves tied together with lead wire. There was also an ancient parchment hidden in a lead box. Once translated by *moriscos* (many were composed in Arabic), these books caused a sensation since they proposed a Christian origin for Granada, a city spurned because it was the last to fall into Christian hands.[15] Barbara Fuchs explains: 'The grenadine apocrypha harked back to the very beginnings of Christianity in Southern Spain, the better to suggest the essential conflation of Christian and Arabic elements in the history of the region' (2001, 114). More specifically, as A.K. Harris asserts, 'The lead books supplement their syncretic theological vision, potentially attractive to both immigrants and Moriscos, with ritual and devotional prescriptions that blended Christian and Muslim practices' (2007, 31). Supposedly written by St James under the command of the Virgin, the texts state unequivocally: 'Y dígoos que los árabes son una de las más excelentes gentes, y su lengua una de las más excelentes lenguas. Eligiólos Dios para ayudar su ley en el último tiempo después de haberle sido grandísimos enemigos' [And I tell you that the Arabs are one of the most excellent of peoples, and their language one of the most excellent of languages. God elected them to help his law in the last days, after they had been great enemies] (Hagerty 1980, 124). The lead books even prophesy a general reconciliation of religions at a council in Cyprus (which had recently fallen to the Turks).

These books tie in quite well with Cervantes' novel. For example, like the *libros plúmbeos,* a large part of the novel or 'history' of Don Quixote is said to have been translated from the Arabic of Cide Hamete to Spanish by a *morisco* at a time when they were supposed to have abandoned their native tongue for Castilian. Readers who doubted the veracity of the *libros plúmbeos* would see Cide Hamete as a false historian, as falsifying reality. Thomas E. Case contends: 'La historia de don Quijote es una burla de la autoridad de textos basados en fuentes falsas. Cervantes sacó esta idea parcial o totalmente de la falsificación de los *Libros plúmbeos* de Granada' [The history of Don Quixote is a satire on the authority of texts based on false sources. Cervantes took this idea in part or fully from the falsification of the *Libros plúmbeos* of Granada] (2002, 21). However, most of the public at the end of the sixteenth and beginning of the seventeenth-centuries believed in the authenticity of these books. Thus, readers who placed their faith in the lead books would link their authority to that of Cide Hamete. The Arab would not be a liar. Instead, he would be bringing new 'revelations' through the humorous characters of Don Quixote and Sancho. Does the novel then include hidden syncretic and esoteric findings? Those reading the text with care would then note that Don Quixote, while a victim of his own anxieties, slowly comes to realize the potential of his multicultural self. Like the lead books, the novel hints at a coming together of the orthodox and the heterodox, of Christianity and the Other. In order to further 'authorize' the claim that Don Quixote is a figure of fate and prophecy, the novel ends not only with the lead box, but with Saturn's procession, as Don Quixote is led home in the planetary chariot. His future adventures may be gleaned from writings in a lead box. Lead is the metal that belongs to the highest of Ptolemaic planets, Saturn. Thus, both the discovery of the *libros plúmbeos* and the saturnine visions of Don Quixote ought to lead the reader to envision new possibilities, even the possibility of *coincidentia oppositorum*, of the harmonizing of opposites.

Don Quixote, then, is a narrative that is constantly breaking limits, going beyond, making use of Charles V's emblem *plus ultra* in order to take the reader to uncharted territories, to a quintessence beyond this world where different revelations come together. The knight metaphorically conquers territories of genre by his mere parodic and destabilizing presence. He obviously overturns the chivalric; he takes the picaresque and makes it his own as he becomes a fugitive from justice, thus transforming the anti-hero into a pseudo-chivalric figure; he enters the pastoral to witness its epic aspirations while at the same time seeking to mirror the Virgilian *cursus*; he turns the Carolingian cycle into a heterodox genre; he uses the Italian romances for his own purposes, using Moorish magic and doing penance for his well-kept secret; he views the sentimental novel in Cardenio and uses its epistolary propensities for unlikely purposes – a letter to a non-existent lady and a second one as a deed for Sancho; he stays away from the conglomerate of *novellas* that crowd around him, rejecting their much needed humidity; he tries to regain protagonism by fighting wineskins/giants in the midst of the tragic tale of the *Curioso impertinente*, thus subverting its tragic thrust; and he mingles and mangles other forms from the hagiographic to technical treatises, and from the ghost story to epics of the defeated. As each set of genres is 'conquered' by breaking its rules, he moves on, creating an empire of broken or metamorphic forms. And each section of the novel forms a conquered set of textual lands from which he moves when caught in excess. In order to move from the Pythagorean structure of the first section to the epic pastoral, the story line crosses the figures of the knight and the Biscayan with their swords held up high. To move from the pastoral landscape, bounded by a fores, to the third section, two other-worldly pillars must be passed, the hill upon which Marcela as goddess stands and the earth that has received the dead Grisóstomo, marked with an epitaph on stone. The third section, one of episodic chivalric adventures commingled with elements of epic, ends at Sierra Morena, as the mountains explode with labyrinthine confusions and interlace which signal the fourth section of the novel. Following Ariadne's thread, the reader and the chivalric pair can navigate their way out. The exit is marked by the last two pillars. Here, it is one object turned into two (helmet/basin) that leads us to the straights of Gibraltar, but turns us back to the beginning, away from territorial *plus ultra*. Although Don Quixote wins the battle of words at the inn or castle, he is placed in an enchanted chariot, in a linear narrative that is homeward bound. Under Saturn's scythe he will sleep at home, dreaming of his freedom from the constraints and anxieties that drove him to knighthood. Holding tight to his newly acquired knowledge, he shows some signs of recovery from his saturnine quest, some signs that the wisdom of Saturn is not obscured by its devilish influences.

While he is taken home, not even realizing where he is, the villagers are all astounded by his remarkable arrival, yellowed with melancholy, reclining on the hay that softens the impact of the rustic cart. This final procession home recalls the funeral procession in memory of the emperor at Brussels, where the Pillars of Hercules, carried by the riderless horse, continue their march forward without a guide. While the knight is at home with the Saracens, the narrative, like Charles V's imperial ambition, comes to an end, having turned back from the excesses of the labyrinth. A second part is promised, much like Philip II promises much. But perhaps his story is already inscribed in the fourth segment of the novel. The excess of writing cannot control an almost boundless empire. Nor can Castilian prevent the proliferation of esoteric Moorish knowledge. Although the many innovative turns of the narrative have come to an end, the narrative, with its many mutations of genre, has also prevailed by attempting a Quixotic feat, to go beyond each impasse, and to venture *plus ultra*, even to the heavens, a space of wandering stars which exert their benefic and baneful influences, affecting the changes in empires and religions, in love and war. But to live with the stars is to comprehend the esoteric, its messages revealed in the esoteric moments of persecuted narratives. As Don Quixote rides in a celestial space removed from clashing civilizations, he can envision his double nature and be at home with Christians and with Western civilization, envisioning their triumphs. Having charted the past of empire and the empire of the word, where genres form a maddening map of conflictive poetics, the knight rests. The empire of the novel, however, will continue without the knight, a riderless horse that is always in search of new challenges.[16]

Notes

1 Pillars of Genre / Ghosts of Empire: An Introduction

1 Natale Conti, although he gives an extensive description of Geryon, seems to be a contrarian on some of these myths. He only gives the name of Eritía in an alternate list of the Hesperides (1988, 490), and he claims that the columns of Hercules were one placed in the East and another in the West 'como confines de sus trabajos . . . en los límites de Libia y Europa' [like confines of his work . . . in the frontier of Libia and Europe] (1988, 489). Only as an alternate story does he state: 'En cambio, los hispanos y los pueblos de Africa pensaron que estaban en Cádiz' [Instead, the Spanish and the villages of Africa thought that they were in Cadiz] (1988, 489). Pérez de Moya, on the other hand, clearly places the second battle with Geryon in the north of Spain. When he triumphed, Hercules built a great tower, the lighthouse in La Coruña (1996, 737–8). He says nothing of the Pillars of Hercules.

2 'On the side facing Spain, at a distance of about 100 yards, is another long island, one mile long and one mile broad, on which the town of Cadiz was previously situated; Ephorus and Philistus call this island Erythea, and Timæus and Silenus call it Aphrodisias, but its native name is the Isle of Juno . . . The island is believed by some people to have been the home of the Geryones whose cattle were carried off by Hercules' (Pliny 1969, 4.22). Hercules claims to have slain Geryon 'by my sole hand' in Seneca's *Hercules oetaeus* (1969, v. 26).

3 Seneca, in *Hercules furens*, has Amphitryon describe the hero's creation of the Straits of Gibraltar: 'When ordered to penetrate the regions of the summer sun scorched kingdoms parched by noonday heat – he split the mountains apart, and by bursting that barrier he made a wide passage for the ocean to rush in' (2002, vv. 235–8).

4 An ancient map derived from the *Tabula Peutingeriana*, tracing the Roman *cursus publicus*, shows the columns in an island. The map was bequeathed to Peutinger in 1508; hence its name. It was copied for Abraham Ortelius and published in 1598.

5 Plato stated that Atlantis was located beyond the Pillars of Hercules.

6 The device, with its French motto *Plus Oultre*, was first painted on the back of a chair in the choir of the Church of St Gududa in Brussels in 1516. The device was created by the physician and humanist from Milan, Luigi Marliano, who was granted the bishopric of Tuy (Pontevedra) as reward (Rosenthal 1973, 202).

7 'The fire steel and flint stone between the columns are symbols of that Order and thus the meaning may be read figuratively as "I promise to lead the order to glory beyond any heretofore known," that is to say, beyond the confines of Europe' (Rosenthal 1971, 218). In 1954, Earl Rosenthal was appointed assistant professor of art at the University·of Chicago, where he remained the rest of his career. His books on the Cathedral of Barcelona and on Charles V's palace in Granada are classical works in art history even today.

8 Frances Yates shows how the 'Sieve Portrait' of Elizabeth I modified Charles V's device: 'There is here a column, marked at its base with an imperial crown, recalling the crowned columns of the famous imperial device' (1975, 116).

9 It is also curious to note that both Charles and Philip carefully prepared their funerals. There is a story that Charles V participated in his own funeral shortly before his death, to make sure all was as he wanted it to be. He was even said to have lain in his own coffin (Eire 1995, 276). His son kept two small candles from Our Lady of Montserrat which were lit as his father passed away; he also had a crucifix held by his father at his death. These were brought to him before his own passing, so as to follow in his father's footsteps (Eire 1995, 277).

10 Philip, like his father, was 'endowed with the square face and low-hung jaw typical of the Habsburg family' (Kamen 1997, 1).

11 In 1878, Díaz de Benjumea referred to critics of the previous century who claimed that Don Quixote 'era el retrato del alma Española, la pintura de Carlos V' [was the portrait of the Spanish soul, the painting of Charles V] (1878, 124). In 1973, Richard L. Predmore called Charles V's challenge of Francis I to single combat a 'challenge worthy of Don Quixote himself' (1973, 15). See also José Antonio Maravall (1991) and De Armas (2006, 113–33).

12 A very useful critique of Huntington's view that the culture of the United States has always been Anglo-Protestant can be found in William Childers's book on Cervantes (2006, 335–6).

13 For example, Cervantes renders homage to the *Lazarillo* in the famous passage in chapter 18 when, asked to look into his master's mouth to see how many teeth he has lost, Don Quixote, under the influence of the balsam of Fierabrás, vomits on Sancho.

14 'pasando una mañana, quando ya el sol quería esclarecer la tierra, por unos valles hondos y escuros que se hazen en la Sierra Morena, vi salir a mi encuentro por entre unos robledales do mi camino se hazía un cavallero, así feroz de presencia como espantoso de vista, cubierto todo de cabello a manera de salvaje' [spending the morning, when the sun wanted to illuminate the earth, in some deep and dark valleys that are found in Sierra Morena, I saw moving forward through some oak trees that marked the road, a gentleman of such ferocious presence and horrid appearance, all hairy in the form of a savage] (1995, 65).

15 The 1605 novel is divided into four parts. The first constituting chapters 1–8, will also form the first narrative segment, and the second from chapters 9–14 will form the second. The third segment starts at the place where the third part begins, but comes to a close much sooner, in chapter 22. Then, chapters 23 through 46 form the fourth segment, and from there until the end we have the fifth.

16 In 1558 Philip II organized funeral ceremonies for Mary Tudor and Mary of Hungary. On 29 December 1559 Philip also organized funeral *exequias* for his father Charles V. This is the event to which we are referring. For a brief description see Anderson (1979, 383–4).

17 Cohen asserts: 'Genre studies is more than another approach to literature or to social institutions or to scientific practices; it analyzes our procedures for acquiring and accumulating knowledge including the changes that such knowledge undergoes . . . To refer to genres is to refer to a group of texts which both have some features in common and others which are individualized' (2003, v).

18 He singles out, for example, the estate poem and the critical epitaph which arose from literary coteries and the system of patronage (2003, 187).

19 'The discourse on genre that is now such an important part of classical studies is far more open than ancient genre theory might have led one to expect. This is so because the discourse is based less on the works of ancient theoreticians than it is on the vastly more complex practice of the ancient poets' (Farrell 2003, 403). He shows that Empedocles was discarded by Aristotle from the epic tradition even though he follows the epic metres (2003, 385). Farrell goes on to study in detail how the love elegy is contaminated with genres such as pastoral, new comedy, and epic.

20 Judith Whitenack explains: 'While many pagans appearing in the romances are "endurecidos" and refuse to convert, it is interesting that the only conversion episode mentioned in *Amadís* is an unsuccessful one. Perhaps this phenomenon is another indication of the work's probable medieval origins . . . We will also remember that in conversions of infidels, as in so many other ways, author Montalvo has Amadís's son Esplandián outdo his father in the sequel' (1993, 66).

21 David Quint has a highly original approach to interlace in Cervantes' novel, splitting the plot between the Dulcinea and the Micomicona narratives and presenting a very useful table of which episode belongs to each type of interlace (2003, 19).

22 Margaret Anne Doody argues that Cervantes was not the creator of the novel. The Greek romances, which impacted Cervantes, can be considered as early novels. And the contemporary novel blurs the distinction between the novel and romance: 'Romance is most often used in literary studies to allude to forms conveying literary pleasure the critic thinks readers would be better off without. It describes works that fail to meet the requirements of realism. But realism has faded away like the Cheshire cat, leaving its smile of reason behind; when novels by admired novelists deal with barons living in trees and with girls born with green hair it is time to drop the pretense that the primary demand of a long work of prose fiction is that it should be realistic' (Doody 1996, 15–16).

23 'First, the shift from epic to novel involves an authorial assertion of femininity in conjunction with the increasingly female public's preference for the more realistic and personal politics of romance over and against the more expansive, heroic, and fantastical tastes of the male scholarly elite' (2007, 60).

24 Burningham asks, for example: 'What do viewers of the Wachowski Brothers' landmark cinematic trilogy bring to a fresh reading of Cervantes' literary masterpiece?' (2008, 2). The links he develops between *The Matrix* and *Don Quixote* illuminate both the baroque and the postmodern.

25 E.C. Riley clearly shows in his *Don Quixote* (1986) how Cervantes' prologue is an attack on Lope's pretentiousness.

26 B.W. Ife argues (1985) that these techniques are used during the sixteenth and seventeenth centuries to overcome Plato's attack on poetry (literature), where the reader or listener identifies with what is read or uttered.

27 There were many other types of satire in the antique world such as Menippean satire, which includes the works of Menippus and Varro. Particularly well-known are Petronius's *Satyricon* and Seneca's *Apocolocyntosis*.

28 This is not to say that parody and humour had not already infiltrated the chivalric genre. José Manuel Lucía, studying works that remained in manuscript form, finds that in Enciso's *Florambel de Lucea*, Duchess Remondina goes mad and although she is rather homely, thinks of herself as the most beautiful damsel on earth. Many knights and gentlemen take advantage of this to play humorous tricks on the lady. Lucía describes it as 'un modelo narrativo con una finalidad humorística: la de un personaje que se encuentra inmerso en la locura de negar su realidad para vivir en una ilusión' [a narrative model with a comic purpose: that of a character who is immersed in the madness of denying her reality in order to live an illusion] (2004, 114). Such a narrative certainly echoes Cervantes' parodic text.

29 'If Don Quixote seated on Rocinante is a figure of the pope holding the reins of the Holy See in Rome, then Sancho Panza mounted on his inseparable gray ass rises as a caricature not only of the papacy in general, but of an individual cardinal seated on a much less exalted throne of his episcopal see as its bishop' (1991, 223). At the same time, Camamis asserts: 'In every chapter that Sancho sleeps a pope dies in the year corresponding to that chapter' (1991, 244).

30 Eric D. Mayer has applied Todorov's analysis to Cervantes' *Novelas ejemplares* (2005, 371–82).

31 Utilized in chapter 17, *alcuza* is a clay jar. Utilized in chapter 40, *zalá* means prayer. This word is used by Zoraida to discuss the Christian prayers that her enslaved nurse taught her.

32 Rogelio Miñana intuits some kind of enigma when he asks what is being hidden when Don Quixote's persona becomes dominant, while the gentleman from La Mancha suddenly disappears (2007, 197).

33 Roberto A. Véguez has discussed the clash of civilizations in the novels, that between Islam and Christianity, citing Samuel P. Huntington so as to relate these struggles to our contemporary world: 'Huntington predicts that the West is bound to have confrontations with two civilizations in the future, the one represented by China, or as he prefers to call it, the Sinic civilization, and the Islamic civilization' (2005, 102).

34 'The fantastic text is not characterized by the simple presence of supernatural phenomena or beings, but by the hesitation which is established in the reader's perception of the events represented . . . if the facts reported are to be explained by a natural or a supernatural cause, if they are illusions or realities' (1977, 156). Of course, no reader actually believes Don Quixote when he claims he has seen ghosts. At the same time, readers may believe that the knight engages on a quest because he is haunted by a secret, a ghostly absence which is never fully revealed.

35 Some claim that the initial story ended with the inquisition of Don Quixote's library. Stagg finds a number of elements that Cervantes could have included in his revisions of the first eight chapters, once he started writing chapter 9 (1964, 463–71).

36 Saracen comes from the Greek term *sarakenós*, meaning people from the Orient. It can also derive from the Aramean, where it meant a person from the desert. They were nomads from Arabian lands to the north. With the advent of Islam and the Christian Crusades, the name came to mean all Islamic peoples from Asia and North Africa. In its most specific definition, the term Saracen was applied during the Middle Ages and the Renaissance to name the Muslims of Sicily and southern Italy. This may be in part why Ariosto uses the term. He could also take the term as it was used since the time of Charlemagne to mean anyone who is not Christian and is thus interchangeable with the term 'pagan.' The same term was applied to Spanish Muslims by chroniclers starting in the eighth century. For example, in the *Crónica profética*, the last section of the *Crónica albeldense* describes how the Saracens themselves have seen in the stars their own defeat at the hands of Alfonso III (Fernández Conde 2000, 269). Even to this day in Sóller, Mallorca, the inhabitants celebrate on 22 April a feast called 'Desembarco de los Sarracenos' [Disembarkation of the Saracens] which commemorates the victory of the native inhabitants against the invaders. There is a small archaeological site in Mallorca, a cave on the hills of Ferrutx, where some twenty Saracens hid after King Jaume I conquered the island. The king eventually found these farmers in 1230 and wrote about this event in his *El llibre dels fets*. See *El País*, Cataluña edition, 15 December 2009.

2 A Pythagorean Parody of Chivalry

1 When Don Quijote meets Maese Pedro the puppeteer, the latter kneels before the knight and intones a parodic praise: 'Estas piernas abrazo, bien así como si abrazara las dos colunas de Hércules, ¡oh resucitador insigne de la ya puesta en olvido andante caballería!' [These legs I embrace, just as if I embraced the two pillars of Hercules, O illustrious reviver of the long-forgotten order of chivalry!] (1978, 2.25.235; 1998, 634).

2 Elsewhere, I have discussed in much greater detail this first narrative unit in Don Quixote. I am thus providing here a short summary. For the full account, see De Armas (2006, 56–70).

3 Parody in the novel includes techniques such as burlesque, irony, hyperbole, mock-epic, ridicule, and satire.

4 Amanda Meixell sees the mixture of these two kinds of magic in Cervantes' play *La casa de los celos*.

5 The Renaissance would have known of Pythagoras's thought through his biographies by Diogenes Laertius and others. From them, people would have learned that for this ancient philosopher, number was the most important principle of the universe. More importantly, Pythagoras believed in the immortality of the soul (the soul as a kind of sphere whose self-motion is likened to an unending circular motion) and passed on this principle to Plato (Celenza 1999, 683–4). For Iamblichus, Pythagoras was a wise seer who was sent to guide the soul from lower to higher things (Celenza 1999, 672). Ficino wished to continue both the prophetic and guiding impulses of Pythagoras. Indeed, Iamblichus's ten-volume work, *On Pythagoreanism*, of which only the first four volumes survived, was amply utilized by Ficino. On the other hand, the notion of metempsychosis is downplayed by Ficino for religious reasons (Celenza 1999, 685–7).

6 José Antonio Madrigal, one of the few critics who has noticed the importance of quaternity in these early chapters, points to the four days needed by Don Quixote to name his horse (1981, 571). He argues that the number four appears at a point in the initiatory rites of the knight when he sees the horse as vehicle for adventure.

7 On Gohory, see Walker (1958, 96–106).

8 Two are from *Amadís de Gaula*: Amadís and Galaor. The other two knights are Palmerín de Inglaterra and the Caballero del Febo (1978, 1.1.73).

9 'pues se imaginaba que, por grandes maestros que le hubiesen curado, o dejaría de tener el rostro y todo el cuerpo lleno de cicatrices y señales' [for he imagined, that notwithstanding the most expert súrgenos had cured him. His face and whole body must still be full of seams and scars] (1978, 1.1.78; 1998, 22).

10 This is my own translation since Jarvis writes that he 'lost his wits' (1998, 23).

11 Paradoxically, a Saturn talisman can be used for longevity. It should include a sapphire, and the figures of an old man, a dragon, and a sickle (1989, 335).

12 For a discussion of the six non-natural elements that can cause imbalance (air, food, sleeping/waking, evacuation, exercise, and the passions), see Heiple (1979).

13 Barbara A. Holdrege explains that one of the links between the Vedas and the Torah has to do with this principle. In the Vedas, for example 'the creator projects name into form' (1996, 127). In other words, the relationship between *nama* and *rupa* is as follows: 'The form is considered to be already

inherent in its natural name and thus represents a more precipitated, consolidated expression of that name' (1996, 110). This is similar to the Torah where the Name of God includes all divine names and is concretized in the words and sentences of the book (1996, 201).

14 Discussing Titian's *Charles V at Mulberg*, Panofsky states that now 'his ungainly mouth [is] set in an expression of unshakable resolve' (1969, 85).

15 As noted in the previous chapter, Simon Dentith contends that parody takes up the style and content of a literary work which it imitates with polemical intent (2000, 9).

16 On the relationship between their love affairs and the amorous action and language of *La Celestina*, see Dasí (2000, http://parnaseo.uv.es/tirant).

17 José Manuel Lucía has studied many of these manuscripts, which must be added to the sum of some sixty-four published romances of chivalry. Interestingly, he argues that the popularity of the romances of chivalry continued in the seventeenth century. What happened is that many of them were not published due to publishing constraints. The economy did not allow for large luxury editions (2004, 37–40).

3 Questioning Quaternities

1 For example, Apollo plays an important role in the *Belianís de Grecia.* The solar god appears in Book 1, as the sun rises on the day of San Juan (1997, 1.90). Although dawn is imminent, Apollo does not want to bring out the sun in Book 2, since there is going to be a terrible battle (1997, 2.399–400).

2 The whole question of Don Quixote as carnival has been studied from Bakhtin (1984, 22–3) to Redondo. The latter sees the knight's initiation as a parody, since Don Quixote becomes a son of the innkeeper and a son of the prostitutes: 'De esta manera la degradación burlesca llega al punto cumbre, pero al mismo tiempo se va delineando la trayectoria vital del personaje principal . . . Don Quijote supera esa degradación por el poder de la imaginación, que transforma la realidad más trivial' [This way the burlesque degradation reaches its peak, but at the same time the central path of the main character is being drawn . . . Don Quijote overcomes this degradation by the power of imagination, that transforms the most trivial of realities] (1998, 304).

3 Yovel concedes that the poor hidalgo in *Lazarillo de Tormes* is almost as repressed as the other: 'Looking further, we see that the poor noble is as much a victim of the value system he represents as are his opposite numbers – the pícaros, the Conversos, the Moriscos, and all those of "inferior blood." When honor is placed in birth as its true source, personality

shrinks to a minimum, indeed to zero, as the origin and carrier of worth' (2009, 270).

4 'Según la leyenda que relata el *Flos sanctorum*, se le habría azotado crudelísimamente antes de desollarlo vivo. Y luego se le habría vuelto a azotar' [According to the legend in *Flos sanctorum*, he was brutally whipped before he was flayed alive. And later was flogged again] (Redondo 1998, 321).

5 Some critics have used this scene as proof for the theory that Cervantes utilized the *Entremés de los romances* as model for his novel. In this interlude, the peasant Bartolo becomes deluded due to excessive reading of the ballads and finds himself in a similar situation as Don Quixote. Indeed, Bartolo also believes that the Marqués de Mantua is coming to help him. There is no question that there are many similarities between the scene in the *Entremés* and that in the novel. However, it is quite possible that the interlude was written as an imitation of Cervantes' episode and not vice versa. For an overview of critical attitudes to this problem, see Stagg (2002).

6 There are four versions of the text. The earliest may be the *Parte de la corónica del ínclito infante don Fernando que ganó a Antequera* which lacks a date. It may be the source for the *Chrónica* of 1561. Then comes the interpolation of 1562 in *La Diana* (reissued in this form a number of times), and finally the tale included in Antonio Villega's *Inventario* (*Miscellany*) of 1565. The author is unknown. See Bollard (2003, 297 note 1).

7 For the emerging maurophilia in Spain see, for example, Cirot (1938), Burshatin (1984), Bollard (2003), and Fuchs (2009).

8 A final point of interest in this episode is that it is a fitting ending to the first set of two adventures since it reverses the Andrés situation. There, Don Quixote had heard laments and gone to help the boy. Here, it is his neighbour who hears the knight's plaints and comes to his rescue.

9 Ovidian metamorphoses include the following transformations from higher to lower: Acteon into a stag, Aretusa into a spring, Adonis, Hyacinth, and Narcissus into flowers, Atalanta and Hipomenes into lions, Cyparissus into a cypress, Daphne into a laurel tree, etc.

10 Although in the past most have agreed that Juanelo is the author of this text, more recently, José A. García-Diego, the editor of Turriano's work, rejects this authorship. He argues that the language of the manuscript suggests that it was written by an Aragonese. It has very few Italianisms and we know that Juanelo spoke Spanish with a strong dose of Italian. Furthermore, there is little said of Toledo where Juanelo presumably wrote the text. However, it is possible to counter these assertions by arguing that Juanelo had a Spaniard write down his ideas.

11 'no viera venir más de veinte dragones cercados de llamas de fego, que
vn carro parecían traer de la misma llama cubierto y en él venían muchas
diformes figuras . . . mas antes llegó el diabólico carro en el qual fueron
puestas las princesas Florisbella, Hermeliana, Policena, con las hermosas
Sirenay Imperia e infanta Matarrossa, con la reyna Aurora' [he saw coming over twenty dragons surrounded by flames, that one charriot looked
like it was made out of fire and in it came many disformed figures . . . even
before the diabolical chariot arrived were the princess Florisbella, Hermeliana, Policena, with the beautiful Sirenay Imperia and princesa Matarrossa,
with the Queen Aurora set in it] (1997, 2.464).

12 The peace at the end of Book 1 is threatened by Amadís's dalliance with
Briolanja, to the detriment of his relationship with Oriana: 'Todo lo que
más desto en este libro primero se dize de los amores de Amadís y desta
Hermosa Reina fue acrecentando como ya se vos dixo; y por esso, como
superfluo y vano se dexará de recontar, pues que no haze al caso' [Every-
thing else that is said in this first book of the love of Amadis and of this
Beautiful Queen grew like it has already been told to you; and therefore,
like everything unnecessary and vain, will be left untold since it does not
further the storyline] (1987, 1.644). The harmony at the end of Book 2 is
shattered when evil counsellors give bad advice to King Lisuarte, while
in Book 3, the culminating problem is the order given by Lisuarte that his
daughter Oriana marry the emperor of Rome.

13 Alvaro Molina claims that in the battle with the Basque, Don Quixote becomes a figure analogous to Saint James and Saint George, the first with
his sword cutting the heads off the Moors and the second with a bloody
arm that becomes a famous relic (2003, 178).

4 An Arab's Audacious Pastoral

1 As is well known, Cleanth Brooks's analysis of Donne's *Canonization* and
Keats's *Ode to a Grecian Urn* were included as two of the eleven essays
in his 1947 collection. They became two of the classic studies of the New
Criticism. In the Keats essay, he argued that the line 'Beauty is truth, truth
beauty' is not sententious and can only be understood if we accept the urn
as speaker (151–66). In a similar manner, Cervantes' first segment can only
be understood if it is viewed in terms of Pythagorean cosmos as it speaks
about the beauty of creation.

2 For a detailed discussion of the links between Ovid and Cervantes, see the
collection of essays *Ovid in the Age of Cervantes* (De Armas 2010).

3 Iamblichus tells us that Pythagoras 'was sent down to men from Apollo's train' (Celenza 1999, 672–3).

4 In his 1988 essay, Prince explains that the disnarrated 'covers all the events that do not happen but, nonetheless, are referred to (in a negative or hypothetical mode) by the narrative text' (1988, 2).

5 In Feliciano de Silva's *Amadis de Grecia* (1530), Darinel is in love with the shepherdess Silvia (who is actually a princess). She spurns him and he becomes an eccentric character. When she marries Anastarax in the *Florisel de Niquea* (1532), Darinel becomes a Neoplatonic lover. In his later novel, *Cuarta parte del Florisel de Niquea* (1551), Rogel de Grecia, disguised as Archileo, woos with pastoral eclogues the empress Archisidea as she abides in her country retreat. See Sydney Cravens (1978, 28–34).

6 'Although pastoral has often been described as escapist and utopian, violence abounds in the genre, especially in the romances' (Damiani and Mujica 1990, 2).

7 'But just as Virgil wished to destroy his unrevised *Aeneid*, so Petrarch expresses dissatisfaction with his *Africa*, a poem sketched in broad design that would remain unfinished in detail' (Kennedy 2002, 149).

8 'Writing like David is profoundly different from writing like Virgil or even Ovid . . . There is no "rota Davidica." If David can indeed outdo Homer, Hesiod, Pindar and the others, then a pious poet – or an ambitious one – would be wise to venture out past pagan hymnody into divine poetry' (Kennedy 2002, 210).

9 'I thus talk of proems, prefaces, and prologues. Pressure also falls too on endings and on intermediate passages of transition or challenge' (Helgerson 1983, 13).

10 Jarvis fails to translate this phrase writing instead that 'no common language can express . . .' (1998, 96).

11 For the epic elements in the novel, see Marasso and McGaha (1980, 34–50). For how Cervantes follows Virgil in Don Quixote and thus imitates his literary career, see De Armas (2002, 268–85).

12 Nelson's study shows links between periods of expansion apogee and decline of the Spanish empire and the pastoral writings that took place under the different periods: 'Continuing a classical (beginning with Theocritus and Virgil) and early-Renaissance (with Jacopo Sannazaro, Juan del Encina and Garcilaso de la Vega) tradition, these pastoral writers took either a laudatory or critical stance towards Imperial Spain' (2007, 244).

13 This critic also established parallels between the highlands of Najd in Arabic poetry and Arcadia in the European tradition.

14 This pagan champion is a descendant of Hector of Troy. He will later convert to Christianity and become and ancestor of the house of d'Este.

15 Of course, the 'view from the wall' is not absent from other literary forms. In Horace's *Odes* (III.2, 6–13), it appears in an epic moment when 'the wife of a warring tyrant and her adult daughter [are] looking from battlements anxious for their prince' (Simpson 2001, 65). Teichoskopia is also found in classical theatre, where we view it, for example, in Euripides' *The Phoenissiae*. Here, an old servant goes with Antigone to the highest point in the house and they watch together the army that threatens Thebes. Euripides follows the ascent with a dialogue where Antigone's many questions elicit detailed responses from the servant, answers that turn into a catalogue of warriors, a type of *enumeratio* which is also found in Helen's teichoskopia in the *Illiad*.

16 'It is an episode in which love and the law are tightly intertwined and which culminates in a variation of the trial scene . . . The conflict, involving injury, restitution, possible revenge, accusations, defense, judgment, and release from culpability, unfolds and is resolved in a decidedly judicial manner' (2005, 78, 79).

17 In its medical context, the term autopsy was first recorded in the *Diccionario de la Real Academia Española* in 1869. For Jonathan Sawday: 'The period between (roughly 1540 and 1640), is, therefore, the period of the discovery of the Vesalian body . . . Guiding the followers of Vesalius was the belief that the human body expressed in miniature the divine workmanship of God, and that its form corresponded to the greater form of the macrocosm' (1995, 23). Sawday finds numerous references to these voyages into the body as related to the discovery of America. Very much like the new continent, the body had to be mapped and 'colonized' (1995, 28). Thus autopsy is still part of the eyewitness account that renders credible voyages to strange lands and body parts.

18 Historians date the fire as starting on 19 June of the year 64. It lasted nine days 'and reduced three of the fourteen regions (regions) of the city to rubble' (Hornblower and Spawforth 1998, 491). In the *Celestina*, Sempronio sings of Nero's fire thus alluding to the fires of passion experienced by his master, Calisto. Indeed, the latter declares: 'Mayor es mi fuego, y menos la piedad de quien yo agora digo' [Greater is the fire, and less the devotion of whom I just said] (Rojas 1993, 92). In the 1615 *Quijote*, Altisidora feigns to be in love with the knight, and asks him not to look at the fires of love in her heart as Nero looked upon the fires of Rome: 'No mires de tu Tarpeya / este incendio que me abraza / Nerón manchego del mundo' [Do not see in your Tarpeya this fire that embraces Nero from La Mancha of the world] (1978, 2.44.373). This part of the poem is not translated.

19 In Tirso's text, after don Juan dishonours Tisbea, she exclaims:

> !Fuego, fuego, que me quemo,
> que mi cabaña se abrasa!
> . . .
> Mi pobre edificio queda
> hecho otra Troya en las llamas,
> que después que faltan Troyas
> quiere Amor quemar cabañas.
>
> [Fire, fire, I'm burning,
> it is burning my shack!
> . . .
> My poor home is
> made into another Troy in the flames,
> since there are no more Troys left
> Love wants to burn down shacks]   (1996, vv. 986–7, 990–3)

As Helen Solterer has shown, the image of conquest which relates woman to city and vice versa was very common during the Middle Ages (1995, 107). Troy is mentioned repeatedly in Cervantes' novel, although not in this context. See, for example, 1978, 1.581 and 2.239, 266, 293, 348.

20 One must wonder at Ambrosio's rhetorical mistakes. Could they be subtle artifices to exonerate Marcela? Much later in the novel, the tale of the 'curioso impertinente' will show two friends in love with the same woman. Could we discover in Ambrosio an incipient desire for Marcela? After all, most of the men present at her speech desire her. Thus Ambrosio's motivation can be questioned. He either unwittingly helps Marcela, or does so given his own feelings for her.

21 'And now early Dawn, leaving the saffron bed of Tithonous, was sprinkling her fresh rays upon the earth. Soon as the queen from her watchtower saw the light within and the fleet move on with even sails, and knew the shores and harbours were void of oarsmen, thrice and four times she truck her comely breast with her hand, and tearing her golden hair . . .' (1. 435; 4.584ff).

22 All three are examples of legendary figures that went against what was considered lawful. Helen went against marital law, Dido went against what was expected of her as widow and Queen of Carthage, and Nero went against what was beneficial for Rome. To be free of society's

marriage expectations, Marcela also removes herself from accepted societal practices.

23 Herman Iventosch (1974) and Ruth El Saffar (1984) underline the resemblances between Marcela and the goddess Diana. Michael McGaha points to Marcela as a new Daphne (1977); and Erna Berndt-Kelley (1989) and Carolyn Nadeau (1995) have argued that Marcela resembles the goddess Astraea.

5 Magics of the Defeated

1 For José Ángel Asunce Arrieta there are three major 'núcleos seriados' [serialized nuclei] forming 'unidades de sentido' [units of sense] (1997, 152). Two of them are in this segment of the novel: the balsam of Fierabrás and Mambrino's helmet.

2 David Quint states: 'Lucan would not supplant Virgil as the great Roman epic poet . . . nor would the Republic return. Lucan did, however, initiate a rival anti-Virgilian tradition of epic' (1993, 133). Don Quixote's adventures in this section of the novel mostly belong to defeat, and include the muleteers, the enamoured princess, the armies of sheep, the dead body, the fulling-hammers, the helmet of Mambrino, and the galley slaves. Only one is truly won, the helmet of Mambrino.

3 Cervantes probably used the Spanish translation of a French prose version, *Hystoria del emperador Carlomagno y de los doze pares de Francia, e de la cruda batalla que huvo Oliveros con Fierabrás*, first published in Seville in 1525. Here, the balsam is located in Jerusalem and is recovered when Oliveros fights the giant and kills him. Although mortally wounded, Oliveros regains health by drinking the balsam. A variation of the balsam can be found in a passage in Gerbert, one of the continuators of Chretien de Troyes' unfinished *Perceval*. See Griffith (1910, 102–4).

4 *Moriscos* were often accused of being practitioners of all kinds of magical arts. See Herrero García (1927, 584–7); Grangel (1953, 117–73); and Díez Fernández and Fernández Aguirre de Cárcer (1992, 33–67).

5 They have collected their evidence from interviews of women in Sephardic communities in areas of the former Ottoman Empire.

6 Rosemary is in many ways a 'heterodox' plant used by gypsies in their magic. Of course the most famous early modern reference to the plant comes from Shakespeare's *Hamlet* where Ophelia offers rosemary for remembrance. J.W. Lever shows that among other things, it restores speech and memory and it 'comforts' the brain (1952, 124). From this perspective, the plant serves to comfort the knight who has been humiliated by too many beatings and defeats.

7 María Elena Arenas Cruz, Javier J. González Martínez, and Santiago Fernández-Mosquera have all found evidence of *evidentia* and particularly of teichoskopia in plays by Rojas Zorrilla, Vélez de Guevara, and Calderón, in which the device is used to narrate major battles or the sieges of cities and fortresses that would be difficult to stage, thus adding epic grandeur and a sense of witnessing to these works. Teichoskopia may simply occur when characters are viewing events from the first or second balcony constructed in back of the stage. Many of these teichoskopic moments simply involve the view from a hilltop (the balcony). Arenas Cruz discusses instances where 'La batalla sucede en el presente y es contada por un personaje que la está viendo desde lejos (desde un monte, desde un muro, desde una torre o incluso escondido). Se corresponde con lo que la Retórica llamaba ticoscopia' [The battle takes place in the present and is told by a character that is viewing it from afar (from a hill, from a wall, from a tower or even hidden). This corresponds with what Rhetoric called teichoskopia] (2005, 250). She analyses, for example, the scene where the *gracioso* Caimán narrates the battle from the top of a hill in Rojas Zorrilla's *Los áspides de Cleopatra* (2005, 253). Fernández-Mosquera notes that even in Calderón's late plays where battles do take place on stage, teichoskopia remains an important device. Magón's harangue to the Carthaginian soldiers, for example, includes a teichoskopia, as he tells them of the advancing Roman army he is viewing as he speaks (2000, 269). Finally, for González Martínez, the tourney in the plays of Luis Vélez de Guevara serves to evoke teichoskopia, since the ladies who comment on the spectacle are found in the balcony above the stage. This is particularly the case in *El amor en vizcaíno* (2005, 78–9).

8 For the epic teichoskopia in this episode, see De Armas (2006, 153–69). For other epic elements in the episode, see McGaha (1991, 149–62).

9 Warriors are often identified with their lands and rivers in the *Aeneid*, as Ismarus comes from Lydia 'where men till rich fields and Patcolus waters them with gold' (1978, 10.141–2). Of course Xanthus, a Trojan river, is repeatedly evoked. See, for example, 1978, 1.473; 3.497; 5.634, 803, 808; 6.88; 10.60.

10 Ajax's confusion appears in Sophocles' *Ajax* and in Apuleius's *The Golden Ass*. The latter is Cervantes' most likely model. See Selig (1983) and McGaha (1991).

11 Don Quixote assures Sancho: 'Todas estas borrascas que nos suceden son señales de que presto ha de serenar el tiempo y han de sucedernos bien las cosas' [All these storms, that fall upon us, are signs that the weather will clear up, and things will go smoothly] (1978, 1.18.225; 1998, 132).

12 Mezentius is an Etruscan king and an ally of Turnus. He appears in the
    tenth book of the *Aeneid*. After Aeneas kills his horse and pins him down,
    he does not beg for mercy, like Turnus would later. There are other epic/
    chivalric similarities between Charles and the Cervantine knight. Charles
    set free his rival, the French king Francis I, taking him at his word. When
    Francis reneged on his promises, Charles lost many of the advantages
    gained at the battle of Pavia. Don Quixote, instead, fails to abide by his
    own sworn statements and he even fails to free Sancho from his blanket-
    ing at the inn. The emperor was said to have won a truly chivalric battle, a
    small force decimating the Protestant army at Muhlberg. Charles lost some
    fifty men while two thousand of the enemies were eliminated and many of
    the leaders captured.
13 'All that night we hide in the woods, enduring monstrous horrors, and
    see not from what cause comes the sound. For neither did the stars show
    their fires, nor was heaven clear with stellar light' (1978, 3.583–5). Marasso
    briefly discusses this episode (1954, 33–5).
14 For a detailed explanation of the talismanic powers found in this episode,
    see De Armas (in press).
15 'Sin embargo, a mí me parece que el yelmo simboliza no el poder men-
    tal de don Quijote como mago, sino más bien su debilidad esencial, que
    resulta de su mente trastornada' [Though, I believe that the helmet sym-
    bolizes not the mental power of Don Quixote as magician but instead his
    esential weakness that comes from his disturbed mind] (McGaha 1981,
    746).
16 Already in 1545 'his health was beginning to break down and he was fre-
    quently bedridden with gout' (Fernández Álvarez 1975, 133). For a com-
    parison between Charles V as portrayed by Titian and Don Quixote, see De
    Armas (2006, 125–33).

6 Clues to a Narrative

1 González Echevarría shows how 'most of don Quijote's crimes take place
   in the *despoblado*; hence toward the end of the novel he and Sancho are
   called by one of the troopers of the Holy brotherhood . . . highway robbers
   or a highwayman, individuals known for assaulting people on the open
   roads' (2005, 64).
2 'The name "Zadig" has taken on such symbolic value that in 1880
   Thomas Huxley, on a lecture to publicize Darwin's discoveries, defined as
   "Zadig's method," that procedure which combined [a number of sciences]
   namely, the ability to forecast retrospectively . . . When causes cannot be

reproduced, there is nothing to do but to deduce them from their effects' (Ginzburg 1989, 117).

3 The appendix to the tale, added by Voltaire in 1652, casts doubt on this future happiness. And, since it is incomplete, the happy ending is left in doubt.

4 Zadig's virtues and knowledge, his evidential or scientific method, and the will of Providence prevail in the best of all possible worlds, the least imperfect of worlds. The tale is said to echo Leibniz's principle of Sufficient Reason and his notion of the best of all possible worlds, that is, the least imperfect (Voltaire 2008 xiv).

5 In the source story for Zadig, clues reveal that a camel or dromedary is blind in one eye, missing a tooth and lame – the last feature recalling the queen's dog.

6 We can recall Ian Watt's famous statement on the pattern of Don Quixote's adventures: 'a visual stimulus; a misinterpretation of the stimulus by Quixote; a realistic correction by Sancho Panza' (1996, 64).

7 For the windmills as a technological invention, see Ivan Jaksic. Charles V's most cherished inventor claimed that windmills were not suited to Spain because the winds there were too strong (De Armas 2006, 146).

8 Windmills of the mind reflected these extreme fluctuations and thus allude to the knight's madness. See, for example, Velázquez's painting of Calabazas, Philip IV's court jester, actually named Juan de Cardenas. He had a misshapen foot, an undersized head, and crossed eyes which point to his instability. Velázquez renders him in Habsburg black, holding a pinwheel (*molinete*) – which is an image that, like the windmill (*molino*), represents folly. See Redondo (1998, 333).

9 Sherlock Holmes tells Watson that he knows he has been to the post office, pointing to the reddish mould in his shoe which is the same as the earth found around the post office where they have taken up the pavement. This, explains Holmes, is mere observation (Doyle 1953, 91). Holmes also claims that it is possible 'by a momentary expression, a twitch of a muscle or a glance of an eye, to fathom a man's inmost thoughts' (1953, 23).

10 In the 24th part of the Amadís de Gaula, the knight defeats Francalón Ciclopes who rode a beast that resembled a dromedary. Not that romances themselves would be inappropriate reading for a sleuth. Sherlock Holmes read 'Sensational Literature' in the search for clues (Doyle 1953, 22). But there would be no clues in the chivalric romances as to present events. And yet, fiction can be read as clues to mysteries that can take place in real life.

11 Watson tells Holmes: 'You have an extraordinary genious for minutiae' (Doyle 1953, 90). As a slave in Egypt, Zadig becomes useful by telling his

master 'the specific gravity per volume of different metals and other commodities' (Voltaire 2008, 137).

12 'The abstract notion of text explains why textual criticism, even while retaining to a large extent its divinatory qualities, had the potential to develop in a rigorously scientific direction' (1989, 107).

13 The story appeared in a collection by Giovanni Sercambi (1537) and later in the work of Christoforo Armeno (the Armenian) published in Venice in 1557 by Michele Tramezzino with the title *Peregrinaggio di tre giovani figliuoli del re Serendippo* (Ginzburg 1989, 116; Remer 1965, 8). Remer believes that Tramezzino was the author, and that Christoforo Armeno is a way to attain anonymity 'because of the ribald character of some of the tales, and the satire on the social order of Venice' (1965, 8). In addition, the original tales might not have come from Persia. Remer asserts: 'There is respectable authority supporting the claim that the tales are of Indian origin' (1965, 36). This story of King Serendippo led Horace Walpole in 1754 'to coin the neologism serendipity to designate 'making of discoveries, by accidents and sagacity, of things which they were not in quest of' (Ginzburg 1989, 116).

14 Walpole's letter states: 'For instance, one of them discovered that a mule blind of the right eye had travelled the same road lately, because the grass was eaten only on the left side, where it was worse than on the right – now do you understand serendipity' (Remer 1965, 6). In the same letter, Walpole goes on to define serendipity as 'accidental sagacity.'

15 For the passage on the camel, see the Italian text (Armeno 2000, 15–19) and the English translation (Remer 1965, 61–5). The word used in the Italian is 'gambello' or camel. The dromedary is a species of camel with only one hump that was domesticated in Persia. Taking as a clue that this is called a 'Persian' story, we may deduce that the prince's camel is a dromedary. In fact, dromedaries were more suited for carrying people and a woman was riding it in the story.

16 Having helped to squelch a conspiracy against him, the emperor held the three brothers in high esteem. He sent them to India to recover a magical mirror that had been stolen from his land (Armeno 2000, 33–4; Remer 1965, 72–3). There, they dealt with the Virgin Queen and helped her banish a huge open hand that appeared at the harbour and took first her people and then their animals (Armeno 2000, 40–52; Remer 1965, 78–85). When they succeeded in this labour and two other mysteries, the queen asked for one of the sons in marriage; he accepted but only after he took the mirror back to the emperor and the news back to his father, King Giaffer of Serendippo. After many adventures and many stories, the tale of the three brothers ends in happiness.

17 Holmes asserts: 'Eliminate all other factors and the one which remains must be the truth' (Doyle 1953, 92).

18 'The constellation of Orion and the bright star of Sirius, guided him with the help of Canopus, southward' (2008, 132).

19 Having succeeded in his first attempt, he tries to look at nature for clues a second time. He looks at the placement of Ursa Minor in the sky to show that dawn is almost three hours away. But Don Quixote tells him that he cannot possibly know this since 'the night is so dark' (1978, 1.20.240; 1998, 144). So, Sancho seems to fake his evidence, as he himself admits, saying that 'fear has many eyes.'

20 Javier Herrero has stated: 'The image of the labyrinth signifies the moral confusion of several lives twisted into the wrong paths through their sins' (1981, 57).

21 Jarvis fails to translate *nudo* as knot, thus leaving out the important image of the thread in this instance (1998, 226).

22 Jarvis fails to translate the numerous images attached to the thread of narrative merely stating: 'resuming the broken thread of the narration' (1998, 230).

23 Herrero describes this scene thusly: 'Rising from the water, her feet and legs bare, and covered with the radiant blondness of her locks, she appears figuratively as a Venus image, or . . . as a pagan nymph' (1981, 56).

24 Horacio Chiong Rivero argues that there is no mistake here since 'don Quijote se propone perseguir a Cardenio, de manera paralela al mito de Teseo, quien se adentra en el laberinto de Dédalo para matar al Minotauro' [Don Quixote decides to pursue Cardenio, in a parallel manner to the myth of Theseus, who enters Daedalus's labyrinth in order to kill the Minataur] (2006, 285). He also argues that 'pues no parece ser tan garrafal equívoco si se considera que el monstruo en el centro del laberinto de Sierra Morena no es el Minotauro, símbolo por excelencia de la lujuria desenfrenada al que Teseo mata, sino más bien la Medusa, monstruo híbrido que Perseo derrota y que emblematiza el peligro de la parálisis latente en todo espejismo de la autorreflexión, de la imitación de la imitación'[it does not appear that it would be such a terrible mistake if one were to consider that the monster in the centre of the labyrinth of Sierra Morena is not the Minotaur, symbol par excellence of the uncontrollable lust that Theseus kills, but instead it is Medusa, hybrid monster that Perseus destroys and that emblematizes the dangers of latent paralysis in all illusions of autoreflection, of the imitation of the imitation] (2006, 295).

25 The urge to have every major character get married at the end also recalls these tales since, in the end Cardenio will marry his Luscinda and Fernando will do his duty and marry below his station.

26 Lathrop shows that Cervantes never uses the expression 'hallar menos.' He uses instead 'hechar menos' (1984, 208). Thus when Sancho misses his ass and says 'hallo menos' (1978, 1.23.279, note 5), this shows the passage is not authored by Cervantes.

27 For Javier Herrero, this Minotaur is the monster of lasciviousness killed by Don Quixote as he slashes wineskins thinking of them as the giant Pandafilando (1981, 55–67). González Echevarría, on the other hand, does not see that the stories in the Sierra Morena are unified by this image and action. Instead, he finds an 'unfinished quality to *Don Quijote*,' while at the same time arguing that 'the underlying unity is found in the relation of the love stories to legal issues' (2005, 76).

28 Horacio Chiong Rivero argues: 'El entramado de hilos narrativos de hecho viene a reflejar la bien proporcionada figura del intrincado laberinto novelesco, tan emblemático de la estética cervantina' [This network of narrative threads in fact comes to reflect the well-proportioned figure of the intricate fictional labyrinth so emblematic of the Cervantine esthetic] (2006, 286). He adds that this shows Cervantes as a new Daedalus constructing a metalabyrinth where both Don Quixote's images and the proliferation of narratives reflect one another (2006, 296).

29 'Cervantes's method of playing one episode of the novel off against another derives from and is inspired in the technique of narrative interlace ("entrelacement") that organizes the great chivalric romances of the Middle Ages' (Quint 2003, 5).

30 Thomas Pavel, turning to the *Curioso impertinente*, emphasizes that Anselmo's desires are vague and useless. They go against his own interests and he does not understand them (2003b, 123). Thus, Pavel compares them to the strange desires of the Princess of Cleves in Madame de La Fayette's novel (129).

31 The webpage claims that it is 'well known for its commitment to excellence, customer service, and dedication in both the American, and Hispanic communities throughout the greater Northwest by providing quality investigations.' They apparently did not derive their name from the characters in fiction, but from the names of the two major investigators: Benito Cervantes and Andy Holmes. This is not to say that they did not revel in this quixotic coincidence. See www.cahi.biz/Home_Page.php.

7 Greek Interlace / Italian Interweaving

1 On Sierra Morena as labyrinth, see J. Herrero (1981), Fajardo (1984), Juárez-Almendros (2004), and Rivero (2006).

2 For Javier Herrero, this Minotaur is the monster of lasciviousness killed by
   Don Quixote as he slashes wineskins thinking of them as the giant Pandafilando (1981, 55–67). González Echevarría, on the other hand, does not see
   that the stories in the Sierra Morena are unified by this image and action.
   Instead, he finds an 'unfinished quality to Don Quijote,' while at the same
   time arguing that 'the underlying unity is found in the relation of the love
   stories to legal issues' (2005, 76).

3 While many Spanish critics insist in calling this genre the Byzantine novel,
   the Greek novel of the Hellenistic period must be differentiated from the
   Byzantine, which was a later development, of lesser originality and vi-
   brancy, and written in verse. For an example of a Byzantine novel, see Joan
   Burton (2004). For an overview of the Greek (and Roman) novel, see Whitmarsh (2008).

4 'porque entre riscos y breñeas / halla el triste desventuras' [bandied betwixt hopes and fears, / By cruel love in wanton play] (1978, 1.26.321).

5 Mary Gossy argues that Dulcinea and Aldonza are two sides of a coin;
   while the first is the femme, the second is the butch.

6 For a fuller discussion of women as territories, including also Oriana and
   Angelica, see De Armas (2001).

7 David Quint uses the notion of interlacing in Don Quixote in a novel way.
   For him, there are two main clusters in the first part of the novel, the Dulcinea cluster and the Micomicona one. He comments: 'In the complex of
   love stories that we have just looked at . . . Cervantes introduces the possibility of mercenary and social motives – only pointedly to discard them.
   He would have us focus instead on how erotic desire in these stories is
   driven by rivalry between men . . . The motive of riches and the rise in social status however inform the second cluster of interlaced stories of Part
   One of Don Quijote, the Princess Micomicona cluster' (2003, 58).

8 See, for example, 1978, 1.50, 52, 71, 73, 83, 113, 152–3, 458, 2.42, 366.

9 On the imitation of Tasso in this episode, see Eisenberg (1984) and De
   Armas (2005).

10 Raymond Immerwahr was one the first critics to study what he calls the
   seven interpolated tales in Don Quixote, in an attempt to show how they
   mirror each other and also have a contrastive structure in terms of the
   obstacles to be surmounted to arrive at amorous happiness. For a recent
   variation on his theories, see David Quint (2003). I would argue that there
   are four types of interpolated stories, and their function depends upon
   their placement within the different segments of the novel as outlined in
   this essay. The first interpolation, that of Grisóstomo and Marcela, serves
   to separate the first from the second narrative segment of the novel. As

discussed above, it also highlights the importance of epic in the second segment. Four lengthy stories, those of Fernando and Dorotea, Cardenio and Lucinda, the captive and Zoraida, and Luis and Clara, are part of the third or 'Byzantine' segment of Cervantes' novel. There is one more story in this section, the Tale of Foolish Curiosity. It is not part of the plot but is read at the inn. The last segment of the novel, just like the second one, includes only one tale, that of Eugenio and Leandra. It does not have a conclusion, being an open ended story that contrasts with the very closed and 'cagey' conclusion of the novel.

11 For the interweaving of the tales of Giges in Herodotus and Cupid and Psyche in Apuleius in order to fashion *El curioso impertinente*, see De Armas (1992a). De Armas Wilson (1987) also foregrounds some of the key models of the novella: the *Orlando furioso*, the tale of Giges from Herodotus, and the tale of the two friends. See also the intriguing essay by Ife on Herodotus and Cervantes (2005).

12 I am referring to Fernando, Anselmo, and Lotario.

13 Perhaps Don Quixote does not fully understand what transpires around him. But the question of love and desire will resurface in part 2 when he decides to visit his lady love. And it is at that point that the tales resonate as he searches his imbalanced imagination for Dulcinea's elusive image.

14 'Composite monarchies were therefore subject to both centripetal and centrifugal forces. Which of these forces emerged the stronger depended on the circumstances. Modern historians, still under the anachronistic spell of the national monarchies concept, have not yet attempted to analyse this problem systematically' (Koenisberger 1994, 172).

8 Palinurus and the Pleiades

1 For a detailed analysis of Cervantes' utilization of Tasso's Armida in fashioning Micomicona, see De Armas (2005). See also Ruis Pérez (1995).

2 There are other models for the Micomicona story. Daniel Eisenberg, for example, tells of an adventure in Feliciano de Silva's *Amadís de Grecia*: 'En una de ellas Amadís mata al gigante Mascarón que ha usurpado el reino de la princesa Malfadea después de violarla y asesinar a sus padre (*AGrecia* I:39–40). Este episodio reune varios de los mismos motivos que el de Dorotea/Micomicona en el *Quijote* (I.29–30)' [In one of them Amadís kills the giant Mascarón who had usurped the kingdom of princess Malfadea after violating her and killing her parents (*AGrecia* I:39–40). This episode brings together several themes from the Dorotea/Micomicona adventure in the *Quixote* (I.29–30)] (2000, 61).

3 On Cervantes' captivity and his fashioning of this tale, see María Antonia Garcés's book (2002). Also, I had the good fortune to serve as reader and look forward to the publication of *Early Modern Dialogues with Islam: Antonio de Sosa's Topography of Algiers (1612)*, edited and translated by María Antonia Garcés and Diana de Armas Wilson.

4 In this assessment she echoes David Quint, whom she cites: 'His [Cervantes'] career reminds us of Spain's great crusade only a few decades in the past – though inasmuch as his story does not end with the great victory at Lepanto, but with the missed opportunity at Navarino, the disaster of the Goleta, and finally captivity in Algiers, it hints at the decline and exhaustion of the nation's military glory' (2003: 61).

5 For an allegorical interpretation of the Captive's Tale, see Camamis, who argues that Zoraida stands not only for the Virgin Mary but also for Christ, who will espouse and save humanity (as represented by the captive). According to Camamis, this interpretation is reinforced when it is agreed that the captive and Zoraida will meet in the garden in order to escape on a Friday, a day that recalls the passion of Christ (1977, 82–3).

6 While Sancho tells his master that the metamorphoses are false: 'a la reina convertida en una dama particular llamada Dorotea' [see the queen converted into a private lady called Dorothea] (1978, 1.37.457; 1998, 331), Don Quixote uses the term metamorphosis to refer to her magical transformation (1978, 1.37.459; 1998, 332).

7 Let us remember that gold coins were one of the clues to the mystery to be solved by Don Quixote and Sancho as they entered Sierra Morena.

8 Robert Stone, analysing the scene when Zoraida enters her first Christian church and sees a myriad of images of the Virgin, explains: 'Cervantes employs a similar device in his tale of the *Licenciado Vidriera*, another impressionable, intelligent and conspicuously fragmented character who visits the shrine of the Virgin of Loretto and seems overwhelmed by the abundance of tokens and *milagros* found there, just as Zoraida is before myriad images of the Mother of God' (2006, np, note 26).

9 Camamis takes it from Jaime Oliver Asín (1947–8).

10 He prefers, instead the association of Zoraida with Zaida 'con el motivo épico de frontera de la *paienne amoureuse* devuelve al relato cervantino a su verdadera dimensión, la de la fusión de datos históricos destinados a hacer verosímil la narración con una tradici'on literaria que hace posible catar el vino anejo vertido en el odre nuevo' [with the frontier epic motif of the amorous pagan, we return to the true dimension of the Cervantine narrative, the fusion of historical data in order to imbue with verisimilitude

a literary tradition, thus making it possible to taste the old wine in a new flask] (2006, 278).

11 Robert Hannah accepts this argument with a modification: 'At the same time, however, it undermines Phillips' case for a link between the constellations and all the agricultural activities on the Shield in the ensuing lines. Of those activities, only ploughing and harvesting would appear to be foreshadowed by the mention of the stars at Iliad 18. 485–89' (1994, np).

12 'The most obvious eighteenth-century novel informed by the principle of an inn was Fielding's *Joseph Andrews* (1742), which preceded Hogarth's print by four years but invoked earlier Hogarth prints in its preface; its ultimate model was *Don Quixote*, the novel *par excellence* where characters and actions converge in inns' (Paulson 1984, 200).

13 Even in the Bible some of these constellations are linked: Orion, the Bear, the Pleiades, and Arcturus can be gleaned from Job 9.9.

9 Don Quixote among the Saracens

1 Alison Weber, for example, complains: 'Although Don Quijote's niece is not precisely "outside the text," Johnson treats her as if she were . . . The location of the self in literature is elusive, and may lie fragmented in characters or scenes, or the interplay between them' (1985, 70, 71). Very much like Eisenberg, she admits that there is value in the book which has some positive qualities, since it 'has given us a sharper vision of the erotic themes of the novel' (1985, 72).

2 In the same issue of the journal, James Iffland praised his 'willingness to change direction and rethink his position' (2007, 6), moving from a psycho-analytic to a material approach.

3 It also appears in the Marxist treatise of Bruno Rizzi, *The Bureaucratization of the World* (1939). In chapter 58 of *Waverly*, entitled 'The Confusion of King Agramant's Camp,' Edward is first warned that the Mac-Yvors believe that he has affronted Flora Bradwardine. When he is shot at, and turns to his enemy's camp, all manner of confusion ensues: 'A hundred tongues were in motion at once. The Baron lectured, the Chieftain stormed, the Highlanders screamed in Gaelic, the horsemen cursed and swore in Lowland Scotch' (1906, 390). In the *Memoirs of the Duchess d'Abrantès* we read: 'It is well-known that there was a complete schism between the chiefs of the army of Egypt; it was the camp of Agramant. Napoleon's party was the most numerous' (1832, 187).

4 This shield was said to have belonged to Hector. It was disputed between Ruggiero and Mandricardo. Representing an eagle with white wings, it

was the insignia of the dukes of Ferrara, Ariosto's patrons. The shield need not appear in Cervantes' novel since its subject of praise is irrelevant for the narrative.

5 Frontino was previously named Frontalatte. This was the horse Brunelo stole from Sacripante and gave to Ruggiero.

6 On the Christian view of the Saracens through the Middle Ages, see John V. Tolan. He shows, for example, how in the ninth century 'Mozarab churchmen played a key role in forging a new royal ideology for the Asturian kings, anointed successors of the Goths of old, destined to drive the Saracen invader from Spain' (2002, 98).

7 Let us recall that the *Prophetic Chronicle* (883), the last section of the *Chronicle of Albeda,* describes how the Saracens themselves have seen in the stars their own defeat at the hands of Alfonso III (Fernández Conde 2000, 269; Tolan 2002, 99); and that thirteen years before the publication of Don Quixote, for example, Petro de la Cavalleria and Martino Alfonso Vivaldo composed their *Tractatus Zelus Christi contra Iudaeos Saracenos et Infideles* (1592).

8 Cervantes retells this story in the 1615 novel, presenting it in greater detail: 'viendo que no le podía llagar con fierro, le levantó del suelo entre los brazos, y le ahogó, acordándose entonces de la muerte que dio Hércules a Anteón, aquel feroz gigante que decían ser hijo de la tierra' [perceiving he could not wound him with steel, he hoisted him from the ground between his arms, and squeezed him to death, recollecting the manner in which Hercules slew Antaeus, that fierce giant, who was said to be a son of the Earth] (1978, 2.32.292; 1998, 682).

9 The only mitigating circumstance might be that the term Saracen was at times used in a more general manner to refer to someone who came from elsewhere (Morrissey 2003, 87).

10 Since the many coloured mice that appear on stage come from one initial family, 'Cervantes se complace aqué en subrayar que los judíos, así como los cristianos descienden todos, al fin y al cabo, de Adán y Eva. ¿Cómo imaginar entonces que una sangre diferente pueda correr en sus venas?' [Cervantes enjoys underlining that all Jews as well as Christians descend, after all, from Adam and Eve. How can you imagine, then, that a different blood courses through their veins?] (Moner 1981, 812).

11 Redondo points to the expression 'tirar la barra' and explains that 'puede tomar el significado de *future* . . . Aldonza se transforma de tal modo en mujer fálica' [it can reflect the meaning of *future* . . . Aldonza is transformed in this way into a phallic woman] (1998, 245).

12 There are exceptions to Cervantes' tolerance, particularly one in the 1615 novel. As Judith Whitenack explains: 'Many modern readers have noted

with dismay, the *morisco* Ricote defends the recent expulsion of his people, forcibly converted generations before, even though he also cites the presence of a few sincere Christians among them' (1993, 70).

13 Graf also points to the fictional story created by Dorotea: 'When Don Quijote castrates the giant threatening Micomicón . . . he figuratively castrates Spanish designs on Africa' (2007, 83).

14 This is a much debated question, which goes back to Americo Castro's *Cervantes y los casticismos españoles* (1966). In recent years, we need think only of Rosa Rossi's book which argues that Cervantes' homosexual and *converso* origins are the causes of his dissidence.

15 Smith shows how Catullus, in *Satire* 12, acts like the beaver that will bite off his genitals (he will give up his treasures in a storm at sea). Thus he is praised for his generosity. But Smith points out that he is a shrewd businessman and 'if the stakes had been less desperate he would not have made the sacrifice' (1989, 292).

10 *Thymos* and the Chariot

1 He will sally forth again in the 1615 novel. But the impulse now is a new one. He is not beset by anxieties of blood purity. In the first part he had disguised it through his pursuit of fame. Now that the first part of his adventures has been made public, he truly seeks to continue this path to fame. He is a less active participant in part 2 not only because others use his image for entertainment, but because his anxieties have died down. He is more quiescent, ready to accept the world (on his own terms).

2 In quoting Fukuyama, I am quite aware that his theories clash with those of his mentor Samuel Huntington, whose book, *The Clash of Civilizations*, helped to shape the title of this volume. In the Afterword to the second paperback edition, Fukuyama explains: 'But there is a fundamental issue that separates us. It is the question of whether the values and institutions developed during the Western Enlightenment are *potentially* universal (as Hegel and Marx thought), or bounded within a cultural horizon (consistent with the views of later philosophers like Nietzsche and Heidegger). Huntington clearly believes that they are not universal. He argues that the kind of political institutions with which we in the West are familiar are the by-product of a certain kind of Western European Christian culture, and will never take root beyond the boundaries of that culture' (2006, 342). I use both Huntington and Fukuyama so that the clash of ideas can bring out new ways of looking at Cervantes' novel. It can also allow us to look at the contemporary world through the lenses of *Don Quixote*.

3 Plato's *Timaeus*, a work deeply influenced by Pythagorean numerology, posits the quintessence, a fifth element out of which the celestial bodies are made.

4 'After about the middle of the seventeenth century, an ever-increasing number of heterodox philosophers who had suffered from persecution published their books not only to communicate their thoughts but also because they desired to contribute to the abolition of persecution as such' (Strauss 1988, 33). Perhaps Cervantes' comic novel can be seen as a precursor to these philosophers who hid their truths less and less, waiting for an age of light. Indeed, *Don Quixote* may even partake of some of the 'dangers' of the classical Socratic dialogues.

5 Each planetary deity often has two or more possible animals to pull their chariot. Luna [Moon] is said to have a dark and a white horse ('quando parece de día denota el cavallo blanco, y quando de noche, el negro'; Pérez de Moya 1996, 638). Others claim that the chariot was led by a mule, while others yet visualize it with two deer (Pérez de Moya 1996, 638). Pérez de Moya lists two horses for Mars, called 'Terror y Pavor' (1996, 549). In many images and paintings he rides a chariot lead by a horse or two horses and is accompanied by a wolf. At times, two wolves lead the chariot (Seznec 1972, 190–2). Many of these images, according to Seznec, are derived from Albricus, an English twelfth-century mythographer.

6 This was the money changer's guild. As Roettgen states: 'The chief responsibility of the *Arte del Cambio* was to guarantee the value of the coinage in circulation' (1997, 254). The *Sala di Udienzia* exhibits paintings of the Virtues as well as Greek and Roman men who exhibited these qualities. There are also Old Testament prophets and classical sibyls. But, there is also a planetary cycle in the vault which many think is unrelated to the main paintings. Each of the gods 'stands or sits enthroned on a car drawn by his or her attendant animals. The wheels of the cars are ornamented with the appropriate constellations' (Roettgen 1997, 260). Saturn has dragons, Jupiter is led by eagles, Mars has two horses, Venus two doves, Mercury two sparrows, and Luna two nymphs. See also Becherer (1997, 283 and 238).

7 Marsilio Ficino, who grappled with the predominant position of Saturn in his chart, ended up by stressing that the planet was bipolar: 'Saturn cannot easily signify the common quality and lot of the human race, but he signifies an individual set apart from others, divine or brutish, blessed or bowed down with the extreme of misery' (1989, 251). This opposition also approximates the portrait of Don Quixote.

8 Describing the agonic and even criminal artist, Rudolf and Margot Witt-kower assert: 'It is clear that the division between a man and his work negates the prevailing Neoplatonic concept according to which a great artist cannot be a bad man' (1969, 181).

9 For the sermon of Martín García, bishop of Barcelona, see Vernet (1974, 23). For a discussion of the impact of Albumasar in Spain up to the times of Lope de Vega, see De Armas (1992a).

10 The mock-prophecy that leads Don Quixote to accept his enchantment is carefully described, along with its implications, by Fajardo (1986, 239ff). He contrasts the name given to the knight 'león manchado' ['Tainted lion' or 'lion of La Mancha'] (1978, 1.46.555; 1998, 432) to the epithet used to refer to the king of Spain in prophecies: 'león coronado' [crowned lion]. It would be interesting to connect the prophecies of 1603–5 with the mock-prophecy given to Don Quixote.

11 Roger Bacon also attributes the birth of Christianity to the conjunction of Saturn and Jupiter. He uses Abu Ma'Sar's theory of conjunctions for his proof (Sidelko 1996, 74). Bacon's belief was condemned. Others who also proclaimed it, such as Peter of Albano and Cecco d'Ascoli, were also condemned by the church (Sidelko 1996, 79).

12 William of Auvergne, bishop of Paris, for example, rejected that religions were born from astrological conjunctions and gave as false examples the following: 'Judaism is with Saturn, Islam with Venus, and Christianity with the Sun' (Sidelko 1996, 79).

13 I prefer my own translation here to that of Jarvis who renders these lines as 'weak and pale' (1998, 456).

14 Abu Ma'Sar explains that Saturn's nature is not only cold and dry (like that of the melancholy person), but also 'fuscus et niger' (Klibansky et al. 1964, 128).

15 It is interesting that many moriscos still spoke Arabic since one of Philip II's goals was to have all speak only Castilian. As Cardaillac has shown, there was much resistance since the moriscos wanted to preserve their tongue (2001, 173).

16 Such an ending leaves open the question: Is the novel complicit with imperial expansionism? I would only say that it searches for new narrative landscapes, for new genres, but that it shows that, like the knight, the empire is ill, that it may not recover.

Works Cited

Abdel-Karim, Gamal. 2006. 'La evidencia islámica en la obra de Cervantes: análisis y valoración.' In *De Cervantes y el Islam*, ed. Nuria Martínez de Castilla Muñoz and Rodolfo Gil Benumeya Grimau. 41–57. Madrid: Sociedad Estatal de Conmemoraciones Culturales.

Abrantès, Laure Junot (Duchess d'). 1832. *Memoirs of the Duchess d'Abrantès*. New York: J. & J. Harper.

Abu Ma'Sar. 2000. *On Historical Astrology: The Book of Religions and Dynasties (On the Great Conjunctions)*. Ed and trans. Keiji Yamamoto and Charles Burnett. 2 vols. Leiden: Brill.

Agrippa, Cornelius. 1987. *Three Books of Occult Philosophy*. London: Chthonios Books.

Albertus Magnus. 1973. *The Book of Secrets of Albertus Magnus of the Virtues of Herbs, Stones and Certain Beasts*. Ed. Michael R. Best and Frank H. Brightman. Oxford: Oxford University Press.

Allen, Richard Hinkley. [1899] 1963. *Star Names: Their Lore and Meaning*. New York: Dover Publications.

Alter, Robert. 1968. *Fielding and the Nature of the Novel*. Cambridge, MA: Harvard University Press.

Anderson, Jaynie. 1979. *Le roy ne meurt jamais: Charles V Obsequies in Italy*. Madrid: Real Colegio de España.

Arenas Cruz, María Elena. 2005. 'Imaginarios campos de batalla en las obras de Rojas Zorrilla.' In *Espacio, tiempo y género en la comedia española*, ed. Felipe B. Pedraza Jiménez, Rafael González Cañal, and Gemma Gómez Rubio. 247–64. Cuenca: Universidad Castilla-La Mancha.

Ariosto, Ludovico. 1983. *Orlando furioso*. Trans. Guido Waldman. Oxford: Oxford University Press.

Aristophanes. 2007. *The Frogs and Other Plays.* Ed. Shomit Dutta. Trans. David Barrett. New York and London: Penguin.

Armeno, Christoforo. 2000. *Peregrinaggio di tre giovani figliuoli del Re di Serendippo.* Ed. Renzo Bragantini. Rome: Salerno.

Armstrong-Roche, Michael. 2009. *Cervantes' Epic Novel: Empire, Religion and the Dream Life of Heroes in Persiles.* Toronto: University of Toronto Press.

Ascunce Arrieta, José Angel. 1997. *Los quijotes del Quijote.* Kassel: Edition Reichenberger.

Asín, Jaime Oliver. 1948. 'La hija de Agi Morato en la obra de Cervantes.' *Boletín de la Real Academia Española* 27:245–339.

Aubier, Dominique. 1966. *Don Quichotte, prophète d'Israël.* Paris: R. Laffont.

Auerbach, Erich. 1968. *Mimesis: The Representation of Reality in Western Literature.* Trans. Williard R. Trask. Princeton: Princeton University Press.

Austin, Norman. 1994. *Helen of Troy and Her Shameless Phantom.* Ithaca: Cornell University Press.

Avalle-Arce, Juan Bautista. 1975. *Nuevos deslindes cervantinos.* Barcelona: Ariel.

Bakhtin, Mikhail. 1984. *Rabelais and His World.* Trans. Helene Iswolsky. Bloomington: Indiana University Press.

Barnés Vázquez, Antonio. 2009. *'Yo he leído en Virgilio': La tradición clásica en el Quijote.* Vigo: Editorial Academia del Hispanismo.

Bassets, Lluís. 2010. 'El Cid se lanza contra los sarracenos.' *El País,* Domingo 5 de septiembre: 13.

Becherer, Joseph Antenucci. 1997. *Pietro Peruggino: Master of the Italian Renaissance.* Grand Rapids, MI: Grand Rapids Art Museum.

Berndt-Kelley, Erna. 1989. 'En torno a la maravillosa visión de la pastora Marcela y otra ficción poética.' In *Actas del IX Congreso de la Asociación Internacional de Hispanistas,* ed. Sebastián Neumeister. 1:267–71. Frankfurt: Vervuert Verlag.

Bjornson, Richard. 1977. *The Picaresque Hero in European Fiction.* Madison: University of Wisconsin Press.

Bloom, Harold. 1994. *The Western Canon: The Books and School of the Ages.* New York: Riverhead Books.

Boccaccio, Giovanni. 1983. *Genealogía de los dioses paganos.* Ed. María Consuelo Álvarez and Rosa María Iglesias. Madrid: Editora Nacional.

Bollard, Kathleen. 2003. 'Re-Reading Heroism in *El Abencerraje.*' *Bulletin of Spanish Studies* 80.3:297–307.

Botello, Jesús. 2009. 'Don Quijote, Felipe II y la tecnología de la escritura.' *Cervantes* 29.1:197–207.

Braudel, Fernand. 1994. *A History of Civilizations.* Trans. Richard Mayne. New York: Penguin Books.

Brooks, Cleanth. 1975. *The Well Wrought Urn: Studies in the Structure of Poetry.* New York: Harcourt, Brace and Co.

Browne, Thomas. 1658. *Pseudodoxia epidemica.* 3rd ed. London: Gun in Pauls Church-Yard.

Brownlee, Marina. 1990. *The Severed Word: Ovid's Heroides and the Novela Sentimental.* Princeton: Princeton University Press.

– 2005. 'Zoraida's White Hand and Cervantes' Rewriting of History.' *Bulletin of Hispanic Studies* 82.5:569–85.

Budner, Keith. 2010. 'Forging Modernity: Vulcan and the Iron Age in Cervantes, Ovid and Vico.' In *Ovid in the Age of Cervantes*, ed. Frederick A. de Armas. 97–115. Toronto: University of Toronto Press.

Bulatkin, Eleanor Webster. 1972. *Structural Arithmetic Metaphor in the Oxford 'Roland.'* Columbus: Ohio State University Press.

Burke, James F. 1974. 'The *Estrella de Sevilla* and the Tradition of Saturnine Melancholy.' *Bulletin of Hispanic Studies* 51.2:137–56.

Burningham, Bruce R. 2008. *Tilting Cervantes: Baroque Reflections on Postmodern Culture.* Nashville, TN: Vanderbilt University Press.

Burshatin, Israel. 1984. 'Power, Discourse, and Metaphor in the *Abencerraje.*' *MLN* 99:139–213.

Burton, Joan B. 2004. A *Byzantine Novel: Drozilla and Charikles by Niketa Eugenianos (12th century).* Wauconda, IL: Bolckazy-Carducci.

Burton, Robert. 1938. *The Anatomy of Melancholy.* Ed. Floyd Dell and Paul Jordan-Smith. New York: Tudor.

Calderón de la Barca, Pedro. 1969. 'Amar después de la muerte o el Tuzaní de la Alpujarra.' In *Obras completas de Don Pedro Calderón de la Barca.* Ed. A. Valbuena Briones. 349–86. Madrid: Aguilar.

Calvino, Italo. 1988. *Six Memos for the Next Millenium.* Cambridge, MA: Harvard University Press.

Camamis, George. 1977. 'El hondo simbolismo de "la hija de Agi morato."' *Cuadernos Hispanoamericanos* 319:71–102.

– 1991. *Beneath the Cloak of Cervantes: The Satanic Prose of Don Quixote de la Mancha.* New York: Senda Nueva de Ediciones.

Campanella, Tommaso. 1982. *La monarquía hispánica.* Ed. P. Mariño. Madrid: Centro de Estudios Constitucionales.

Campos Moreno, Araceli. 2001. 'El ritmo de las oraciones, ensalmos y conjuros mágicos novohispanos.' *Revista de literaturas populares* 1.1:69–93.

Canavaggio, Jean. 1990. *Cervantes.* Trans. J.R. Jones. New York: W.W. Norton.

Cardaillac, Louis. 2001. 'Felipe II y los moriscos.' In *Mélanges Luce López-Baralt*, ed. Abdeljelil Temimi. 1:169–81. Zaghouan: Fondation Temimi.

Caro Baroja, Julio. 1967. *Vidas mágicas e inquisición.* 2 vols. Madrid: Taurus.

Carrasco Urgoiti, Soledad. 2006. 'Presencia de la mujer morisca en la narrative cervantina.' In *De Cervantes y el Islam*, ed. Nuria Martínez de Castilla Muñoz and Rodolfo Gil Benumeya Grimau. 117–33. Madrid: Sociedad Estatal de Conmemoraciones Culturales.

Cascardi, Anthony J. 1997. *Ideologies of History in the Spanish Golden Age*. University Park: Pennsylvania State University Press.

– 2002. '*Don Quixote* and the Invention of the Novel.' In *The Cambridge Companion to Cervantes*, ed. Anthony J. Cascardi. 58–79. Cambridge: Cambridge University Press.

Case, Thomas E. 2002. 'Cide Hamete Benengeli y los libros plúmbeos.' *Cervantes* 22.2:9–24.

Castro, Américo. 1966. *Cervantes y los casticismos españoles*. Madrid: Alfaguara.

Celenza, Christopher S. 1999. 'Pythagoras in the Renaissance: The Case of Marsilio Ficino.' *Renaissance Quarterly* 52:667–711.

Cervantes, Miguel de. 1998. *Don Quixote de la Mancha*. Ed. E.C. Riley. Trans. Charles Jarvis. Oxford: Oxford University Press.

– 1833. *El ingenioso hidalgo don Quijote de la Mancha*. Ed. Diego Clemencín. Madrid: Aguado.

– 1978. *El ingenioso hidalgo don Quijote de la Mancha*. Ed. Luis Andrés Murillo. 2 vols. Madrid: Castalia.

– 1982. *Entremeses*. Ed. Nicholas Spadaccini. Madrid: Cátedra.

– 1995. *La Galatea*. Ed. Francisco López Estrada and María Teresa López García Bedoy. Madrid: Cátedra.

– 1999. *Don Quijote de la Mancha*. Ed. Francisco Rico. 3rd ed. 2 vols. Barcelona: Instituto Cervantes.

Chambers, Ross. 1999. *Loiterature*. Lincoln: University of Nebraska Press.

Champlin, Edward. 2003. *Nero*. Cambridge, MA, and London: The Belknap Press of Harvard University Press.

Cheney, Patrick. 2002. ' "Novells of his devise": Chaucerian and Virgilian Career Paths in Spenser's *Februarie* Eclogue.' In *European Literary Careers: The Author from Antiquity to the Renaissance*, ed. Patrick Cheney and Frederick A. de Armas. 231–67. Toronto: University of Toronto Press.

Childers, William. 2006. *Transnational Cervantes*. Toronto: University of Toronto Press.

Cirot, G. 1938. 'La maurophilie littéraire en Espagne.' *Bulletin Hispanique* 40:280–96; 433–47.

Ciruelo, Pedro. 1978. *Reprouacion de las supersticiones y hechizerias*. Ed. Alva V. Ebersole. Valencia: Albatros-Hispanófila.

Close, Anthony. 2007. 'The Liberation of the Galley Slaves and the Ethos of *Don Quijote*'s Part I.' *Cervantes* 27.1:11–30.

Cohen, Ralph. 2003. Introduction. *New Literary History* 34.2:v–xv.

Conti, Natale. 1988. *Mitología*. Ed. and trans. Rosa María Iglesias Montiel and María Consuelo Álvarez Morán. Murcia: Universidad de Murcia.

Coolidge, J.S. 1965. 'Great Things and Small: The Virgilian Progression.' *Comparative Literature* 17:1–23.

Corral, Eloy Martín. 2002. *La imagen del magreb en España: Una perspectiva histórica siglos XVI–XX*. Barcelona: Ediciones Bellaterra.

Covarrubias, Sebastián de. 1987. *Tesoro de la lengua Castellana o Española*. Ed. Martín de Riquer. Barcelona: Alta Fulla.

Cravens, Sydney. 1978. 'Feliciano de Silva and His Romances of Chivalry in *Don Quijote*.' *Inti: Revista de literatura hispánica* 7:28–34.

Cruz, Anne J. 1999. *Discourses of Poverty: Social Reform and the Picaresque Novel in Early Modern Spain*. Toronto: University of Toronto Press.

– 2007. 'Remembering Carroll Johnson.' *Cervantes* 27.1:7–10.

Cuadra, Pino Valera, ed. 2000. *La leyenda de la doncella Carcayona*. Alicante: Universidad de Alicante.

Curtius, Ernst R. 1953. *European Literature and the Latin Middle Ages*. Trans. Willard R. Trask. New York: Harper & Row.

Damiani, Bruno, and Barbara Mujica. 1990. *Et in Arcadia Ego: Essays on Death in the Pastoral Novel*. Lanham, NY, and London: University Press of America.

Dasí, Emilio José Sales. 2000. 'Ecos celestinescos en el Lisuarte de Grecia de Feliciano de Silva.' *Tirant* 3: http://parnaseo.uv.es/tirant.

De Armas, Frederick A. 1992a. 'Interpolation and Invisibility: From Herodotus to Cervantes' *Don Quixote*.' *Journal of the Fantastic in the Arts* 4:8–28.

– 1992b. 'Saturn in Conjunction: From Albumasar to Lope de Vega.' In *Saturn from Antiquity to the Renaissance*, ed. Massimo Ciavolella and Amilcare A. Iannucci. 151–72. University of Toronto Italian Studies 8. Ottawa: Dovehouse.

– 2001. 'Painting Dulcinea: Italian Art and the Art of Memory in Don Quijote.' *Yearbook for Comparative and General Literature* 49:3–19.

– 2002. 'Cervantes and the Virgilian Wheel: The Portrayal of a Literary Career.' In *European Literary Careers: The Author from Antiquity to the Renaissance*, ed. Patrick Cheney and Frederick A. de Armas. 268–85. Toronto: University of Toronto Press.

– 2005. 'La magia de Micomicona: Geopolítica y cautiverio en Heliodoro, Tasso y Cervantes.' *Voz y Letra* 16:23–34.

– 2006. *Quixotic Frescoes: Cervantes and Italian Renaissance Art*. Toronto: University of Toronto Press.

– ed. 2010. *Ovid in the Age of Cervantes*. Toronto: University of Toronto Press.

– (in press). 'La fragua de Vulcano: Ansiedades talismánicas y extravíos ec-frásticos en *Don Quijote* I.12.' In *Cervantes y su mundo VII*, ed. C. Hsu. Kassel: Editio Reichenberger.

De Armas Wilson, Diana. 1987. 'Passing the Love of Women: The Intertextuality of *El curioso impertinente*.' *Cervantes* 7:9–28.

– 1994. 'Homage to Apuleius: Cervantes' Avenging Psyche.' In *The Search for the Ancient Novel*, ed. James Tatum. 88–100. Baltimore: Johns Hopkins University Press.

De la Cavalleria, Petro, and Martin Alfonso Vivaldo. 1592. *Tractatus Zelus Christi contra Iudaeos Saracenos et Infideles*. Venice: Baretium de Baretiis.

Dentith, Simon. 2000. *Parody*. London and New York: Routledge.

Derrida, Jacques. 1980. 'The Law of Genre.' *Critical Inquiry* 7.1:55–81.

– 1994. *Specters of Marx: The State of the Debt, the Work of Mourning, and the New International*. Trans. Peggy Kamuf. Intro. Bernd Magnus and Stephen Cullenberg. New York and London: Routledge.

Díaz de Benjumea. Nicolás. [1878] 1986. *La verdad sobre el Quijote*. Madrid: Gaspar; Barcelona: Ediciones Ronda.

Díez Fernández, José-Ignacio, and Luisa Fernández Aguirre de Carcer. 1992. 'Contexto histórico y tratamiento literario de la hechicería morisca y judía en el *Persiles*.' *Cervantes* 12.2:33–63.

Donato, Clorinda. 1986. 'The Rhetorical Tapestry: A Model for Perspective Reality in *Orlando Furioso* and *Don Quijote*.' *Comitatus: A Journal of Medieval and Renaissance Studies* 17.1:12–21.

Doody, Margaret Anne. 1996. *The True Story of the Novel*. West Lafayette, IN: Purdue University Press.

Doyle, Arthur Conan. 1953. *The Complete Sherlock Holmes*. Garden City, NY: Doubleday.

Dudley, Edward. 1972. 'Don Quixote as Magus: The Rhetoric of Interpolation.' *Bulletin of Hispanic Studies* 49:355–68.

Durán, Manuel. 1995. 'From Fool's Gold to Real Gold: Don Quixote and the Golden Helmet.' In *Studies in Honor of Donald W. Bleznick*, ed. D.V. Galván, Anita K. Stoll, and P. Brown Yin. 17–31. Newark, DE: Juan de la Cuesta.

Eire, Carlos M.N. 1995. *From Madrid to Purgatory: The Art and Craft of Dying in Sixteenth-Century Spain*. Cambridge: Cambridge University Press.

Eisenberg, Daniel. 1983. 'Review of Carroll B. Johnson's *Madness and Lust: A Psychoanalytic Approach to Don Quijote*.' *Journal of Hispanic Philology* 7:155–7.

– 1984. 'Cervantes and Tasso Reexamined.' *Kentucky Romance Quarterly* 31:305–17.

– 2000. 'Amadís de Gaula reivindicado por Feliciano de Silva.' *Nueva Revista de Filología Hispánica* 48.1:51–69.

Eisenberg, Daniel and Thomas Lathrop. 2009. 'Debate Eisenberg-Lathrop: Los "errores" en Don Quijote.' In *USA Cervantes: 39 Cervantistas en Estados Unidos,* ed. Gorgina Dopico Black and Francisco Layna Ranz. 1193–1220. Madrid: CSIC and Polifemo.

Elliott, J.H. 2009. *Spain, Europe and the Wider World 1500–1800.* New Haven and London: Yale University Press.

El Saffar, Ruth. 1984. *Beyond Fiction: The Recovery of the Feminine in the Novels of Cervantes.* Berkeley, Los Angeles, and London: University of California Press.

Empson, William. [1974] 1935. *Some Versions of Pastoral.* New York: New Directions.

Espinora, Nicolás. 1556. *La segunda parte de Orlando.* Madrid: Nucio.

Fajardo, Salvador J. 1984. 'The Sierra Morena as Labyrinth in *Don Quixote* I.' *MLN* 99.2:214–34.

– 1986. 'The Enchanted Return: On the Conclusion of *Don Quijote* I.' *Journal of Modern and Renaissance Studies* 16:233–51.

– 2002. Review of José Ángel Ascunce Arrieta's *Los quijotes del Quijote.' Cervantes* 22.2:547–9.

Farrel, Joseph. 2003. 'Classical Genre in Theory and Practice.' *New Literary History* 34.3:383–408.

Fernández, Jerónimo. 1997. *Hystoria del magnanimo, valiente e invencible cavallero don Belianís de Grecia.* Ed. Lilia E.F. de Orduna. 2 vols. Kassel: Edition Reichenberger.

Fernández Alvarez, Manuel. 1975. *Charles V: Elected Emperor and Hereditary Ruler.* London: Thames and Hudson.

Fernández Conde, Francisco Javier. 2000. *La religiosidad medieval en España.* Vol. 1, *Alta edad media (s. vii–x).* Oviedo: Universidad de Oviedo.

Fernández Mosquera, Santiago. 2000. 'Sobre la funcionalidad del relato ticoscópico en Calderón.' In *Ayer y hoy de Calderón,* ed. José María Ruano de la Haza and J. Pérez Magallón. 259–75. Madrid: Castalia.

Ficino, Marsilio. 1989. *Three Books of Life.* Ed. Carol V. Kaske and John R. Clark. Binghamton, NY: Medieval and Renaissance Texts and Studies.

Finello, Dominick. 1994. *Pastoral Themes and Forms in Cervantes's Fiction.* Lewisburg, PA: Bucknell University Press.

– 1998. *Cervantes: Essays on Social and Literary Polemics.* London: Tamesis.

Foucault, Michel. 1970. *The Order of Things: Archeology of the Human Sciences.* New York: Random House.

Fowler, Alastair. 2003. 'The Formation of Genres in the Renaissance and After.' *New Literary History* 34.2:185–200.

Franklin, H. Bruce. 1961. ' "Apparent Symbol and Despotic Command": Melville's *Benito Cereno.' The New England Quarterly* 34.4:462–77.

Freud, Sigmund. 1959. *Inhibitions, Symptoms and Anxiety.* Ed. James Strachey. Trans. Aliz Strachey. New York and London: W.W. Norton.

Fuchs, Barbara. 2001. *Mimesis and Empire: The New World, Islam and European Identities.* Cambridge: Cambridge University Press.

– 2009. *Exotic Nation: Maurophilia and the Construction of Early Modern Spain.* Philadelphia: University of Pennsylvania Press.

Fukuyama, Francis. 2006. *The End of History and the Last Man.* New York: Free Press.

Garcés, María Antonia. 2002. *Cervantes in Algiers: A Captive's Tale.* Nashville, TN: Vanderbilt University Press.

– 2009. ' "Grande amigo mío": Cervantes y los renegados.' In *USA Cervantes: 39 Cervantistas en Estados Unidos,* ed. Georgina Dopico Black and Francisco Layna Ranz. 545–82. Madrid: CSIC and Polifemo.

Garcés, María Antonia, and Diana de Armas Wilson, eds. *Early Modern Dialogues with Islam: Antonio de Sosa's Topography of Algiers (1612).* Manuscript.

García, Martha. 2005. 'Zoraida en el cuento del Cautivo: Un caso de Otredad.' *Anuario de Estudios Cervantinos* 2:77–88.

Garrett, Erin Webster. 2000. 'Recycling Zoraida: The Muslim Heroine in Mary Shelley's *Frankenstein.' Cervantes* 20.1:133–56.

Gerli, E. Michael. 1995. *Refiguring Authority: Reading, Writing and Rewriting in Cervantes.* Lexington: University of Kentucky Press.

Giles, Ryan D. 2009. ' "Del día que fue conde": The Parodic Remaking of the Count of Barcelona in the *Poema de mio Cid.' La corónica* 38.1:121–38.

Ginzburg, Carlo. 1989. *Clues, Myths, and the Historical Method.* Trans. John and Anne C. Tedeschi. Baltimore, MD.: Johns Hopkins University Press.

González Echevarría, Roberto. 2005. *Love and the Law in Cervantes.* New Haven, CT, and London: Yale University Press.

González Martínez, Javier J. 2005. 'Ticoscopia, espacio y tiempo de los torneos caballerescoes en Luis Vélez.' In *Espacio, tiempo y género en la comedia española,* ed. Felipe B. Pedraza Jiménez, Rafael González Cañal, and Gemma Gómez Rubio. 73–92. Cuenca: Universidad Castilla-La Mancha.

Gorlée, Dinda L. 1988. 'Signs of Magic in Don Quixote de la Mancha.' *Neophilologus* 72.1:56–65.

Gossy, Mary. 1995. 'Aldonza as Butch: Narrative and the Play of Gender in Don Quixote.' In *¿Entiendes? Queer Readings, Hispanic Writings,* ed. Emilie Bergmann and Paul Julian Smith. 17–28. Durham, NC: Duke University Press.

Graf, Eric. 2004. 'Martin and the Ghosts of the Papacy: *Don Quijote* 1.19 between Sulpicius Severus and Thomas Hobbes.' *MLN* 119.5:949–78.

– 2007. *Cervantes and Modernity: Four Essays on Don Quixote.* Lewisburg, PA: Bucknell University Press.

Grafton, Anthony. 1999. *Cardano's Cosmos: The Worlds and Works of a Renais-sance Astrologer.* Cambridge, MA: Harvard University Press.

Granjel, Luis S. 1953. *Aspectos médicos de la literatura antisupersticiosa española de los siglos XVI y XVII.* Salamanca: Universidad de Salamanca.

Greene, Thomas M. 1982. *The Light in Troy: Imitation and Discovery in Renais-sance Poetry.* New Haven, CT: Yale University Press.

Greenblatt, Stephen. 1986. 'Psychoanalysis and Renaissance Culture.' In *Liter-ary Theory/Renaissance Texts,* ed. Patricia Parker and David Quint. 210–23. Baltimore and London: Johns Hopkins University Press.

Griffith, R.H. 1910. 'The Magic Balm of Gerbert and Fierabras, and a Query.' *MLN* 25.4:102–4.

Hagerty, Miguel José. 1980. *Los libros plúmbeos del Sacromonte.* Madrid: Nacional.

Hahn, Juergen. 1972. '*El curioso impertinente* and Don Quijote's Symbolic Struggle against Curiositas.' *Bulletin of Hispanic Studies* 49:128–40.

Hannah, Robert. 1994. 'The Constellations on Achilles' Shield (*Iliad* 18: 485–89).' *Electronic Antiquities* 2.4: http://scholar.lib.vt.edu/ejournals/ElAnt/V2N4/hannah.html

Harris, A.K. 2007. *From Muslim to Christian Granada: Inventing a City's Past in Early Modern Spain.* Baltimore, MD: John Hopkins University Press.

Hart, Thomas R. 1989. *Cervantes and Ariosto: Renewing Fiction.* Princeton, NJ: Princeton University Press.

Hasbrouck, Michael D. 1992. 'Posesión demoníaca, locura y exorcismo en el *Quijote.*' *Cervantes* 12.2:117–22.

Hattaway, Michael. [1982] 2005. *Elizabethan Popular Theatre: Plays in Perfor-mance.* London: Routledge.

Heiple, Daniel L. 1979. 'Renaissance Medical Psychology in *Don Qiujote.*' *Ide-ologies and Literature* 2:65–72.

– 1991. 'Protofeminist Reactions to Huarte's Mysogyny in Lope de Vega's *La prueba de los ingenios* and María de Zayas's *Novelas amorosas y ejemplares.*' In *The Perception of Women in Spanish Theater of the Golden Age,* ed. Anita K. Stoll and Dawn L. Smith. 121–34. Lewisburg, PA: Bucknell University Press.

Helgerson, Richard. 1983. *Self-Crowned Laureates: Spenser, Jonson, Milton and the Literary System.* Berkeley and Los Angeles: University of California Press.

Heninger, S.K. 1974. *Touches of Sweet Harmony: Pythagorean Cosmology and Re-naissance Poetics.* San Marino, CA: The Huntington Library.

Herrero, J. 1981. 'Sierra Morena as Labyrinth: From Wildness to Christian Knighthood' *Forum for Modern Language Studies* 17.1:55–67.

Herrero García, Miguel. [1927] 1966. *Idea de los espanoles del siglo XVII.* Madrid: Gredos.

Hesiod. 2004. *Theogony, Works and Days, Shield.* Trans. Apostolos N. Athanassakis. Baltimore, MD: Johns Hopkins University Press.

Higuera, Henry. 1995. *Eros and Empire: Politics and Christianity in* Don Quixote.
·London: Rowman and Littlefield.

Holdrege, Barbara A. 1996. *Veda and Torah: Transcending the Textuality of Scrip-
ture.* Albany: State University of New York Press.

Homer. *The Iliad.* 1898. Trans. A.T. Murray. 2 vols. Cambridge, MA: Harvard
University Press.

Hornblower, Simon, and Antony Spawforth. 1998. *The Oxford Companion to
Classical Civilization.* Oxford: Oxford University Press.

Huntington, Samuel P. 1996. *The Clash of Civilizations and the Remaking of World
Order.* New York: Simon and Schuster.

Hutcheon, Linda. 1985. *A Theory of Parody: The Teachings of Twentieth-Century
Art Forms.* London: Methuen.

Ife, B.W. 1985. *Reading and Fiction in Golden Age Spain: A Platonist Critique and
Some Picaresque Replies.* Cambridge: Cambridge University Press.

– 2005. 'Cervantes, Herodotus and the Eternal Triangle: Another Look at the
Sources of *El curioso impertinente.*' *Bulletin of Hispanic Studies* 82.5:671–81.

Iffland, James. 2007. Preface. *Cervantes* 27.1:5–6.

Immerwahr, R. 1958. 'Structural Symmetry in the Episodic Narratives of *Don
Quijote,* Part I.' *Comparative Literature* 10:121–35.

Iriarte, Mauricio de. 1948. *El doctor Huarte de San Juan y su 'Examen de ingenios':
Contribución a la historia de la Psicología Diferencial.* Madrid: Consejo Superior
de Investigaciones Científicas.

Iventosch, Hermann. 1963. 'Dulcinea, nombre pastoral.' *Nueva Revista de
Filología Hispánica* 17:60–81.

– 1974. 'Cervantes and Courtly Love: The Grisóstomo-Marcela Episode of Don
Quixote.' *PMLA* 89:64–76.

Jaksic, Iván. 1994. 'Don Quijote's Encounter with Technology.' *Cervantes*
14:75–96.

Jardine, Lisa. 1996. *Worldly Goods: A New History of the Renaissance.* New York:
Macmillan.

Johnson, Carroll B. 1982. 'Organic Unity in Unlikely Places: *Don Quijote* I,
39–41,' *Cervantes* 2.2:133–54.

– 1983. *Madness and Lust: A Psychoanalytical Approach to Don Quixote.* Berkeley
and Los Angeles: University of California Press.

– 2000. *Cervantes and the Material World.* Urbana: University of Illinois Press.

– 2004. 'Dressing Don Quijote: Of Quixotes and Quixotes.' *Cervantes*
24.1:11–21.

Johnson, W.R. 1984. 'Virgil's Bees: The Ancient Romans' View of Rome.' In *Roman Images*, ed. Annabel Patterson. 1–22. Baltimore, MD: Johns Hopkins University Press.

Juárez-Almendros, E. 2004. 'Travestismo, Transferencias, Trueques e Inversiones en la Sierra Morena.' *Cervantes* 24.1:39–64.

Junot, Laure. 1831. *Memoirs of the Duchess d'Abrantes.* Vol. 1. London: Henry Colburn and Richard Bentley.

Kallendorf, Hilaire. 2003. *Exorcism and Its Texts: Subjectivity in Early Modern England and Spain.* Toronto: University of Toronto Press.

Kamen, Henry. 1986. 'Una crisis de conciencia en la edad de oro en España: Inquisición contra "limpieza de sangre."' *Bulletin Hispanique* 88:322–56.

– 1997. *Philip of Spain.* New Haven, CT, and London: Yale University Press.

Kennedy, William J. 2002. 'Versions of a Career: Petrarch and His Renaissance Commentators.' In *European Literary Careers: The Author from Antiquity to the Renaissance*, ed. Patrick Cheney and Frederick A. de Armas. 146–64. Toronto: University of Toronto Press.

Kirschner, Teresa. 1981. '*El retablo de las maravillas* de Cervantes o la dramatización del miedo.' In *Cervantes: Su obra y su mundo*, ed. Manuel Criado de Val. 819–27. Madrid: Edi-6.

Klibansky, Raymond, Edwin Panofsky, and Franz Saxl. 1964. *Saturn and Melancholy.* London: Thomas Nelson.

Koenisberger, H.G. 1994. 'The Politics of Philip II.' In *Politics, Religion and Diplomacy in Early Modern Europe: Essays in Honor of De Lamar Jensen*, ed. Malcom R. Throp and Arthur J. Slavin. 171–89. Kirksville: Sixteenth Century Essays and Studies 27.

Lathrop, Thomas. 1984. '¿Por qué Cervantes no incluyó el robo del rucio?' *Anales Cervantinos* 22:207–12.

Lazarillo de Tormes. 1976. Ed. Joseph V. Ricapito. Madrid: Cátedra.

Leahy, Chad. 2008. 'Lascivas o esquivas? La identidad geográfica y sexual de las yeguas gallegas en *Don Quijote* (I.15).' *Cervantes* 28.2:89–118.

Lever, J.W. 1952. 'Three Notes on Shakespeare's Plants.' *The Review of English Studies* 3:117–29.

Lévy, Isaac Jack, and Rosemay Lévy Zumwalt. 2002. *Ritual Medical Lore of Sephardic Women: Sweetening the Spirits, Healing the Sick.* Urbana: University of Illinois Press.

Lí, Andrés de. 1999. *Repertorio de los tiempos.* Ed. Laura Delbrugge. London: Tamesis.

Lipking, Lawrence. 1981. *The Life of the Poet: Beginning and Ending Poetic Careers.* Chicago: University of Chicago Press.

Looney, Dennis. 1996. *Compromising the Classics: Romance Narrative in the Italian Renaissance*. Detroit, MI: Wayne State University Press.

Lucía, José Manuel. 2004. *De los libros de caballerías manuscritos al Quijote*. Madrid: SIAL Ediciones.

Lukács, George. 1971. *The Theory of the Novel*. Trans. Anne Bostock. Cambridge: Massachusetts Institute of Technology Press.

Madrigal, José Antonio. 1981. 'El símbolo y su función temática en los primeros capítulos de *Don Quijote*.' In *Cervantes: Su obra y su mundo*, ed. Manuel Criado de Val. 569–74. Madrid: Edi-6.

Maggi, Armando. 2001. *Satan's Rhetoric: A Study of Renaissance Demonology*. Chicago and London: University of Chicago Press.

Maiorino, Giancarlo. 2003. *The Picaresque Art of Survival and the Practice of Everyday Life in Lazarillo de Tormes*. University Park: Pennsylvania State University Press.

Makki, Mahmud Ali. 2006. 'La visión del Islam en en *Quijote*.' In *De Cervantes y el Islam*, ed. Nuria Martínez de Castilla Muñoz and Rodolfo Gil Benumeya Grimau. 223–46. Madrid: Sociedad Estatal de Conmemoraciones Culturales.

Maldonado de Guevara, Francisco. 1954. 'Molinos de viento, tres meditaciones.' *Anales Cervantinos* 4:77–100.

Mancing, Howard. 2001. 'Bendito Sea Alá: A New Edition of Don Belianís de Grecia.' *Cervantes* 21.1:111–15.

Marasso, Arturo. 1954. *Cervantes: La invención del Quijote*. Buenos Aires: Hachette.

Maravall, José Antonio. 1991. *Utopia and Counterutopia in the* Quixote. Trans. Robert W. Felkel. Detroit, MI: Wayne State University Press.

Marcilly, Charles, and Saadeddine Bencheneb. 1996. 'Qui était Cide Hamete Benengeli?' In *Mélange à la mémoire de Jean Sarrailh*. 97–116. Paris: Centre de recherches de l'institute d'etudes hispaniques.

Martínez Ruiz, Juan. 1985. 'Ensalmos curativos del manuscrito árabe *Misceláneo de Salomón* de Ocaña (Toledo), en el marco de convivencia de las Tres Culturas.' In *II Congreso Internacional 'Encuentro de las Tres Culturas' (Toledo, 3–6 octubre 1983)*. 217–22. Toledo: Ayuntamiento de Toledo.

Martín Morán, José Manuel. 1986. 'Los escenarios teatrales del Quijote.' *Anales Cervantinos* 24:27–46.

Mayer, Eric D. 2005. 'The Secret of Narrative: A Structural Analysis of Cervantes's *Novelas ejemplares*.' *Neophilologus* 89.3:371–82.

McDonough, Christopher M. 2003. 'The Swallows in Cleopatra's Ship.' *The Classical World* 96.3:251–8.

McGaha, Michael. 1977. 'The Sources and Meaning of the Grisóstomo-Marcela Episode in the 1605 *Quijote*.' *Anales Cervantinos* 16:1–37.

– 1980. 'Cervantes and Virgil.' In *Cervantes and the Renaissance,* ed. Michael Mc-Gaha. 34–50. Newark, DE: Juan de la Cuesta.

– 1981. 'Fuentes y sentido del episodio del "yelmo de Mambrino" en el *Quijote* de 1605.' In *Cervantes: Su vida y su mundo,* ed. Manuel Criado de Val. 743–7. Madrid: Edi-6.

– 1991. 'Intertextuality as a Guide to the Interpretation of the Battle of the Sheep (*Don Quixote* 1.18).' In *On Cervantes: Essays for L.A. Murillo,* ed. James A. Parr. 149–62. Newark, DE: Juan de la Cuesta.

McKendrick, Melveena. 1974. *Women and Society in the Spanish Drama of the Golden Age: A Study of the 'mujer varonil.'* Cambridge: Cambridge University Press.

Meixell, Amanda S. 2004. 'The *Espíritu de Merlin,* Renaissance Magic, and the Limitations of Being Human in *La casa de los celos.'* *Cervantes* 24.2:93–118.

Mendeloff, Henry. 1975. 'The Maritornes Episode: A Cervantine Bedroom Farce.' *Romance Notes* 16:753–9.

Mexía, Pedro. 1989. *Silva de varia lección.* Ed. Antonio Castro. 2 vols. Madrid: Cátedra.

Miller, J. Hillis. 1992. *Ariadne's Thread: Story Lines.* New Haven, CT: Yale University Press.

Miller, William. [1926] 1969. *Trebizond: The Last Greek Empire of the Byzantine Era 1204–1461.* Chicago: Argonaut.

Miñana, Rogelio. 2007. *Monstruos que hablan: el discurso de la monstruosidad en Cervantes.* North Carolina Studies in the Romance Languages and Literatures. Chapel Hill: University of North Carolina Press.

Molina, Álvaro. 2003. 'Santos y quebrantos: auge y ocaso de la violencia sagrada en Don Quijote II, LVIII.' In *Estas primicias del ingenio: Jóvenes cervantistas en Chicago,* ed. Francisco Caudet and Kerry Wilks. 155–84. Madrid: Castalia.

Moner, Michel. 1981. 'Las maravillosas figures de *El retablo de las maravillas.'* In *Cervantes: Su obra y su mundo,* ed. Manuel Criado de Val. 809–17. Madrid: Edi-6.

Montaner Frutos, Alberto. 2005. 'La derrota compuesta del cautivo (*Quijote* XLI).' *Anales Cervantinos* 37:45–106.

– 2006. 'Zara/Zoraida y la Cava Rumia: Historia, leyenda e invención.' In *De Cervantes y el Islam,* ed. Nuria Martínez de Castilla Muñoz and Rodolfo Gil Benumeya Grimau. 247–80. Madrid: Sociedad Estatal de Conmemoraciones Culturales.

Morrissey, Robert. 2003. *Charlemagne and France: A Thousand Years of Mythology.* Trans. Catherine Tihanyi. Notre Dame, IN: University of Notre Dame Press.

Murillo, Luis Andrés. 1983. 'Cervantes' Tale of the Captive Captain.' In *Florilegium Hispanicum: Medieval and Golden Age Studies Presented to Dorothy Clotelle Clarke*, ed. John S. Geary. 229–43. Madison, WI: Hispanic Seminary of Medieval Studies.

Murrin, Michael. 1994. *History and Warfare in Renaissance Epic*. Chicago: University of Chicago Press.

Nadeau, Carolyn A. 1995. 'Evoking Astraea: The Speeches of Marcela and Dorotea in *Don Quijote*, I.' *Neophilologus* 79:53–61.

– 2002. *Women of the Prologues: Imitation, Myth and Magic in Don Quixote, I*. Lewisburg, PA: Bucknell University Press.

Nelson, Benjamin J. 2007. 'Tending to Empire: The Spanish Pastoral Novel and Its Reflection upon Imperial Spain.' Dissertation. University of Chicago.

Ovid. *Metamorphoses*. 1998. Trans. A.D. Melville. Oxford: Oxford University Press.

Panofsky, Erwin. 1969. *Problems in Titian: Mostly Iconographic*. New York: New York University Press.

Pardo Tomás, José. 1991. *Ciencia y censura: La Inquisición Española y los libros científicos en los siglos XVI y XVII*. Madrid: Consejo de Investigaciones Científicas.

Parker, Geoffrey. 1998. *The Grand Strategy of Philip II*. New Haven, CT, and London: Yale University Press.

Parr, James A. 2009. 'Aspectos formales del Quijote.' In *USA Cervantes: 39 Cervantistas en Estados Unidos*, ed. Georgina Dopico Black and Francisco Layna Ranz. 931–49. Madrid: Consejo de Investigaciones Cientificas y Polifemo.

Patterson, Annabelle. 1987. *Pastoral and Ideology: Virgil to Valéry*. Berkeley and Los Angeles: University of California Press.

Paulson, Ronald. 1984. 'Country Inn Yard at Election Time: A Problem in Interpretation.' *The Yearbook of English Studies. Satire Special Number: Essays in Memory of Robert C. Elliott 1914–1981*. 14:196–208.

Pavel, Thomas. 2003a. 'Literary Genres as Norms and Good Habits.' *New Literary History* 34.2:201–10.

– 2003b. *La pensée du roman*. Paris: Gallimard.

– In press. 'Cervantes' Don Quixote: Ambition and Talent.' *Strumenti Critici*.

Pérez de Moya, Juan. 1996. *Comparaciones o similes para los vicios y virtudes: Philosophía secreta*. Madrid: Biblioteca Castro.

Perry, Mary Elizabeth. 2005. *Moriscos and the Politics of Religion in Early Modern Spain*. Princeton, NJ: Princeton University Press.

Phillips, J.H. 1980. 'The Constellations on Achilles' Shield (*Iliad* 18. 485–489).' *Liverpool Classical Monthly* 5.8:179–80.

Plato. 1974. *Republic*. Trans. G.M.A. Grube. Indianapolis, IN: Hackett.

Pliny. 1969. *Natural History*. Trans. H. Rackham. Vols 2, 3. Cambridge, MA: Harvard University Press.

Predmore, Richard L. 1973. *Cervantes*. New York: Dodd, Mead.

Presberg, Charles. 2001. *Adventures in Paradox: Don Quixote and the Western Tradition*. University Park, PA: Pennsylvania State University Press.

Prescott, Anne Lake. 2002. 'Divine Poetry as a Career Move: The Complexities and Consolations of Following David.' In *European Literary Careers: The Author from Antiquity to the Renaissance*, ed. Patrick Cheney and Frederick A. de Armas. 206–30. Toronto: University of Toronto Press.

Prescott, William Hickling, and John Foster Kirk. 1882. *History of the Reign of Philip the Second, King of Spain*. Vol. 1. Philadelphia: J.B. Lippincott.

Prince, Gerald. 1988. 'The Disnarrated.' *Style* 22.1:1–8.

Quinn, Mary B. 2008. 'Handless Maidens, Modern Texts: A New Reading of Cervantes's The Captive's Tale.' *MLN* 123.2:213–29.

Quint, David. 1993. *Epic and Empire: Politics and Generic Form from Virgil to Milton*. Princeton, NJ: Princeton University Press.

– 2003. *Cervantes's Novel of Modern Times: A New Reading of Don Quijote*. Princeton, NJ: Princeton University Press.

Quintilian. 2001. *The Orator's Education*. Trans. Donald A. Russell. 5 vols. Loeb Classical Library. Cambridge, MA: Harvard University Press.

Rabín, Lisa. 1994. 'The Reluctant Companion of Empire: Petrarch and Dulcinea in *Don Quixote de la Mancha*.' *Cervantes* 14:81–92.

Redondo, Augustín. 1998. *Otra manera de leer el Quijote: Historia, tradiciones culturales y literatura*. Madrid: Castalia.

Reichenberger, Kurt. 2005. *Cervantes and the Hermeneutics of Satire*. Kassel: Edition Reichenberger.

Remer, Theodore G. 1965. *Serendipity and the Three Princes: From the Peregrinaggio of 1557*. Norman: University of Oklahoma Press.

Riley, Edward C. 1962. *Teoría de la novela en Cervantes*. Madrid: Taurus.

– 1986. *Don Quixote*. London: Allen and Unwin.

Rivero, Horacio C. 2006. 'A imitación del hilo del laberinto de Perseo: El nexo narrativo de las ficciones laberinticas en Sierra Morena.' *MLN* 121.2:278–98.

Rizzi, Bruno. 1985. *The Bureaucratisation of the World*. Trans. Adam Westoby. London: Tavistock.

Rodríguez de Montalvo, Garci. 1987. *Amadís de Gaula*. Ed. Juan Manuel Chaco Blecua. Madrid: Castalia.

Roettgen, Steffi. 1997. *Italian Frescoes: The Flowering of the Renaissance 1470–1510*. New York, London, and Paris: Abbeville Press.

Rojas, Fernando de. 1993. *La Celestina*. Ed. Dorothy Severin. Madrid: Cátedra.

Rose, Margaret. 1979. *Parody/Metafiction: An Analysis of Parody as a Critical Mirror to the Writing and Reception of Fiction.* London: Croom Helm.

Rosenmeyer, Thomas G. 1969. *The Green Cabinet: Theocritus and the European Pastoral Lyric.* Berkeley and Los Angeles: University of California Press.

Rosenthal, E. 1971. 'Plus Ultra, Non plus Ultra, and the Columnar Device of Emperor Charles V.' *Journal of the Warburg and Courtauld Institutes* 34:204–28.

– 1973. 'The Invention of the Columnar Device of Emperor Charles V at the Court of Burgundy in Flanders in 1516.' *Journal of the Warburg and Courtauld Institutes* 36:198–230.

Rossi, Rosa. 2003. *Tras las huellas de Cervantes: Perfil inédito del autor del Quijote.* Trans. Juan Ramón Capella. Madrid: Trotta.

Rowland, Beryl. 1973. *Animals with Human Faces: A Guide to Animal Symbolism.* Knoxville: University of Tennessee Press.

Ruiz Pérez, Pedro. 1995. 'La hipóstasis de Armida: Dorotea y Micomicona.' *Cervantes* 15:147–63.

Samsó, Julio. 2009. 'La *Urŷūza* de Ibn Abī l-Riŷāl y su comentario por Ibn Qunfud: Astrología e historia en el Magrib en los siglos XI y XIV (I).' *Al-Qanṭara* 30.1:7–39.

San Pedro, Diego de. 1995. *Cárcel de amor: Arnalte y Lucenda; Sermón.* Ed. Joséw Francisco Ruiz Casanova. Madrid: Cátedra.

Sawday, Jonathan. 1995. *The Body Emblazoned: Dissection and the Human Body in Renaissance Culture.* London and New York: Routledge.

Saylor, Charles F. 1978. '*Belli Spes Inproba:* The Theme of Walls in Lucan's Pharsalia VI.' *Transactions of the American Philological Association* 108:243–57.

Scobie, A. 1976. '*El curioso impertinente* and Auleius.' *Romanishce Forschungen* 88:75–6.

Scott, Walter. 1906. *Waverly or 'Tis Sixty Years Since.* Ed. Ernest Rhys. London: J.M. Dent.

Selig, Karl Ludwig. 1983. 'Apuleius and Cervantes: *Don Quijote* (I, XVIII).' In *Auereum Saeculum Hispanum,* ed. Karl-Hermann Korner and Dietrich Briesemeister. 285–7. Wiesbaden: Franz Steiner.

Seneca. 1969. *Tragedies II.* Ed. and trans. F.J. Miller. Cambridge, MA: Harvard University Press.

– 2002. *Tragedies.* Ed. and trans. J.G. Fitch. Cambridge, MA: Harvard University Press.

Seznec, Jean. 1972. *The Survival of the Pagan Gods.* Trans. Barbara F. Sessions. Princeton, NJ: Princeton University Press.

Sidelko, Paul L. 1996. 'The Condemnation of Roger Bacon.' *Journal of Medieval History* 22.1:69–81.

Simpson, Charles. 2001. 'Teichoskopia and Autopatheia in Horace *Odes* 1–3.' *Revue Belge de Philologie et d'Histoire* 70:65–8.

Smith, Warren S. 1989. 'Greed and Sacrifice in Juvenal's Twelfth Satire.' *Transactions of the American Philological Association* 119:287–98.

Solá-Solé, Josep. M. 1981. 'Sobre el Quejana de *Don Quijote.*' In *Cervantes: Su obra y su mundo*, ed. Manuel Criado de Val. 717–22. Madrid: Edi-6.

Solterer, Helen. 1995. *The Master and Minverva: Disputing Women in French Medieval Culture.* Berkeley and Los Angeles: University of California Press.

Stagg, Geoffrey. 1964. 'Sobre el plan primitivo del Quijote.' In *Actas del primer congreso de la Asociación Internacional de Hispanistas*, ed. Frank Pierce and Cyril A. Jones. 463–71. Oxford: Dolphin Book.

– 2002. '*Don Quijote* and the *Entremés de los romances*: A Retrospective.' *Cervantes* 22.2:129–50.

Stetkevych, Jaroslav. 1993. *The Zephyrs of Najd: The Poetics of Nostalgia in the Classical Arabic Nasīb.* Chicago: University of Chicago Press.

Stirling, William. 1851. 'The Cloister Life of Emperor Charles V.' *Fraser's Magazine* 43:528–44.

Stone, Robert. 2006. 'Unsettling Details: The Canonized Mooress in the Quixote.' *Dissidences: Hispanic Journal of Theory and Criticism* 2.1: http://www.dissidences/CervantesMooress.html.

Strauss, Leo. 1988. *Persecution and the Art of Writing.* Chicago and London: University of Chicago Press.

Strong, Roy. 1984. *Art and Power: Renaissance Festivals 1450–1650.* Woodbridge: Boydell.

Suetonius. 2000. *Lives of the Caesars.* Trans. Catherine Edwards. Oxford: Oxford University Press.

Sullivan, Henry W. 1996. *Grotesque Purgatory: A Study of Cervantes's Don Quixote, Part II.* University Park: Pennsylvania State University Press.

Syverson-Stork, J. 1986. *Theatrical Aspects of the Novel: A Study of 'Don Quixote.'* Valencia: Albatros-Hispanófila.

Tanner, Marie. 1993. *The Last Descendants of Aeneas: The Hapsburgs and the Mythic Image of the Emperor.* New Haven, CT: Yale University Press.

Tasso, Torquato. 2000. *Jerusalem Delivered.* Trans. Anthony M. Esolen. Baltimore, MD: Johns Hopkins University Press.

Tirso de Molina. 1996. *El burlador de Sevilla.* Ed. Alfredo Rodríguez López-Vázquez. Madrid: Cátedra.

Todorov, Tzvetan. 1977. *The Poetics of Prose.* Trans. Richard Howard. New York: Cornell University Press.

Tolan, John V. 2002. *Saracens: Islam in the Medieval European Imagination.* New York: Columbia University Press.

Traister, Barbara Howard. 1984. *Heavenly Necromancers: The Magician in English Renaissance Drama*. Columbia: University of Missouri Press.

Trueblood, Alan S. 1973. *Experience and Artistic Expression in Lope de Vega: The Making of La Dorotea*. Cambridge, MA: Harvard University Press.

Turriano, Juanelo. 1983. *The Twenty-One Books of Devices and of Machines*. Ed. José A. García Diego. Madrid: Colegio de Ingenieros de Caminos, Canales y Puertos.

Vaganay, Hughes. 1937. 'Une source du "Cautivo" de Cervantes.' *Bulletin Hispanique* 39:153–4.

Véguez, Roberto A. 2001. 'Un millón de Ave Marías: El rosario en *Don Quijote*.' *Cervantes* 21.2:81–108.

– 2005. '*Don Quijote* and 9/11: The Clash of Civilizations and the Birth of the Modern Novel.' *Hispania* 88.1:101–13.

Vernet, J. 1974. *Astrología y astronomía en el Renacimiento*. Barcelona: Ariel.

Virgil. 1978. *Eclogues. Georgics. Aeneid*. Trans. H.R. Fairclough. 2 vols. Cambridge, MA: Harvard University Press.

Voltaire. 2008. 'Zadig.' In *Candide and Other Stories*. 107–77. Ed. and Trans. Roger Pearson. Oxford: Oxford University Press.

Walker, D.P. 1958. *Spiritual and Demonic Magic: From Ficino to Campanella*. London: Warburg Institute.

Watt, Ian. 1996. *Myths of Modern Individualism: Faust, Don Quixote, Don Juan, Robinson Crusoe*. Cambridge: Cambridge University Press.

Weber, Alison. 1985. 'Review of Carroll B. Johnson's *Johnson's Madness and Lust: A Psychoanalytic Approach to Don Quijote*.' *Cervantes* 5.1:60–72.

– 1991. 'Padres e hijas: Una lectura intertextual de la historia del cautivo.' In *Actas del II coloquio internacional de la Asociación de Cervantistas*. 425–31. Barcelona: Anthropos.

Weimer, Christopher. 1996. 'A Cervantine Reading of Conan Doyle: A Cervantine Reading of a Study in Scarlet.' In *Sherlock Holmes: Victorian Sleuth to Modern Hero*, ed. Charles R. Putney, Joseph A. Cutshall, and Sallie Sugarman. 196–210. Lanham, MD, and London: Scarecrow Press.

Wethey, Harold. 1971. *The Paintings of Titian*. Vol. 2. London: Phaidon.

Whitenack, Judith A. 1993. 'Don Quixote and the Romances of Chivalry Once Again: Converted *Paganos* and Enamoured *Magas*.' *Cervantes* 13.2:61–91.

Whitmarsh, Tim. 2008. *The Cambridge Companion to the Greek and Roman Novel*. Cambridge: Cambridge University Press.

Williamson, Edwin. 1984. *The Halfway House of Fiction: Don Quixote and Arthurian Romance*. Oxford: Clarendon Press.

Wittkower, Rudolf, and Margot Wittkower. 1969. *Born under Saturn: The Character and Conduct of Artists; A Documented History from Antiquity to the French Revolution.* New York: Random House.

Yates Frances A. 1975. *Astraea: The Imperial Theme in the Sixteenth Century.* London: Routledge and Keagan Paul.

Yovel, Yirmiyahu. 2009. *The Other Within: The Marranos; Split Identity and Emerging Modernity.* Princeton, NJ: Princeton University Press.

Ziomek, Henryk. 1984. *A History of Spanish Golden Age Drama.* Lexington: University Press of Kentucky.

Index